# Learning Large Lessons

## The Evolving Roles of Ground Power and Air Power in the Post–Cold War Era

David E. Johnson

Prepared for the United States Air Force

PROJECT AIR FORCE

The research described in this report was sponsored by the United States
Air Force under Contract F49642-01-C-0003. Further information may
be obtained from the Strategic Planning Division, Directorate of Plans,
Hq USAF.

**Library of Congress Cataloging-in-Publication Data**

Johnson, David E., 1950–
    Learning large lessons : the evolving roles of ground power and air power in the
    post-Cold War era / David E. Johnson.
      p. cm.
    Includes bibliographical references.
    "MG-405."
    ISBN 0-8330-3876-1 (pbk. : alk. paper)
    1. United States—Armed Forces. 2. Military doctrine—United States. 3. United
States—Armed Forces—Operations other than war. 4. Air power—United States. 5.
Unified operations (Military science) 6. Operational art (Military science)  I. Title.

UA23.J57 2006
355.4'20973—dc22

                                                                    2005030914

The RAND Corporation is a nonprofit research organization providing
objective analysis and effective solutions that address the challenges
facing the public and private sectors around the world. RAND's
publications do not necessarily reflect the opinions of its research clients
and sponsors.

**RAND®** is a registered trademark.

*Cover photo: Several of the generals who developed and employed
the air-ground cooperation system for the U.S. 12th Army Group during World
War II in Western Europe at Fort Ehrenbreitstein, Koblenz,
Germany on April 6, 1945. From left to right: Lieutenant General George S.
Patton, Jr., 3d Army; Major General Otto Paul "Opie" Weyland, XIX Tactical
Air Command; General Omar N. Bradley, 12th Army Group; Major General Hoyt S.
Vandenberg, Ninth Air Force; Lieutenant General Courtney H. Hodges, First
Army; and Major General Elwood R. "Pete" Quesada, IX Tactical Air Command.
U.S. Army photograph, collection of the Dwight D. Eisenhower
Presidential Library and Museum, courtesy of the U.S. National Park Service.*

Published 2007 by the RAND Corporation
1776 Main Street, P.O. Box 2138, Santa Monica, CA 90407-2138
1200 South Hayes Street, Arlington, VA 22202-5050
4570 Fifth Avenue, Suite 600, Pittsburgh, PA 15213-2665
RAND URL: http://www.rand.org/
To order RAND documents or to obtain additional information, contact
Distribution Services: Telephone: (310) 451-7002;
Fax: (310) 451-6915; Email: order@rand.org

# Preface

This monograph poses the hypothesis that U.S. post–Cold War military operations have witnessed a shift in the relative roles of ground power and air power in warfighting, but the joint warfighting potential of this shift is not being fully realized. It examines five military operations—Iraq (1991), Bosnia (1995), Kosovo (1999), Afghanistan (2001), and Iraq (2003)—to test this hypothesis. In the process, this study examines the continuing service dominance in U.S. joint warfighting concepts and the fact that warfighting success does not necessarily achieve a strategic political end state that supports U.S. long-term interests. A revision of the original monograph published in 2006, this edition incorporates recent changes to joint and service doctrines and adds an index.

The research reported here was sponsored by Christopher Bowie, Deputy Director, Air Force Strategic Planning, Deputy Chief of Staff for Plans and Programs, Headquarters U.S. Air Force (AF/XPX). It was conducted within the Strategy and Doctrine Program of RAND Project AIR FORCE. The monograph should be of interest to policymakers in the Department of Defense, the Joint Chiefs of Staff, and the U.S. Joint Forces Command, and to those in the armed services concerned with concept development, doctrine, and weapon system acquisition.

## RAND Project AIR FORCE

RAND Project AIR FORCE (PAF), a division of the RAND Corporation, is the U.S. Air Force's federally funded research and development center for studies and analyses. PAF provides the Air Force with independent analyses of policy alternatives affecting the development, employment, combat readiness, and support of current and future aerospace forces. Research is conducted in four programs: Aerospace Force Development; Manpower, Personnel, and Training; Resource Management; and Strategy and Doctrine.

Additional information about PAF is available on our Web site at http://www.rand.org/paf.

# Contents

# Figure and Tables

## Figure

## Tables

# Summary

The roles of ground and air power have shifted in U.S. post–Cold War warfighting operations. However, the two services largely responsible for promulgating the relevant doctrines, creating effective organizations, and procuring equipment for the changing battlefield in the domains of land and air—the U.S. Army and the U.S. Air Force—do not appear to be fully incorporating the lessons of post–Cold War operations. Thus, the joint warfighting potential of comprehensive ground-air integration is not being fully realized. Indeed, the Army and the Air Force (and the other services) have tended to view the conflicts of the post–Cold War period through their specific institutional prisms.

Additionally, all the U.S. military services have focused the vast majority of their attention on warfighting, to the exclusion of other types of military operations that are increasingly central to achieving national security objectives. These mind-sets must change if the U.S. armed forces are to provide the capabilities most needed to protect and advance national interests in the future.

## Principal Conclusions

At the warfighting level of military operations, air power has proven to be capable of performing a mission—deep strike operations—that the Army has long believed the Air Force either could not or would not reliably perform. Army doctrine envisions deep operations as a key element in its corps-level campaigns at the operational level of war. However, the two systems the Army has for striking deep—the AH-64

Apache helicopter and the Army Tactical Missile System (ATACMS)—have not shown themselves to be as effective as fixed-wing aircraft in conducting deep operations. Consequently, by seeking to control operations in large areas of operation beyond the frontline battlefield, the Army limits the effectiveness and responsiveness of more capable air power weapons in the prosecution of the overall joint campaign. (See pp. 157–174.)

The effective combination of ground and air power in an integrated theater campaign is not a service issue; it is a joint warfighting issue. At present, however, joint doctrine mainly defers to service doctrine. If, however, air power can largely supplant ground power in deep operations, the implications for both joint doctrine and service capabilities are significant. Although the subject is beyond the scope of this study, the capability of fixed-wing aircraft raises questions about the roles of the attack helicopter on the battlefield and the control, and possibly the utility, of ATACMS in deep operations. (See pp. 191–200.)

Despite the warfighting prowess of the U.S. military, its forces have been less effective across the full range of military operations.[1] This realm is largely and intrinsically ground centric. It is also the strategic realm in which post-warfighting victory is secured for the nation. Given the effectiveness of air power in deep operations, perhaps the time has come to assess whether the Army's structure should be substantially altered to bolster its effectiveness in this all-important realm. Resources for this redesign should come in part from existing or envisioned deep operations capabilities—from across the services—that air power can provide more effectively. (See pp. 200–207.)

Although the period since the end of the Cold War has witnessed a significant number of MOOTW, the "war" dimension of the range of military operations is where the Army and the Air Force have generally focused their institutional efforts, which are reflected in their doctrines, organizations, and equipment. Consequently, this study analyzed the

---

[1]   See U.S. Joint Chiefs of Staff, JP 3-0, *Joint Operations*, 2006, p. iii, which discontinues the "use of the term and acronym 'military operations other than war (MOOTW).'" This study retains the term in all but the final chapter, because it was the organizing doctrinal construct for the range of military operations for the conflicts described in this study.

following post–Cold War conflicts: Iraq (1991), Bosnia (1995), Kosovo (1999), Afghanistan (2001), and Iraq (2003). The analysis was limited to identifying the responses of the ground-centric and the air-centric communities to what happened in these wars and, where appropriate, a more integrated assessment of these wars. Table S.1 depicts the results of the case analysis.

## Findings About the Relative Warfighting Roles of Ground and Air Power

Individually and in toto, these cases suggest that a shift has occurred in the relative warfighting roles of ground and air power. This shift was most apparent in Operation Iraqi Freedom (OIF). Several conclusions emerge from the assessment of that war:

- The strategic and operational levels of warfighting against large conventional enemy forces were dominated by flexible, all-weather, precision-strike air power, enabled by intelligence, surveillance, and reconnaissance (ISR). (See pp. 111–116 and 123–128.)
- The tactical level of war and the exploitation of the operational effects of air power were the primary domains of ground power. Despite significant increases in ISR-enabled situational awareness at the strategic and operational levels, uncertainty at the tactical and close combat levels of war endures. (See pp. 116–117.)
- Successful major combat operations did not necessarily achieve a strategic political end state or conflict resolution. A protracted postwar U.S. presence in military support to stability, security, transition, and reconstruction (SSTR) is the norm. (See pp. 200–207.)
- The Army and the Air Force experience the greatest interservice tension over the relative roles of ground and air power in warfighting. This tension largely results from how joint doctrine designates and defines areas of operation (AOs) and how the Army views deep operations. Generally, AOs are expansive to support an aggressive surface scheme of maneuver and to enable the maxi-

**Table S.1**
**Case Assessment Results**

| Case | Ground Centric | Air Centric | Integrated | End State |
|---|---|---|---|---|
| Iraq, 1991 | Ground campaign decisive after air softened Iraqi forces. | Air power set the conditions for overwhelming success—all but won the war. | Air campaign significantly weakened an incompetent opponent who was defeated by ground power. | Containment and sanctions for 10+ years; OIF |
| Bosnia | Croat-Muslim ground offensive principally responsible for Serb concessions. | Decisive and precise air power forced Serb concessions. | Combination of ground threat and air attack and low stakes for Serbs resulted in concessions; rapidity yields false expectations about Serb will to resist. | MOOTW |
| Kosovo | Threat of a ground invasion caused Milosevic to yield; center of gravity Serb Forces in Kosovo; a minor view held that KLA influenced decision. | Air power forced Milosevic to yield after stepping up modest initial campaign; center of gravity "downtown"—what Milosevic valued; attacking forces in Kosovo a waste of bombs. | Air attack against infrastructure targets changed the political dynamic. This use of air power, coupled with diplomatic isolation (Russians) and NATO unity, caused Milosevic to yield. Ground threat a future consideration and may have influenced to a lesser degree. | MOOTW |

**Table S.1—Continued**

| Case | Ground Centric | Air Centric | Integrated | End State |
|---|---|---|---|---|
| Afghanistan | Anti-Taliban Afghan ground forces, enabled by air power, overcame Taliban and al Qaeda. CAS not responsive during Operation Anaconda, when U.S. ground forces necessary to root out remnants. | Air power decisive in giving Anti-Taliban Afghans the edge. Also key in Operation Anaconda in protecting U.S. ground forces. | Air power decisive in giving Afghans the edge, but U.S. ground forces needed to do the searches and rooting out that surrogate Afghan forces did not want to do. Air power critical in Operation Anaconda. | MOOTW |
| Iraq, 2003 | "Shock and awe" did not obviate the need for ground combat; "boots on the ground" were needed to destroy Saddam's regime and occupy Iraq. Nevertheless, air power was a key enabler in achieving these objectives. | Air power set the conditions for rapid success on the ground, despite being in a supporting role. However, control of the FSCL by ground commanders limited air power's contribution in the "deep battle" (as defined by the Army and Marine Corps). | Air power precluded effective positioning and employment of Iraqi ground forces even in bad weather or darkness, often shattering units before they could close with coalition ground forces. This not only reduced the costs, risks, and duration of the coalition campaign to remove Saddam's regime but largely left coalition ground units to mop up the remnants of shattered enemy formations in close battle where friction persisted unabated. | MOOTW |

mum use of the organic capabilities of the surface components. The Army's doctrine tends to retain control over a large AO so that a corps can control and shape the battlespace for its fight and employ its organic assets (ATACMS and attack helicopters) to the limits of their capability. Not surprisingly, Army operational commanders want to control the resources used in their AOs. This is accomplished by establishing fire support coordination measures—for example, the fire support coordination line (FSCL) within the corps or combined/joint force land component commander AOs that are permissive for Army systems but restrictive for the systems of other components. Using air power short of the FSCL can be inefficient because of coordination requirements. (See pp. 140–141.)

In reality, despite improved joint "interdependence," U.S. military operations remain an amalgamation of component operations, designed for optimal employment of organic capabilities (See pp. 140–145).

If these conclusions are correct, the question that logically follows is: How are they influencing joint, Army, and Air Force concepts and doctrine? The record of joint, Army, and Air Force "learning" in this area is mixed, essentially for three reasons:

- Joint doctrine defers to surface components in the establishment of AOs. (See p. 141.)
- The Army's retention of control of large AOs in support of its preferred warfighting role—offensive operations at the operational level—constrains the potential effectiveness of joint fires across the theater of operations. (See pp. 192–193.)
- The Air Force's continued push of its decades-long quest for equality (some would say preeminence) creates tension between it and the other services, most notably with the Army. (See pp. 189–191.)

Nevertheless, the effectiveness of air power at the operational level of war is clear. Also clear is that the United States must prepare for potentially sterner tests than it has faced since the end of the Cold War. It is also obvious that U.S. military transformation plans and programs to meet the challenges of the future must reflect the reality that U.S. air forces have repeatedly demonstrated the ability to dominate adversaries at the operational level of warfighting and the fact that Army deep attack systems—in the current inventory or that planned for the future—are not adequate to the task of shaping the large ground AOs called for in Army doctrine. Consequently, the task of shaping the theater—strategically and operationally—should be an air component function, and joint and service doctrines and programs should change accordingly. However, a clear transformation challenge for the United States remains: to ensure that air power can operate effectively against future, first-class opponents, who will undoubtedly pose significantly more formidable challenges to its employment than has been the case in the post–Cold War conflicts discussed in this study.

Evolving joint operating concepts for major combat operations should adapt themselves to this reality. Absent significant reform, however, the joint system will continue to produce concepts that are an amalgamation of service doctrines and capabilities, rather than demanding that the services develop capabilities specifically designed to support joint doctrine.[2] Therefore, the final warfighting recommendation of this study is that joint doctrine—and the processes by which it is derived and promulgated—must be overhauled. As its stands now, joint doctrine frequently reflects a consensus view rather than a truly integrated joint perspective. Service doctrines and capabilities—even if redundant or conflicting—are often accommodated. (See pp. 197–200.)

A signal example of this reality is the FSCL, as employed by the Army in both Gulf wars, which is permissive to ground component

---

[2]  An alternative perspective views interservice rivalry as a positive force. See Stephen Peter Rosen, "Service Redundancy: Waste or Hidden Capability?" *Joint Force Quarterly*, Summer 1993. Rosen argues, "The defense establishment should not turn a blind eye to the warp in which creative competition among the services can encourage the development of new capabilities in even a period of fiscal constraint."

commanders (and established by the land component commander) but restrictive to the employment of air power. The FSCL, however, is merely symptomatic of the Army's desire to control a large battlespace to execute its operational doctrine. This limits the employment and effectiveness of fixed-wing air power—which is more effective than organic Army systems for deep operations—in operations short of the FSCL but forward of the range of divisional indirect fire systems. An essential first step in reforming joint doctrine is to eliminate the principle that joint doctrine must defer to that of the services. At present, guidance to joint commanders is that "JFCs [joint force commanders] should allow Service tactical and operational assets and groupings to function generally as they were designed."[3] Rather, the guidance should stipulate that the services should organize and equip themselves in ways that provide the JFC capabilities and organizations that best realize the theaterwide campaign plan by providing integrated fire and maneuver. A lesser but still critical step would be to withhold to the JFC the authority to establish all fire support coordinating measures that could affect the theater campaign plan. These measures would begin the process of building a new American warfighting construct that is truly joint and not a collection of service perspectives.

Thus, in the future, the principal roles of the Army (and the Marine Corps) in joint theater warfighting would be to employ its overwhelming tactical dominance to

- force enemy reaction at the operational and strategic levels by forcing concentration or movement, thus making him vulnerable to air attack (see p. 193)
- close with and finish enemy tactical remnants, exploit success, and seize and hold ground (see p. 194)
- deal with the post-conflict security environment until the desired end state is reached (see p. 194)

---

[3]  U.S. Joint Chiefs of Staff, JP 3-31, *Command and Control for Joint Land Operations*, 2004, p. III-2.

Air power roles should be to

- shape the theater at the operational and strategic levels (see p. 194
- provide close air support (CAS); intelligence, surveillance, and reconnaissance (ISR); and lift to support ground combat operations (see p. 194)
- provide CAS, ISR, and lift for ground force operations to secure and stabilize the theater (see p. 194).

Again, accepting and implementing these doctrinal changes will be particularly difficult for the Army, given its focus on operational-level warfighting.

The ongoing interservice relationships discussed in this study have deep cultural and institutional origins. The fact that these "service ways of doing things" have persisted for the nearly two decades since the passage of Goldwater-Nichols Department of Defense Reorganization Act of 1986 shows the deep-rooted nature of service cultures and bureaucracies. It would seem self-evident that service doctrines should be subordinated to the central idea that *the supported commander is the joint force commander* and that the components exist to support his warfight and efforts to resolve conflict.

Clearly, the issues identified in this study demand joint solutions. Fortunately, processes are in place within the Department of Defense (DoD) to implement the necessary reforms. The Joint Staff and the U.S. Joint Forces Command have the authorities to promulgate joint doctrine and to experiment with new operational concepts, and they should exercise them more rigorously. Regarding enhanced cooperation and integration between the Army and the Air Force specifically, a historical example worthy of emulation is the period between 1973 and 1990. During these years, the Army–Air Force peacetime partnership, although perhaps anomalous in the context of their overall historical relationship, was as strong as it has ever been, as the two services worked together to defend NATO. Nevertheless, any meaningful change to service warfighting doctrines and organizations will likely be met with strong service resistance. One should recall that the last significant attempt at sweeping joint reform—Goldwater-Nichols—was bitterly resisted by the services as an infringement of their prerogatives.

## Recommendations for Reforms Beyond Warfighting

However, another issue looms large in American security affairs. What has emerged in the American way of war is an unmatched capacity to conduct operations and win battles. This capacity is reflected in the 2004 *National Military Strategy,* which

> directs a force sized to defend the homeland, deter forward in and from four regions, and conduct two, overlapping 'swift defeat' campaigns. Even when committed to a limited number of lesser contingencies, the force must be able to 'win decisively' in one of the two campaigns.[4]

Winning decisively in a military campaign is a warfighting, operational capability. Unfortunately, it is not a recipe for strategic victory, as evidenced by the fact that U.S. forces remain in Kosovo, Afghanistan, and Iraq with no end in sight. In the words of Antulio Echevarria, "the new American way of war . . . appears geared to fight wars as if they were battles and, thus, confuses the winning of campaigns or small-scale actions with the winning of war."[5] Echevarria recommends that American "political and military leaders must habituate themselves to thinking more thoroughly about how to turn combat successes into favorable strategic outcomes."[6] Thus, the supreme irony of this study's assessment of the relative relationship of American air and ground power is tied to this reality: In a world where the United States is the sole remaining superpower, its operational prowess and immense

---

[4] U.S. Joint Chiefs of Staff, *National Military Strategy of the United States: A Strategy for Today; A Vision for Tomorrow,* 2004, p. 18.

[5] Antulio Echevarria II, *Toward an American Way of War,* Carlisle Barracks, Pa.: Strategic Studies Institute, U.S. Army War College, 2004, p. vi.

[6] Echevarria (2004), p. vii.

technological advantages do not necessarily guarantee an outcome that is favorable to U.S. strategic interests. As events in Kosovo, Afghanistan, and Iraq have shown, substantial and often specialized investments, particularly in ground forces, are required to turn warfighting successes into the desired strategic political end states and the realization of national policy objectives.

Improving service capabilities to translate successful warfighting operations into the achievement of national goals will be at least as difficult as addressing competing service warfighting perspectives. However, within DoD there is an emerging sense that in the future the United States will require capabilities beyond those optimized for warfighting.

The Army will be the service expected to provide these new capabilities. To its credit, the Army is energetically adapting to the situations in which it now finds itself. It is creating more combat brigades and more specialized units (e.g., civil affairs and military police). Furthermore, tactics, techniques, and procedures are being developed and implemented to respond to the tactical lessons the Army in the field is learning. Nevertheless, a review of the Army's concepts for the future reveals a remarkable consistency in the belief that well-trained combat forces can perform any task.

Warfighting is at the core of the Army's culture. In the three decades since the end of the Vietnam War, the Army has become the world's preeminent conventional ground force. Nevertheless, its doctrine, training, organizational, materiel, and leader development efforts have remained focused almost exclusively on warfighting combat operations, based on the enduring belief that its principal responsibility is to fight and win America's wars and that other operations can be dealt with by an Army prepared for warfighting. This results in a dominant cultural belief that effective combat units can adapt to any challenge across the range of military operations.

Although the other services share the Army's focus on warfighting, the Army will be expected—as it always has been—to take the lead in dealing with non-warfighting missions. Nevertheless, given the Army's long history of focusing on conventional conflict, it will likely be difficult for the Army to enact the reforms needed to improve its capabilities across the range of military operations. (See pp. 151–157 and 179–181.)

Therefore, the final conclusion of this study is that many of the lessons learned about the relative roles of air and ground power since the end of the Cold War have been interpreted within service frameworks. Much work remains to attain a true American joint warfighting system, including objectively assessing the "lessons." Even more work is needed to adapt American warfighting prowess to capabilities to achieve strategic national objectives. Reform will be difficult, but these reforms must proceed apace to ensure that the United States has the capacity to deal with the strategic realities of the twenty-first century.

# Acknowledgments

Many individuals contributed their time and intellectual energy to the evolution of this study to its present form.

First, I thank my RAND colleagues. Karl P. Mueller, the study's project leader, read several drafts of the manuscript and made many thoughtful comments and suggestions. Natalie W. Crawford, Richard E. Darilek, John Gordon IV, Andrew Hoehn, Stephen T. Hosmer, Jody Jacobs, Thomas L. McNaugher, David Shlapak, Michael Spirtas, John Stillion, Alan Vick, Peter A. Wilson, and Laurinda L. Zeman all offered valuable advice about the concepts examined in the study. Jerry Sollinger gave the draft manuscript his usual masterful treatment. The monograph's editors, Phillip Wirtz and Phyllis Gilmore, and the Publications staff at RAND did what they always do so well, again.

Second, I deeply appreciate contributions to the study by many individuals outside RAND, including Colonel John V. Allison (U.S. Air Force), Colonel Chelsea Chae (U.S. Army), Robert E. Everson, Major General David Fastabend (U.S. Army), Colonel Gregory P. Gass (U.S. Army), Lieutenant Colonel Michael Johnson (U.S. Army), Colonel Robert C. Johnson (U.S. Army), General Ronald E. Keys (U.S. Air Force) and members of his staff at Air Combat Command, Andrew F. Krepinevich, Brigadier General Michael Longoria (U.S. Air Force), Brigadier General Stephen D. Mundt (U.S. Army), Colonel Matthew D. Neuenswander (U.S. Air Force), Lieutenant General David H. Petraeus (U.S. Army), Major General David C. Ralston (U.S. Army), Major General Bentley B. Rayburn, Colonel Rickey E. Smith (U.S.

Army), Colonel David Sutherland (U.S. Army), Brigadier General Robin Swan (U.S. Army), Barry Watts, Lieutenant General Stephen G. Wood (U.S. Air Force), and Brigadier General R. Mike Worden (U.S. Air Force). They, and many others too numerous to list, provided important insights during briefings on the study. Several of these individuals also invested a great deal of time in reading and commenting on various drafts of the monograph.

Third, I want to thank the students and faculty who participated in seminars on the study at the U.S. Air Force School of Advanced Air and Space Studies and the U.S. Army Command and General Staff College. In accordance with their reputation, these individuals engaged in a vigorous and valuable debate with me about this study.

Fourth, this revised edition of the study was informed by many thoughtful responses to the original version by participants at the Fall 2006 U.S. Air Force CORONA Conference, chaired by Secretary of the Air Force Michael W. Wynne and Air Force Chief of Staff General T. Michael Moseley. I also express my appreciation to General Moseley for including the study on the October 2006 Chief of Staff Air Force Reading List.

Finally, the study's reviewers—Adam Grissom, Francis G. Hoffman, David A. Ochmanek, and James T. Quinlivan—each provided thorough and very useful reviews.

The efforts of all these individuals contributed immeasurably to the final product that is this monograph. I owe them all an enormous debt of gratitude.

# Abbreviations

| | |
|---|---|
| ACC | air component commander |
| ACE | aviation combat element |
| AFDD | Air Force Doctrine Document |
| AFDO | Advanced Full Dimensional Operations |
| AFM | Air Force Manual |
| AHB | Attack Helicopter Battalion |
| AHR | Attack Helicopter Regiment |
| AO | area of operation |
| ATACMS | Army Tactical Missile System |
| ATO | air tasking order |
| AWPD-1 | Air War Plans Division, Plan 1 |
| BACS | Balkan Air Campaign Study |
| BCL | battlefield coordination line |
| BCT | brigade combat team |
| BUR | Bottom-Up Review |
| $C^3$ | command, control, and communications |

| C4ISR | command, control, communications, computers, intelligence, surveillance, and reconnaissance |
| CAOC | combined air operations center |
| CAS | close air support |
| CENTCOM | Central Command |
| CFACC | combined forces air component commander |
| CJTF | combined joint task force |
| DoD | Department of Defense |
| DOTMLPF | doctrine, organization, training, materiel, leadership, personnel, facilities |
| FCS | Future Combat System |
| FEBA | forward edge of the battle area |
| FM | Field Manual |
| FSCL | fire support coordination line |
| GPS | Global Positioning System |
| ID | Infantry Division |
| IFOR | Implementation Force |
| ISR | intelligence, surveillance, and reconnaissance |
| JDAM | Joint Direct Attack Munition |
| JFACC | joint force air component commander |
| JFC | joint force commander |
| JFLCC | joint force land component commander |
| JSTARS | Joint Surveillance Target Attack Radar System |
| KLA | Kosovo Liberation Army |

| KTO | Kuwaiti Theater of Operations |
| LCC | land component commander |
| MAGTF | Marine air-ground task force |
| MCDP | Marine Corps Doctrinal Publication |
| MLRS | Multiple Launch Rocket System |
| MOOTW | military operations other than war |
| NATO | North Atlantic Treaty Organization |
| NEO | noncombatant evacuation operations |
| OEF | Operation Enduring Freedom |
| OIF | Operation Iraqi Freedom |
| RPG | rocket-propelled grenade |
| SACEUR | Supreme Allied Commander |
| SEAD | suppression of enemy air defenses |
| SOF | special operations forces |
| TF | task force |
| UA | unit of action |
| UAV | unmanned aerial vehicles |
| UE | unit of employment |
| USAF | United States Air Force |
| WMD | weapons of mass destruction |

# CHAPTER ONE

# Introduction

You may fly over a land forever; you may bomb it, atomize it, pulverize it, and wipe it clean of life—but if you desire to defend it, protect it, and keep it for civilization, you must do this on the ground, the way the Roman legions did, by putting your young men into the mud.

*—T. R. Fehrenbach*[1]

The airplane is the only weapon which can engage with equal facility, land, sea, and other air forces for the destruction of the enemy's will to fight.

*—Major General Frank A. Andrews, 1938*[2]

[T]he air-armor team is a most powerful combination in the breakthrough and exploitation. . . . The use of this coordinated force, in combat, should be habitual.

*—Omar Bradley's 12th Army Group*[3]

This monograph poses the hypothesis that post–Cold War operations have witnessed a shift in the roles of ground and air power in war-

---

[1]  T. R. Fehrenbach, *This Kind of War: A Study in Unpreparedness*, New York: MacMillan, 1963, p. 427.

[2]  U.S. Department of the Air Force, AFM 1-1, *Basic Aerospace Doctrine of the United States Air Force*, 1984, p. 3-1.

[3]  12th Army Group, *12th Army Group Report of Operations, Vol. 11: Antiaircraft Artillery, Armored Artillery, Chemical Warfare, and Signal Sections*, 1945, p. 61. This "lessons learned" report was prepared at the conclusion of World War II in Europe.

fighting.[4] Note that "warfighting" is not "conflict resolution," a point that will be addressed at the end of this monograph. Rather, it refers to conventional major combat operations. The two services largely responsible for promulgating the relevant doctrines, creating effective organizations, and procuring equipment for the changing conflict environment in the domains of land and air—the U.S. Army and the U.S. Air Force—do not appear to be fully incorporating the lessons learned from post–Cold War operations. Thus, the joint warfighting potential of comprehensive ground-air integration is not being fully realized. Indeed, the Army and the Air Force seem to have viewed the conflicts of the post–Cold War period through prisms that often favor their specific institutional imperatives. [5]

## Study Scope and Methodology

### Study Scope: The Range of Military Operations and Focused Learning

This monograph focuses on how the Army and Air Force have viewed five "war" cases during the post–Cold War era and what lessons they

---

[4]  Throughout this monograph, reference to "air power" is inclusive of "space" and "aerospace" power.

[5]  See Department of Defense (DoD) Directive 5100.1, "Functions of the Department of Defense and Its Major Components," August 1, 2002. This directive specifies the functions of the military departments and establishes the central roles of the Army and Air Force in preparing for sustained ground and air operations. It specifies that "[t]he Army is responsible for the preparation of land forces necessary for the effective prosecution of war and military operations short of war" (6.6.1, p. 16). The first listed primary function of the Army is "[t]o organize, train, and equip forces for the conduct of prompt and sustained combat operations on land—specifically, to defeat enemy land forces and to seize, occupy, and defend land areas" (6.6.1.2.1, p. 16). Regarding the Air Force, the directive states that "[t]he Air Force is responsible for the preparation of the air and space forces necessary for the effective prosecution of war and military operations short of war" (6.6.3.1, p. 23). The first listed primary function is

> [t]o organize, train, equip, and provide forces for the conduct of prompt and sustained offensive and defensive combat operations in the air and space—specifically, forces to defend the United States against air and space attack in accordance with doctrines established by the JCS, gain and maintain general air and space supremacy, defeat enemy air and space forces, conduct space operations, control vital air areas, and establish local air and space superiority. (6.6.3.2.1, p. 24)

have drawn from them. Before moving into the case analysis, the study briefly examines the historical relationship between the Army and the Air Force before the end of the Cold War.

The case assessments focus on Army and Air Force lessons learned from conflicts in the post–Cold War period, despite the fact that all of the cases under examination occurred subsequent to the passage of the Goldwater-Nichols Department of Defense Reorganization Act of 1986, which prompted the introduction of joint doctrine. In reality, joint warfighting doctrine is largely an amalgamation of service doctrines, subject to interpretation in the event of execution by the regional combatant commander. Consequently, prevailing views about ground and air power are largely informed by the services, enabled by service capabilities, and influenced in application by the views of combatant commanders and their subordinates. Finally, this monograph offers concluding thoughts about the changing roles of ground and air power relative to each other and what lessons are *not* being learned in the larger realm of conflict resolution.

War cases have been isolated as the area of analysis because warfighting is the activity that largely influences the behavior of the services. This warfighting focus dominates, despite the fact that joint doctrine notes the requirement for the U.S. armed forces to be prepared to "meet various challenges, protect national interests, and achieve strategic goals in a variety of ways, depending on the nature of the strategic environment."[6] This strategic environment translates into a "range of military operations," delineated in Joint Publication (JP) 3-0, *Doctrine for Joint Operations*, and depicted in Table 1.1.

---

[6]  U.S. Joint Chiefs of Staff, JP 3-0, *Doctrine for Joint Operations*, 2001, p. I-2. U.S. Joint Chiefs of Staff, Joint Publication (JP) 3-0, *Joint Operations*, Washington, D.C., 2006, p. xxii. *Warfighting* is used throughout this study to connote major operations and campaigns involving large-scale combat (p. I-14). JP 3-0 (p. xxii) notes:

> Major operations and campaigns are the most **complex** and require the greatest diligence in planning and execution due to the time, effort, and national resources committed. They normally will include some level of **offense and defense** (e.g., interdiction, maneuver, forcible entry, fire support, counterair, computer network defense, and base defense). [Emphasis in the original.]

Army and Air Force doctrines, although they address the full range of military operations (also termed the "spectrum of conflict"), clearly focus on the "war" category, as they have done throughout the post–World War I era. The Army's current Field Manual (FM) 3-0, *Operations*, is quite explicit in this regard:

> Army forces are the decisive component of land warfare in joint and multinational operations. The Army organizes, trains, and equips its forces to fight and win the nation's wars and achieve directed national objectives. Fighting and winning the nation's wars is the foundation of Army service—the Army's nonnegotiable contract with the American people and its enduring obligation to the nation.[7]

**Table 1.1**
**The Range of Military Operations**

| Military Operations | | General U.S. Goal | Examples |
|---|---|---|---|
| Combat | War | Fight and win | Large-scale combat operations: attack; defend; blockades |
| Combat / Noncombat | Military operations other than war | Deter war and resolve conflict | Peace enforcement; noncombatant evacuation operations (NEO) strikes; raids; show of force; counterterrorism; peacekeeping; counterinsurgency |
| Noncombat | | Promote peace and support U.S. civil authorities | Antiterrorism; disaster relief; peacebuilding; nation assistance; domestic support; counterdrug; NEO |

SOURCE: JP 3-0 (2001), p. I-2. See U.S. Joint Chiefs of Staff, JP 3-0 (2006), p. iii, which discontinues the "use of the term and acronym 'military operations other than war (MOOTW).'" The new JP 3-0 also delineates the types of military operations: Major Operations; Homeland Defense; Civil Support; Strikes; Raids; Show of Force; Enforcement of Sanctions; Protection of Shipping; Freedom of Navigation; Peace Operations; Support to Insurgency, Counterinsurgency Operations, Combating Terrorism, Noncombatant Evacuation Operations; Recovery Operations; Consequence Management; Foreign Humanitarian Assistance; Nation Assistance; Arms Control and Disarmament; and Routine, Recurring Military Activities. This monograph retains MOOTW in all but the final chapter, because it was the organizing doctrinal construct for the range of military operations for the conflicts described in this study.

---

[7]  U.S. Department of the Army, FM 3-0, *Operations*, 2001, p. 1-2.

FM 3-0 retains the tenet, first introduced in the U.S. Army's 1923 *Field Service Regulations* (which will be discussed later), that an army prepared for war can handle any other military operation as a lesser-included case, stating: "The Army's warfighting focus produces a full spectrum force that meets the needs of joint force commanders (JFCs) in war, conflict, and peace."[8] Furthermore, a warfighting focus is central even to training for full-spectrum operations: "Battle-focused training on combat tasks prepares soldiers, units, and leaders to deploy, fight, and win."[9]

Air Force doctrine also focuses on warfighting. Air Force Doctrine Document (AFDD) 1, *Air Force Basic Doctrine*, specifies that "[t]he role of the Air Force is to organize, train, and equip aviation forces 'primarily for prompt and sustained offensive and defensive air operations.'"[10]

Although the period since the end of the Cold War has witnessed significant conflict, the "war" dimension of the range of military operations is where the Army and the Air Force have generally focused their institutional efforts, which are reflected in their doctrines, organizations, and equipment. The stakes are high in this area in terms of budget share and service prestige. Consequently, the war dimension is also the focus of the "lesson learning" within military institutions and the locus of interservice tension. Table 1.2 shows the most notable conflicts the United States has been engaged in since the end of the Cold War.

In the table, the conflicts with an "X" in the right-hand column included large-scale combat operations for the Army, the Air Force, or both. These conflicts have "lessons" that have been interpreted quite differently by the Army and the Air Force, resulting in disagreements

---

[8]  U.S. Department of the Army, FM 3-0 (2001), p. 1-3.

[9]  U.S. Department of the Army, FM 3-0 (2001), p. 1-17.

[10]  U.S. Department of the Air Force, AFDD 1, *Air Force Basic Doctrine*, 2003, p. 35.

**Table 1.2**
**Post–Cold War Conflict Cases**

| Case | Type | Ground vs. Air Tension |
|------|------|----------------|
| Panama | Strike (regime takedown) | |
| Iraq, 1991 | Regional conventional war | X |
| Somalia | Humanitarian assistance; peace enforcement | |
| Haiti | Strike; peace enforcement | |
| Rwanda | Humanitarian assistance | |
| Bosnia | Limited conventional conflict; peace enforcement | X |
| Kosovo | Limited conventional conflict; peace enforcement | X |
| Afghanistan | Limited conventional conflict; peace enforcement; counterinsurgency; counterterrorism | X |
| Iraq, 2003 | Regional conventional war; counterinsurgency; counterterrorism | X |

NOTE: The typology in the "Type" column of this figure is adapted from the range of military operations specified in JP 3-0, *Doctrine for Joint Operations* (1995, 2001). For a discussion of the types of operations in the range of military operations and their implications for conventional coercion, see David E. Johnson, Karl P. Mueller, and William H. Taft V, *Conventional Coercion Across the Spectrum of Operations: The Utility of U.S. Military Forces in the Emerging Security Environment*, Santa Monica, Calif.: RAND Corporation, MR-1494-A, 2002.

between the two services. The other operations—Panama, Somalia, Haiti, and Rwanda—were limited and created little Army–Air Force friction about how they should best be addressed.[11] These "less-than-

---

[11] Panama is something of an exception. Although there was apparently little Army–Air Force tension, there was friction among the Army, Navy, and Marine Corps. See Brooks L. Bash, "Leadership and Parochialism: An Enduring Reality?" *Joint Force Quarterly*, Summer 1999, p. 65. Bash notes that the decision by Chairman of the Joint Chiefs of Staff Colin Powell to rely mainly on Army forces to invade Panama in 1989 reflected his background and preferences. A "risky and unnecessary" airborne operation was mounted, over the objections of the Chief of Naval Operations, Admiral David Trost, who "believed troops could be landed without opposition. He also felt that the primary reason for the airdrop was to allow thousands of Army soldiers to earn combat jump wings." The Marine Corps Commandant, General Al Gray, also believed that the operation reflected Powell's Army view, because "the

war" conflicts have also largely been treated as "lesser-included cases" by both services and have mainly provided tactics, techniques, and procedures to inform existing doctrines or provide negative lessons, as in the case of Somalia.

## Study Methodology

The next chapter briefly examines the historical Army–Air Force relationship. The following four chapters of this monograph assess five wars: Iraq (1991) and Bosnia (1995) in Chapter Three, Kosovo (1999) in Chapter Four, Afghanistan (2001) in Chapter Five, and Iraq (2003) in Chapter Six. The analysis is limited to identifying the responses of the ground-centric community and the air-centric community to what happened in these wars, the lessons learned, and, where appropriate, a more integrated assessment of the wars. For the ground-centric and air-centric views, the approach used was to characterize what "credible advocates" (those who define the outer limits of service conventional wisdom) were saying about these cases, so long as those people were within the bounds of what the institution regarded as mainstream. For the assessment of what actually happened, the research used academic and public sources not rooted in a specific ground or air perspective. The analysis focused on providing answers to the following questions:

- What are the causes of interservice tension at the war end of the range of military operations?
- Are Army and Air Force lessons learned being shaped by service influences that are inhibiting true learning and improvements in joint warfighting capabilities?
- Are single-service doctrinal paradigms sufficient to capture these lessons, or do they call for a fundamental rethinking and shift of the roles of air and ground power in warfighting? What would be the implications of such a shift in the realms of joint doctrine, service roles and missions, service programs, and service cultures?

---

selected course of action was primarily Army and did not include Marine assets suited for a forced entry."

The concluding chapter offers recommendations about approaches to resolving Army–Air Force warfighting tensions and thoughts about the need for broader joint and service doctrine for conflict resolution.

# CHAPTER TWO

# The Relationship Between American Ground Power and Air Power Before the End of the Cold War

Historically, tension has existed between the Army and the Air Force over the relative roles of ground and air power. The origins of this tension date to the period between the two World Wars, when the Air Force was a branch of the Army. Throughout the interwar period, U.S. Army airmen fought to establish air power as a decisive instrument and to gain their independence from what they considered a conservative Army hierarchy that was incapable of realizing the potential of air power as anything other than long-range artillery relegated to supporting the ground effort. The views of the airmen were not without basis or bias.

During the 1920s and 1930s, Army leaders were focused on incorporating the lessons of World War I into Army doctrine and organization. They viewed ground combat as the decisive arena of warfare and believed that the "mission of the infantry is the general mission of the entire force."[1] And the mission of the Army was clear: "The ultimate objective of all military operations is the destruction of the enemy's armed forces by battle. Decisive defeat in battle breaks the enemy's will

---

[1] U.S. War Department, *Field Service Regulations, United States Army, 1923*, Washington, D.C.: U.S. Government Printing Office, 1924, p. 11. This version of the Army's *Field Service Regulations* was in effect until 1939. For a thoughtful discussion of the development of U.S. Army doctrine between the two World Wars, see William O. Odom, *After the Trenches: The Transformation of U.S. Army Doctrine, 1918–1939*, College Station, Tex.: Texas A&M University Press, 1999.

to war and forces him to sue for peace."[2] Furthermore, the regulations also stressed that "[d]ecisive results are obtained only by the offensive."[3] In the minds of the ground Army leadership, given these fundamental doctrinal tenets, "the other arms and services existed only to aid the infantry."[4]

The post–World War I period also witnessed the transformation of the U.S. Army from a frontier constabulary to a modern army. In the aftermath of the Great War, the Army embraced a key principle that would guide its fundamental institutional decisions to this day: An Army designed for the worst case can handle all other types of operations as lesser-included cases. The Army codified this tenet in its *Field Service Regulations*, which stated that the Army would focus on preparing to fight "an opponent organized for war on modern principles and equipped with all the means of modern war," because "An army capable of waging successful war under these conditions will prove adequate to any less grave emergency with which it may be confronted."[5]

The Army air component's doctrine evolved along radically different lines than that of the ground forces. During the interwar period, the Army Air Corps developed a theory of strategic bombing that focused not on enemy armies but on an opposing nation's ability to wage war. Brigadier General Haywood S. Hansell, one of the architects of U.S. strategic bombing doctrine, later summed up this view when he noted that "modern nations cannot wage war if their industries are

---

[2]   U.S. War Department (1924), p. 77.

[3]   U.S. War Department (1924), p. 77. Significant continuity exists between the 1923 *Field Service Regulations* and the Army's 2001 FM 3-0, *Operations*, which states: "The offense is the decisive form of war. Offensive operations aim to destroy or defeat an enemy. Their purpose is to impose US will on the enemy and achieve decisive victory" (p. 7-2).

[4]   David E. Johnson, *Fast Tanks and Heavy Bombers: Innovation in the U.S. Army, 1917–1945*, Ithaca, N.Y.: Cornell University Press, 1998, p. 96.

[5]   U.S. War Department (1924), p. iii. See also U.S. Department of the Army, FM 3-0 (2001), pp. vii, 1–3. The resilience of this notion of the lesser-included case is reflected in current Army doctrine, which states: "The doctrine holds warfighting as the Army's primary focus and recognizes that the ability of Army forces to dominate land warfare also provides the ability to dominate any situation in military operations other than war" (p. vii), and "The Army's warfighting focus produces a full spectrum force that meets the needs of joint force commanders (JFCs) in war, conflict, and peace" (p. 1-3).

destroyed." Therefore, "air warfare is . . . a method of destroying the enemy's ability to wage war. It is primarily a means of striking a major blow toward winning a war, rather than a direct auxiliary to surface warfare."[6]

In 1941, a group of air officers presented a plan to President Franklin D. Roosevelt that captured the essence of American air power doctrine. The officers' plan, Air War Plans Division, Plan 1 (AWPD-1), postulated that American air power could have a decisive influence on the outcome of the war against Germany by destroying its industrial war-making capacity, restricting Axis air operations, and creating the conditions for and supporting a ground invasion of Germany.[7] The confidence of the air officers was reflected in a bold assertion in AWPD-1: "[I]f the air offensive is successful, a land offensive may not be necessary."[8] Nevertheless, the officers noted that the promise of American air power could only be realized if it were *given priority over all other national production requirements.*[9]

When the United States entered World War II, General George C. Marshall, the Army Chief of Staff, reorganized the Army into three components: Army Ground Forces, Army Air Forces, and Army Service Forces. This new arrangement implicitly recognized the autonomy, if not the independence, of the Air Force. Indeed, in 1943, the Army published FM 100-2, *Command and Employment of Air Power*, which explicitly recognized the new relationship between Army ground and air forces: "LAND POWER AND AIR POWER ARE CO-EQUAL AND INTERDEPENDENT FORCES; NEITHER IS AN AUX-

---

[6]  Brigadier General Haywood S. Hansell, "The Development of the United States Concept of Bombardment Operations," lecture presented at the Air War College, February 16, 1951 (published by Maxwell Air Force Base, Ala.: Airpower Research Institute), p. 7.

[7]  Johnson (1998), pp. 169–170.

[8]  "AWPD/1, Munitions Requirements of the Army Air Forces to Defeat Our Potential Enemies," table 2, section 2, part 3, appendix 2, p. 2, in Joint Board 355, Serial 707, National Archives Microfilm Publication M1080, Washington, D.C.: National Archives, undated.

[9]  "AWPD/1, Munitions Requirements of the Army Air Forces to Defeat Our Potential Enemies," p. 3. Emphasis in the original. See also Johnson (1998), p. 171. The resource issue was significant. The plan envisioned 251 combat groups with more than 63,000 aircraft and some 2 million officers and men.

ILIARY OF THE OTHER."[10] Moreover, the new manual defined command relationships that are clearly recognizable in current joint doctrine:

> CONTROL OF AVAILABLE AIR POWER MUST BE CENTRALIZED AND COMMAND MUST BE THROUGH THE AIR FORCE COMMANDER IF THIS INHERENT FLEXIBILITY AND ABILITY TO DELIVER A DECISIVE BLOW ARE TO BE FULLY EXPLOITED. THEREFORE, THE COMMAND OF AIR AND GROUND FORCES IN A THEATER OF OPERATIONS WILL BE VESTED IN THE SUPERIOR COMMANDER CHARGED WITH THE ACTUAL CONDUCT OF OPERATIONS IN THE THEATER, WHO WILL EXERCISE COMMAND OF AIR FORCES THROUGH THE AIR FORCE COMMANDER AND COMMAND OF GROUND FORCES THROUGH THE GROUND FORCE COMMANDER.[11]

What developed during and after World War II were two institutions with fundamentally different views of warfare. The Army was convinced that conventional ground forces were the critical war-winning factor; the Air Force believed that air power was the key to victory. In World War II, and during subsequent major conflicts, each service largely fought independently. This is not to say that the Army and the Air Force have not effectively integrated their capabilities in the past. Nevertheless, the most effective "systems" of cooperation were generally developed in the field—not by the institutions responsible for training, organizing, or equipping forces—because the need was so great. Perhaps the most compelling example of this development of closely integrated air-ground capabilities can be found in the experience of General Omar Bradley's 12th Army Group in Europe during World War II. A photograph of several of the ground and air com-

---

[10] U.S. War Department, FM 100-2, *Command and Employment of Air Power*, Washington, D.C.: U.S. Government Printing Office, 1943, p. 1. Capitalization in the original.

[11] U.S. War Department (1943), p. 2. Capitalization in the original.

manders responsible for this integration appears on the cover of this study. Their example is instructive:

> A postwar review of operations in the European theater asserted that the Army's failure to develop air-ground doctrine meant that means of cooperation had to be invented extemporaneously in the field. In the combat theaters, ground and air commanders were forced to create ad hoc procedures for tactical air power because their superiors provid ed no centralized direction. . . . The final after-action report of General Omar Bradley's 12th Army Group emphasized that "the air-armor team is a most powerful combination in the breakthrough and exploitation. . . . The use of this coordinated force, in combat, should be habitual." Thus, although air support of ground operations played an important role in the Allied drive into Germany and procedures were continually improved, the initiative came from below. In the combat zones, where Americans were dying, intraservice agendas were discarded and field expedients were devised to overcome institutional agendas.[12]

At the risk of oversimplification, it might be said that the Army fought tactical battles to the range of its organic artillery. The Air Force focused on strategic and interdiction efforts while providing tactical close air support (CAS) to ground forces. This bi-service approach to warfare is perhaps best illustrated in the performance of the Army and the Air Force in the Korean and Vietnam wars, during which the Army focused on closing with and destroying enemy forces, while the Air Force concentrated on strategic targets in the homeland of the enemy and sought to interdict forces and logistics beyond the influence of the Army.[13]

---

[12] Johnson (1998), p. 226; see 12th Army Group (1945), p. 61, for its report quote. World War II in Europe was perhaps the last time the United States fought an opponent of such competence that operational success depended on the integration of cross-service capabilities.

[13] Numerous sources assess the post–World War II Army and Air Force, but a few stand out. For an appreciation of service cultures, see Carl H. Builder, *The Masks of War: American Styles in Strategy and Analysis*, Baltimore, Md.: Johns Hopkins University Press, 1989. For the Army, see Russell F. Weigley, *The American Way of War: A History of United States*

In the aftermath of the Vietnam War, the focus of the U.S. military shifted to NATO and the defense of Western Europe from attack by the Warsaw Pact. For the Army, in particular, the change in focus was fundamental, as witnessed in the first edition of its *Operations* manual published after the Vietnam War:

> Battle in Central Europe against forces of the Warsaw Pact is the most demanding mission the US Army could be assigned. Because the US Army is structured primarily for that contingency and has large forces deployed in that area, this manual is designed mainly to deal with the realities of such operations. The principles set forth in this manual, however, apply also to military operations anywhere in the world.[14]

The Air Force also looked to Europe and kept "its eyes fixed . . . on grand strategic warfare against enemies with similar industrial and military institutions."[15] Thus, like the Army, the Air Force focused on preparing for war against the Soviet Union, confident that if it could meet this most difficult challenge, it could handle lesser opponents.

The post-Vietnam era also witnessed a period of Army–Air Force cooperation that was unprecedented and focused on dealing with the

*Military Strategy and Policy*, Bloomington, Ind.: Indiana University Press, 1977; Russell F. Weigley, *History of the United States Army*, Bloomington, Ind.: Indiana University Press, 1984; Jonathan M. House, *Combined Arms Warfare in the Twentieth Century: Modern War Studies*, Lawrence, Kan.: University Press of Kansas, 2001; John B. Wilson, *Maneuver and Firepower: The Evolution of Divisions and Separate Brigades*, Washington, D.C.: U.S. Army Center of Military History, 1998. For the Air Force, see the useful review essay, David R. Mets, "Bomber Barons, Bureaucrats, and Budgets: Your Professional Reading on the Theory and Doctrine of Strategic Air Attack," *Airpower Journal*, Summer 1996, pp. 76–93. See also Benjamin Franklin Cooling, ed., *Case Studies in the Development of Close Air Support*, Washington, D.C.: Office of Air Force History, 1990; William W. Momyer, *Airpower in Three Wars*, Maxwell Air Force Base: Air University Press, 1978; and Robert A. Pape, *Bombing to Win: Air Power and Coercion in War*, Ithaca, N.Y.: Cornell University Press, 1996.

[14] U.S. Department of the Army, FM 100-5, *Operations*, 1976, pp. 1–2.

[15] Earl H. Tilford, Jr., "Air Power in Vietnam: The Hubris of Power," in Lawrence E. Grinter and Peter M. Dunn, eds., *The American War in Vietnam: Lessons, Legacies, and Implications for Future Conflicts*, Seaport, Conn.: Greenwood, 1987, p. 81.

multi-echeloned threat that Warsaw Pact forces posed to NATO. Historian Harold R. Winton notes that, between 1973 and 1990,

> [t]he NATO defense mission gave each service a clear and *unifying* mission. The ability to defeat a Warsaw Pact invasion of Western Europe below the nuclear threshold was . . . the single most significant criterion of operational effectiveness for both services. When the Army and the Air Force looked at this challenge, each realized it needed the other. While it was true that the Army dependence on the Air Force was greater than vice versa, it could not be denied that to suppress hostile air defenses, the Air Force needed Army help. Furthermore, in order to make manifest its contribution to the national defense, the Air Force had to demonstrate its ability to destroy Soviet tanks as well as Soviet MiGs.[16]

Army and Air Force doctrines of the period reflected a new level of interservice collaboration, but this cooperation only went so far. The 1986 version of FM 100-5, *Operations*, was the ultimate expression of the Army's AirLand Battle concepts. The manual, as all post-Vietnam Army *Operations* manuals, focused on warfighting: "AirLand Battle doctrine focuses primarily on mid- to high-intensity warfare." Nevertheless, it was in keeping with the 1923 *Field Service Regulations*, since it implied that mastering the most difficult NATO case prepared the Army for any lesser-included cases, noting: "[T]he tenets of AirLand Battle apply equally to the military operations characteristic of low

---

[16] Harold R. Winton, "Partnership and Tension: The Army and the Air Force Between Vietnam and Desert Shield," *Parameters*, Spring 1996. Winton also notes: "The relative cohesion and strength of the Army–Air Force partnership from 1973 to 1990 can be attributed in rough priority to: the unifying effect of the NATO defense mission; the close cooperation of personalities at or near the top of each service; a leadership shift in the Air Force that put fighter rather than bomber pilots in the majority of influential positions; and the clarity of the Army's vision of how it intended to fight a future war that tended to pull the Air Force in its wake" (p. 11). Perhaps the best source for this period of Army–Air Force cooperation is Richard G. Davis, *The 31 Initiatives: A Study in Air Force–Army Cooperation*, Washington, D.C.: Office of Air Force History, 1987. See also Terrance J. McCaffrey III, *What Happened to BAI? Army and Air Force Battlefield Doctrine from Pre–Desert Storm to 2001*, thesis, School of Advanced Airpower Studies, Air University, 2002.

intensity war."[17] The 1986 manual also acknowledged the importance of strategic air attack "directed against the heartland" that would "normally produce direct effects on an enemy nation or alliance." Nevertheless, the preeminence of the enemy's ground forces was stressed, because the contribution of strategic air attacks

> may be delayed because of the inherent momentum of forces actively engaged in combat and those reserve forces ready to enter the action. Consequently, an air commander must exploit the devastating firepower of air power to disrupt that momentum and place an enemy's land forces at risk.[18]

The March 1984 version of Air Force Manual (AFM) 1-1, *Basic Aerospace Doctrine of the United States Air Force*, was the final doctrinal manual published by the Air Force before the end of the Cold War. The manual stressed that "since 1943, several fundamental beliefs have remained imbedded in Air Force doctrine":

> Airpower can exploit speed, range, and flexibility, better than land and seas [sic] forces, and therefore, it must be allowed to operate independently of these forces. These characteristics are most fully realized when air is controlled centrally but executed decentrally.[19]

The manual also noted the basic roles of ground and air power:

> The basic objective of **land** forces is to win the land battle—to gain and/or maintain control of vital territories. Land forces may neutralize, destroy or capture enemy land forces in this effort. To invade, occupy, or defend vital areas, our aerospace forces must render enemy aerospace power ineffective, which is a necessary step in ultimately eliminating the enemy's combat effectiveness on land.

---

[17] U.S. Department of the Army, FM 100-5, *Operations*, 1986, p. 6.

[18] U.S. Department of the Army, FM 100-5 (1986), p. 47.

[19] U.S. Department of the Air Force, AFM 1-1 (1984), p. A-6. Appendix A of this manual, "Evolution of Basic Doctrine," contains a concise and useful discussion of the development of U.S. Air Force doctrine.

The basic objective of **aerospace** forces is to win the aerospace battle—to gain and/or maintain control of the aerospace environment and to take decisive actions immediately and directly against an enemy's warfighting capacity. These actions include neutralizing or destroying the enemy's forces, his command and control mechanisms, and his sustaining warfighting capacity. As a critical element of the interdependent land-naval-aerospace team, aerospace power can be the decisive force in warfare.[20]

Thus, although both the Army and the Air Force recognized a degree of mutual interdependence, they both clung tenaciously to the institutional imperative that their service was decisive in winning wars. Interservice collaboration, however, began to unravel as the Cold War came to a close.

Winton is again useful in explaining the deterioration of the Army–Air Force relationship. He believes that the cooperative environment between the Army and the Air Force began to come apart for two reasons. First, as the Army continued to develop its AirLand Battle concepts, it focused on the operational level of war.[21] In so doing, the Army began to extend the depth of the battlespace it wanted to control to take advantage of the capabilities of the long-range weapons it was fielding. Winton explains the effects new Army capabilities, and

---

[20] U.S. Department of the Air Force, AFM 1-1 (1984), p. 1-3. Emphasis in the original. See also Glenn A. Kent and David A. Ochmanek, *Defining the Role of Airpower in Joint Missions*, Santa Monica, Calif.: RAND Corporation, MR-927-AF, 1998, p. 9, in which the authors note, "This formulation constrains air power to, at most, a subsidiary role in defeating enemy surface forces."

[21] See U.S. Department of the Army, FM 100-5, *Operations*, 1982, pp. 2–3. This manual promulgated AirLand Battle and defined the operational level of war:

> The operational level of war uses available military resources to attain strategic goals within a theater of war. Most simply, it is the theory of larger unit operations. It also involves planning and conducting campaigns. Campaigns are sustained operations designed to defeat an enemy force in a specified space and time with simultaneous and sequential battles. The disposition of forces, selection of objectives, and actions taken to weaken or to out maneuver the enemy all set the terms of the next battle and exploit tactical gains. They are all part of the operational level of war. In AirLand Battle doctrine, this level includes the marshalling of forces and logistical support, providing direction to ground and air maneuver, applying conventional and nuclear fires in depth, and employing unconventional and psychological warfare.

the emerging doctrines for their employment, had on Army–Air Force cooperation:

> [B]y developing extended-range systems that allowed the corps commander to fight the deep battle, the Army had raised the question of how the effects of these systems would be coordinated with air operations. The immediate focus of this issue was the placement of and procedures surrounding the fire support coordination line (FSCL). The FSCL, originally known as the no-bomb line, was developed during World War II as a coordination measure to reduce, if not eliminate, the chance that aircraft might drop ordnance on friendly troops. It was defined as a line short of which the release of air weapons required the prior clearance of a ground commander, and it applied primarily to aircrews returning from interdiction and armed reconnaissance missions with unexpended ordnance who wanted to be able to take advantage of targets of opportunity without endangering friendly ground forces. The FSCL was normally placed at the range limit of friendly artillery. As long as this range was in the neighborhood of 10–15 kilometers beyond the friendly front lines, this placement did not present much of a problem, because air strikes within that range would, perforce, be coordinated with ground forces. However, with the advent of the multiple-launch rocket system and later ATACMS [Army Tactical Missile System], the Army had weapons that could reach out to roughly 30 and 100 kilometers respectively. Additionally, the corps deep attack manual envisioned Apache helicopter attacks to a depth of 70–100 kilometers beyond the front lines. These newly developed capabilities placed the Army and the Air Force at loggerheads. If, on the one hand, the FSCL was pushed out to the depths of new Army weapons, it would significantly interfere with Air Force interdiction efforts and could potentially allow enemy forces to escape attack by friendly air formations. If, on the other hand, the FSCL was kept relatively close to the friendly front lines, the corps commander would lose freedom of action in the employment of his fire support assets if he was required to coordinate fires beyond

the FSCL with the Air Force prior to execution. This conundrum defied mutually satisfactory resolution.[22]

The second development Winton cites in the fraying of the Army–Air Force relationship in the late 1980s was the publication of Colonel John Warden's *The Air Campaign*. In this book, Colonel Warden focused on air power at the operational level, positing, "The air campaign may be the primary or supporting effort in a theater."[23] Warden's book "suggested an air power-centered approach to warfare that had perhaps not fully matured at the time of publication." Eventually, as a member of the Air Staff, Colonel Warden refined his ideas and developed a targeting construct that focused on targeting "in decreasing order of significance . . . leadership, organic essentials, infrastructure, population, and fielded forces." Thus, Warden served as a catalyst for the emerging view within the Air Force at the end of the Cold War that "the application of air power could, and perhaps even should, be thought of as being independent of ground operations."[24]

As the Cold War era drew to a close, and the unifying effect of the NATO defense mission ended, the Army and the Air Force had two areas of contention: "the amount of influence that senior ground commanders should have over Air Force interdiction operations, and the mechanisms for coordinating the effects of fixed-wing air and extended-range Army systems."[25] Both services, however, had operational doctrines that served as the basis for organizing, equipping, and training their own forces. These doctrines also provided a baseline against which lessons would be learned and incorporated into Army and Air Force doctrine in the aftermath of the various conflicts of the post–Cold War period.

---

[22] Winton (1996), p. 10.

[23] John A. Warden III, *The Air Campaign: Planning for Combat*, Washington, D.C.: National Defense University Press, 1988, p. 153.

[24] Winton (1996), p. 10.

[25] Winton (1996), p. 11. See also Davis (1987). The peacetime Army–Air Force cooperation in preparing to defend NATO seems to have been an anomaly. The normal state of the peacetime relationship is one in which "the services seem often to fall back on their broader agenda for preparation for future war" (p. v).

# CHAPTER THREE

# Iraq, 1991

## Background

Operation Desert Storm was the pivotal moment in reigniting the debate about the relative roles of ground and air power that had largely abated during the final years of the Cold War. As the *Gulf War Air Power Survey Summary Report* presciently noted, "Whether this remarkable outcome presages a new relationship between air forces and ground forces will, no doubt, be debated for years to come."[1]

On August 2, 1990, Iraqi forces invaded Kuwait and quickly overran the country. By August 6, the Iraqis were consolidating their gains and had more than 200,000 soldiers and some 2,000 tanks in Kuwait. Iraqi President Saddam Hussein declared the annexation of Kuwait as Iraq's 19th province on August 8. He also began massing forces along the Kuwaiti border with Saudi Arabia.[2]

The international community responded quickly. In a series of resolutions, the UN Security Council condemned the invasion, called for the unconditional withdrawal of Iraqi troops from Kuwait, and imposed sanctions and an embargo on Iraq.

The United States also acted. On August 2, President George H. W. Bush issued Executive Orders 12722 and 12723, declaring a national emergency, imposing trade sanctions on Iraq, and freezing

---

[1] Thomas A. Keaney and Eliot A. Cohen, *Gulf War Air Power Survey Summary Report*, U.S. Government Printing Office, 1993, p. 246.

[2] U.S. Department of Defense, *Conduct of the Persian Gulf War: Final Report to Congress*, U.S. Government Printing Office, 1992, pp. 3–4.

Iraqi and Kuwaiti assets. The Joint Staff and the U.S. Central Command (CENTCOM) began reviewing and revising war plans (Operational Plan 1002-90) and planning for the defense of Saudi Arabia. On August 3, U.S. Naval forces began deploying to Southwest Asia, and on August 4, General Norman Schwarzkopf, CENTCOM commander, and Lieutenant General Charles Horner, CENTCOM air component commander, presented a concept for the defense of Saudi Arabia to President Bush at Camp David.

On August 5, President Bush vowed that the Iraqi invasion of Kuwait "will not stand" and demanded a complete Iraqi withdrawal from Kuwait. This demand was central to a framework of U.S. objectives regarding the region in the aftermath of the Iraqi invasion, defined by August 6 as

- Immediate, unconditional, and complete withdrawal of all Iraqi forces from Kuwait;
- Restoration of Kuwait's legitimate government;
- Ensuring the stability and security of Saudi Arabia and the Persian Gulf; and
- Ensuring the safety and protection of the lives of American citizens abroad.[3]

On August 6, President Bush ordered that combat forces be deployed to the Gulf, and on August 7, Maritime Prepositioning Squadrons at Diego Garcia, a brigade from the 82nd Airborne Division, and U.S. Air Force fighters started deploying to Saudi Arabia. These forces began Operation Desert Shield in an effort to thicken the defense of Saudi Arabia, a process that continued until early October. In October, President Bush called for military options in the event sanctions would not convince Saddam to leave Kuwait.[4] The plan for what became Operation Desert Storm had several significant goals:

---

[3]   Anthony H. Cordesman and Abraham R. Wagner, *The Lessons of Modern War*, Vol. IV, *The Gulf War*, Boulder, Colo.: Westview Press, 1996, p. 53.

[4]   U.S. Department of Defense (1992), pp. 34–35, 65.

[T]o eject Iraq's forces from Kuwait. . . . to destroy Iraqi ability to threaten regional peace and stability. The coalition would accomplish this by attacking carefully selected targets, but leave most of the basic economic infrastructure of the country intact. Collectively, these actions would weaken Saddam Hussein's regime and set the stage for a stable regional military balance.[5]

These goals translated into six military objectives in the operations order for Desert Storm: Attack Iraqi political/military leadership and command and control; gain and maintain air superiority; sever Iraqi supply lines; destroy chemical, biological, and nuclear capability; destroy Republican Guard forces; and liberate Kuwait City.[6]

The plan for Operation Desert Storm envisioned accomplishing these military objectives in a four-phased campaign: Phase I—Strategic Air Campaign; Phase II—Air Supremacy in KTO (Kuwaiti Theater of Operations); Phase III—Battlefield Preparation; and Phase IV—Offensive Ground Campaign.[7]

Air power was a key to all four phases of the campaign, and focused on 12 target sets: strategic air defenses; chemical, nuclear, and biological facilities; leadership; command, control, and communications sites; electric power; oil facilities; railroads and bridges; airfields; naval ports and facilities; military support facilities; Scud [missile] facilities; and Republican Guards.[8] These target sets were selected to accomplish the following objectives:

- Gain and maintain air supremacy to permit unhindered air and ground operations.

---

[5] U.S. Department of Defense (1992), p. 74.

[6] Thomas A. Keaney and Eliot Cohen, *Revolution in Warfare? Air Power in the Persian Gulf*, Annapolis, Md.: Naval Institute Press, 1995, pp. 32–33.

[7] U.S. Department of Defense (1992), p. 74.

[8] Keaney and Cohen (1995), p. 35. See also pp. 22–44 for an interesting discussion of the evolution of the air campaign, including the contribution of Colonel John Warden and Checkmate to the overall plan. See also Richard T. Reynolds, *Heart of the Storm: The Genesis of the Air Campaign Against Iraq*, Maxwell Air Force Base, Ala.: Air University Press, 1995, particularly on how Warden's strategic air campaign, "Instant Thunder," plan was incorporated into the actual air campaign by General Horner.

- Isolate and incapacitate the Iraqi regime.
- Destroy Iraq's known NBC warfare capability.
- Eliminate Iraq's offensive military capability by destroying key military production, infrastructure, and power capabilities.
- Render the Iraqi army and its mechanized equipment in Kuwait ineffective, causing its collapse.[9]

Additionally, for the first time in U.S. warfighting history, a joint force air component commander (JFACC), Lieutenant General Horner, was designated and responsible for "planning, coordination, allocation, and tasking of apportioned sorties and capabilities" for the combatant commander.[10]

The air campaign began on January 17, 1991. By that time, coalition air forces "comprised more than one thousand fixed-wing attack aircraft and another eight hundred air defense fighters and electronic combat aircraft to prosecute the air campaign."[11] The first three phases of the campaign plan continued until Phase IV, the offensive ground campaign, began on February 24, 2001. The ground campaign

> envisioned a supporting attack along the Kuwait–Saudi Arabia border by the I Marine Expeditionary Force (I MEF) and Arab Coalition Forces . . . to hold most forward Iraqi divisions in place. Simultaneously, two Army corps, augmented with French and United Kingdom (UK) divisions—more than 200,000 soldiers—would sweep west of the Iraqi defenses, strike deep into Iraq, cut Iraqi lines of communication (LOC) and destroy the Republican Guards forces in the KTO.[12]

Within 100 hours of the inception of ground operations, the war was over.

---

[9] U.S. Department of Defense (1992), p. 75.

[10] U.S. Department of Defense (1992), p. 179.

[11] Keaney and Cohen (1995), p. 43.

[12] U.S. Department of Defense (1992), p. 227.

## Lessons: The Ground-Centric View

The Army's official history of the war—*Certain Victory: The U.S. Army in the Gulf War*—captures in several sentences the ground perspective on "lessons learned":

> Iraq's operational center of gravity, the Republican Guard, and to a lesser extent, the heavy divisions of the regular army, remained a viable fighting force in spite of significant physical damage caused by air attack because their will to fight was not broken. Only by vanquishing an enemy and displacing him on the ground can a military force break the enemy's will and ensure ultimate victory.

Given this "truth," the report went on to note the principal lesson of the war: "**Maintaining an immediately deployable capability for decisive land combat to end a conventional conflict successfully is the single most enduring imperative of the Gulf War.**"[13] Summing up, Certain Victory stressed that this "was a lesson that has been repeated with unbroken fidelity through all of America's wars" and then closed with a quote that frequently finds its way into Army doctrinal publications, from T. R. Fehrenbach's *This Kind of War: A Study in Unpreparedness*:

> You may fly over a land forever; you may bomb it, atomize it, pulverize it, and wipe it clean of life—but if you desire to defend it, protect it, and keep it for civilization, you must do this on the ground, the way the Roman legions did, by putting your young men into the mud.[14]

---

[13] Robert H. Scales, Terry L. Johnson, and Thomas P. Odom, *Certain Victory: The US Army in the Gulf War*, Washington, D.C.: Office of the Chief of Staff, United States Army, 1993, pp. 359–360. Emphasis in the original.

[14] Scales, Johnson, and Odom (1993), p. 360. The Fehrenbach quote shows up frequently in Army discussions of the immutability of the value of land power. A recent example is in the current FM 3-0, *Operations* (2001), pp. 1–2.

To underscore this point, *Certain Victory* stressed that "Desert Storm confirmed that the nature of war has not changed. At its heart is control of resources, people, and territory, and the strategic core of joint warfare is ultimately decisive land combat."[15] Clearly, from this perspective, ground power was the supported force, albeit supported in unprecedented fashion by air power. As one postwar assessment noted, "The Gulf War confirmed the Air Force's ever-increasing ability to destroy military things and people. But air power had not demonstrated an ability to change governments."[16] A retrospective assessment by General Barry McCaffrey, an Army division commander during the war, captures the ground-centric perspective quite eloquently:

> During one hundred hours of ground combat, preceded by the most stunning air campaign in history, seven Army and two Marine combat divisions in concert with coalition ground forces turned the fourth-largest army in the world into the second-largest army inside Iraq. This allied force used maneuver, deception, speed, and carefully targeted violence, which not only achieved its military objectives and cut short what could have become a protracted struggle . . . . This victory was possible because of a revolution in military affairs that was largely unseen by the American people until the lopsided victory in the Persian Gulf revealed its dimensions and power.[17]

## Lessons: The Air-Centric View

An article by James A. Mowbray, an Air War College professor, succinctly captures the air-centric perspective on the Gulf War:

> The Gulf War brought to the fore the technology, tactics, techniques, and operational methods on which the Air Force had

---

[15] Scales, Johnson, and Odom (1993), p. 388.

[16] Michael R. Gordon and Bernard E. Trainor, *The Generals' War: The Inside Story of the Conflict in the Gulf*, Boston: Little, Brown and Company, 1995, p. 474.

[17] Barry R. McCaffrey, "Lessons of Desert Storm," *Joint Force Quarterly*, Winter 2000–2001, p 13.

been working since the Vietnam War. Precision guided munitions, precision navigation systems like the global positioning
system (GPS), and day-night all-weather operations allowed the
Air Force to fly, fight, and win in the face of the worst weather in
the Middle East in more than a decade. That technology helped
to win the fastest, lowest casualty, most devastatingly destructive one-sided war in recorded history. Air Force capabilities had
come of age.[18]

Others, however, were more pointed in their view of the contribution of air power to victory in the Gulf. Air Force Chief of Staff General Merrill A. McPeak claimed that "This is the first time in history
that a field army has been defeated by air power."[19] Similarly, the Air
Force historian, Richard P. Hallion, echoed McPeak's view, writing:

Today, air power is the dominant form of military power. Does
this mean that all future wars will be won solely by air power?
Not at all. But what it does mean is that air power has clearly
proven its ability not merely to be *decisive* in war—after all, it
had demonstrated decisiveness in the Second World War and, to
a degree, as early as the First World War—but to be the *determi-
nant of victory* in war.[20]

## Areas of Ground-Air Tension

### Who Won the War?

Areas of ground-air tension over the lessons of the Gulf War were inevitable, given the polarity of the views of the two camps. The principal

---

[18] James A. Mowbray, "Air Force Doctrine Problems 1926–Present," *Airpower Journal*,
Winter 1995.

[19] Mark Clodfelter, "Of Demons, Storms, and Thunder: A Preliminary Look at Vietnam's
Impact on the Persian Gulf Air Campaign," *Airpower Journal*, Winter 1991, p. 17, quoted
in James A. Winnefield, Preston Niblack, and Dana J. Johnson, *A League of Airmen: U.S.
Air Power in the Gulf War*, Santa Monica, Calif.: RAND Corporation, MR-343-A, 1994,
p. 277.

[20] Richard P. Hallion, *Storm Over Iraq: Air Power and the Gulf War*, Washington, D.C.:
Smithsonian Institution Press, 1992, p. 264. Emphasis in the original.

issue was the role of ground versus air power in a war. Ground power advocates, as noted earlier, were adamant that "boots on the ground" were the decisive factor; air power was a supporting, albeit important, capability subordinate to the decisive ground campaign. Again, *Certain Victory* is instructive. Although acknowledging the contribution of air power to the victory—"coalition air forces so dominated the air that enemy ground forces were largely prohibited from maneuvering and only dared to reposition at night or in bad weather"—the book cites the war-winning element to be ground power:

> Yet the air operation, even though it lasted 41 days, failed to break the will of the Republican Guard, to stop it from responding to the Great Wheel, or to prevent it from retiring some of its elements to safety. . . . [A] first-rate unit with high morale and good leadership can reconstitute its fighting strength if the destruction occurs gradually through attrition rather than suddenly through decisive, unrelenting close-in combat.[21]

The 1995 Army posture statement continued to echo this refrain:

> Wars are won on the ground. Success or failure of the land battle typically equates to national success or failure. The culminating or decisive action of a war is most often conducted by land forces. . . . The application of military force on land is an action an adversary cannot ignore; it forces decision.[22]

If the Army's assertions were correct, then it logically followed that "the most legitimate role for air power is in support of land warfare."[23]

Air power advocates were essentially of two minds before, during, and after the Gulf War. General Charles G. Boyd noted this intra–Air Force tension:

---

[21] Scales, Johnson, and Odom (1993), p. 368.

[22] U.S. Department of the Army, *A Statement on the Posture of the United States Army:Fiscal Year 1996*, 1995, pp. 26–27, quoted in Richard P. Hallion, "Airpower and the Changing Nature of Warfare," *Joint Force Quarterly*, Autumn/Winter 1997–1998, p. 42.

[23] Hallion (1997–1998), p. 42.

Airmen, long uneasy about the lingering inconclusiveness of past applications of their form of military power, now had what they believed to be an example of air power decisiveness so indisputably successful as to close the case forever.

Within the United States Air Force, among those who thought about the uses of air power, there were two basic groups of airmen. The first—smaller and less influential—held to the views of early air pioneers in their belief that air power was best applied in a comprehensive, unitary way to achieve strategic results. The second—much more dominant—had come to think of air power in its tactical applications as a supportive element of a larger surface (land or maritime) campaign.

Thinking in terms of strategic air campaigns, members of the first group found their inclinations reinforced by Col John Warden's book, *The Air Campaign: Planning for Combat*, published in 1988. Over the years, the second group increasingly concentrated on refining specific mission capabilities (close air support, interdiction, air refueling, etc.) that could be offered to a joint force commander for his allocation decisions. Members of this group rarely thought in terms of comprehensive air campaigns to achieve strategic objectives. . . . Both groups found agreement in their love of the airplane and their search for acceptance as equal partners with their older sister services.

General Boyd continued to note that there was "a hot and often bitter debate . . . within the Air Force on the eve of Operation Desert Storm over the very issue of the strategic air campaign and the question of whether air power would be used in that form." He stakes out his own position—one that would become increasingly influential in the Air Force:

> In the end, of course, the Gulf War did in fact include a strategic air campaign, and the very least that one could say about it was that by so thoroughly destroying the Iraqis' capability to wage warfare, it permitted a relatively bloodless war-concluding ground operation by coalition army forces. The most one could

say about the air campaign was that it—in and of itself—won the war.[24]

Thus, the post–Desert Storm internal Air Force debate had two major groups. One group believed that concentrating air attacks on the enemy's "strategic centers of gravity" (e.g., leadership, command and control, and economic infrastructure) would induce "paralysis" in the enemy state and render its military forces impotent and irrelevant. A second group believed that, while attacks on targets such as these could be useful in disrupting the enemy and, perhaps, providing some coercive leverage, air power had to contribute directly to defeating the enemy's fielded forces as part of a joint campaign. The first group was the minority element and was overruled in the conduct of the actual air campaign during Desert Storm, yet emerged as the more influential group within the Air Force in the war's aftermath.

This fundamental dispute about the relative roles of ground and air power was more than a mere theoretical argument. In the aftermath of the Gulf War, the U.S. armed forces continued their massive post–Cold War downsizing. The issue of the relative contributions of ground and air power to the victory in the Gulf War was one fraught with institutional consequences for the budget wars that would begin after the war. A report by the House Armed Services Committee was explicit in this regard:

> Operation *Desert Storm* will now be the yardstick against which the most significant military hardware and policy questions for the future will be measured. The instinctive question will no longer be "What did the failures of Vietnam teach us about this or that?" but rather "How well did we do against Iraq with this technology or with that doctrine?"[25]

---

[24] The quotes are from General Boyd's foreword in Reynolds (1995), pp. xi–xii. For a discussion of the various viewpoints on the role of air power in the Gulf War, see Winnefeld, Niblack, and Johnson (1994), pp. 259–288.

[25] Les Aspin and William L. Dickinson, *Defense for a New Era: Lessons of the Persian Gulf War*, Washington, D.C.: U.S. Government Printing Office, 1992, pp. 5–6.

General Boyd foresaw the coming budget wars, noting his concern that "air power's effect on the outcome of the war would become increasingly controversial as non–Air Force institutions realized that their own resources would likely diminish if airmen's conclusions were accepted."[26]

Thus, the conditions were set for future wars to be assessed by institutionally motivated judgments about the relative decisiveness of ground or air power in their resolution. Nevertheless, the bar was higher for air power advocates at the close of the war, because of the "traditions dating across millennia emphasizing that victory can only come on the battlefield."[27] Furthermore, there was concern about "The danger that air power advocates will oversell in the Washington arena its major accomplishments, and that its detractors will undersell it . . . for their own doctrinal or other reasons grounded in vested interests." The authors of this statement went on to quote Mark Clodfelter from an article in which he observed that "we must avoid creating a new spectre that judges success or failure in future wars according to whether or not the Air Force was the most decisive factor."[28] As we shall see later, Clodfelter's argument would go largely unheeded by both ground and air power advocates.

In the end, the arguments about the relative roles of ground and air power are important largely for how they polarized the perspectives of both camps. In the aftermath of the war, the Army and the Air Force would look inward, while joint doctrine would largely continue to be an amalgamation of service perspectives, with, as will be shown later, something of a ground emphasis. Thus, the reality of what happened has often been "spun" for bureaucratic, rather than "learning," purposes.

Still, it is important to note that a middle ground exists that is probably closer to reality in explaining the outcome of the war than that proffered by either the ground or air advocates. One such early

---

[26] Reynolds (1995), p. xii.

[27] Hallion (1997–1998), p. 42.

[28] See Winnefeld, Niblack, and Johnson (1994), pp. 287–288. The Clodfelter quote is from Clodfelter (1991), p. 31.

appraisal was in the 1993 book *Desert Storm: The Gulf War and What We Learned*. This volume's authors wrote that

> Even if it is not true, as USAF general Merrill McPeak suggested, that the air campaign against Iraq was the first time in history that a field army was defeated by air power, it is widely agreed that in this case it created the conditions for a rapid, low-casualty ground phase.[29]

In 1996, the Air Force Chief of Staff, General Ronald R. Fogleman, seemed to echo this view:

> Airpower is a strategic force in that it offers the opportunity to defeat an enemy's strategy—some times [sic] directly but most often in concert with other forces.
>
> In Desert Storm, we hit hard, smart, and deep; and we put few people at risk. We had a theater commander in chief in Gen H. Norman Schwarzkopf, who understood the asymmetrical application of power. Airpower decisively changed the military balance and enabled the coalition to close with Iraqi land forces after gaining tremendous advantages over them.[30]

A decade after the war, Benjamin S. Lambeth offered this similarly dispassionate appraisal:

> Desert Storm confirmed what high-tech weapons, coupled with competent leadership and good training, can do against less-endowed forces. Yet ultimately the war was not about systems or technology, although some weapons and combat support systems were star performers. It was more about consensus building and the formulation of national goals, diplomacy and leadership in pursuit of those goals, and planning and coordinated action by professionals in employing military power, notably air power, to

---

[29] Michael J. Mazarr, Don M. Snider, and James A. Blackwell, Jr., *Desert Storm: The Gulf War and What We Learned*, Boulder, Colo.: Westview Press, 1993, p. 124.

[30] Ronald R. Fogleman, "Aerospace Doctrine: More Than Just a Theory," *Airpower Journal*, Summer 1996, p. 45.

achieve them once negotiations and economic sanctions failed. Insofar as Desert Storm heralded a revolution in the American way of war, it was the fusion of all these ingredients in a winning combination.[31]

Stephen Hosmer, however, provided one of the most comprehensive assessments of the effect the air campaign had on the success of the ground campaign during the 1991 Gulf War:

In addition to maintaining air supremacy over the KTO, reducing Iraqi armor and artillery inventories in the KTO, softening the breach areas, restricting Iraqi supply, and most important, reducing the size of the Iraqi force opposing the Coalition,[32] the air campaign

---

[31] Benjamin S. Lambeth, "Storm Over the Desert: A New Assessment," *Joint Force Quarterly*, Winter 2000–2001, p. 34. See also Cordesman and Wagner (1996), p. 945. Cordesman and Wagner provide the following assessment:

*Focused and effective interdiction bombing*: While the Coalition strategic bombing effort had limitations, most aspects of offensive air power were highly successful. The interdiction effort was successful in most respects. The Coalition organized effectively to use its deep-strike capabilities to carry out a rapid and effective pattern of focused strategic bombing where planning was sufficiently well coupled to intelligence and meaningful strategic objectives so that such strikes achieved the major military objectives that the planners set. At the same time, targeting, force allocation, and precision-kill capabilities had advanced to the point where interdiction bombing and strikes were far more lethal and strategically useful than in previous conflicts.

*Expansion of the battlefield—"Deep Strike"*: As part of its effort to offset the Warsaw Pact's superiority, US tactics and technology emphasized using AirLand battle capabilities to extend the battlefield far beyond the immediate forward edge of the battle area. The Coalition exploited the resulting mix of targeting capabilities, improved air strike capabilities, and land force capabilities in ways that played an important role in attriting Iraqi ground forces during the air phase of the war, and which helped the Coalition break through Iraqi defenses and exploit the breakthrough. This achievement is particularly striking in view of the fact that the US was not yet ready to employ some "deep strike" targeting technologies and precision-strike systems designed to fight the Warsaw Pact that were still in development.

[32] For the level attrition desired and achieved against Iraqi forces, see Diane T. Putney, *Airpower Advantage: Planning the Gulf War Air Campaign, 1989–1991*, Washington, D.C.: Air Force History and Museums Program, 2004, pp. 356, 362. Putney notes, "The CINC-CENT's directions to achieve the 50 percent attrition against the Republican Guard and then against the regular army units drove the wartime targeting process" (p. 356). Furthermore, this directive was largely achieved: "Schwarzkopf's color-coded charts showed almost all Iraqi frontline divisions at less than 50 percent effectiveness, while the rear divisions, including the Republican Guard, were above the 75 percent level. Even though the

- denied the Iraqis the use of their own offensive and defensive air
- deterred Iraqi aerial battlefield surveillance, reconnaissance; deterred Iraqi signal intelligence (SIGINT)
- degraded Iraqi battlefield $C^3$ [command, control, and communications], particularly at the brigade and battalion level
- provided close air support to Coalition ground forces
- interdicted maneuvering, deployed, and withdrawing Iraqi armored forces.

The weakened Iraqi opposition to the Coalition ground campaign attested to the success of the air campaign. As a result of poor Iraqi motivation and morale, the ground campaign encountered the following battlefield situation:

- light opposition from Iraqi frontline units in breach areas
- limited opposition from Iraqi rear area units
- the surrender of some Republican Guard and other heavy division units without a fight
- the nonengagement of many Iraqi units in the fighting
- the abandonment of much Iraqi equipment
- low Coalition personnel and materiel losses
- high surrenders and low casualties on the Iraqi side.[33]

### Lesser-Included Tensions

Aside from the "who won the war" question centering on the relative contributions of ground and air power, several other areas of contention arose during the Gulf War that would surface again in future conflicts. Two merit further elaboration in a discussion of lessons learned: the role of the JFACC and control of the operational battlespace.

**The Joint Force Air Component Commander.** As already noted, the Gulf War marked the first operational employment of a JFACC. As

---

50-percent goal had not been consistently achieved, the ground war was launched the next day" (p. 362).

[33] Stephen T. Hosmer, *Effects of the Coalition Air Campaign Against Iraqi Ground Forces in the Gulf War*, Santa Monica, Calif.: RAND Corporation, MR-305/1-AF, 2002, pp. xvii–xviii.

JFACC, Lieutenant General Charles Horner was responsible for running the air war, including "planning, coordinating, allocating, and assigning personnel to theater air operations derived from General Schwarzkopf's apportionment decisions."[34] General Horner "exercised his authority through the air tasking order (ATO), which provided detailed directions—with some exceptions—for all Coalition flight operations."[35]

The ATO supported an air campaign that was, in the view of many Army, Navy, and Marine Corps officers, an Air Force–dominated process that reflected Air Force conceptions about the appropriate use of air power.[36] The air planners designed an air campaign that reflected their doctrine of "centralized control of air power and attacks against targets critical to the overall campaign."[37] The other U.S. service components did not believe that the system run by General Horner addressed all of their requirements and believed that it forced "Air Force approaches" on them.[38] Army and Marine Corps commanders complained that the ATO process was cumbersome and unresponsive. As well, the targets they wanted to hit were being ignored because they fell outside the ATO targets picked by the Air Force and were designed for "weakening the enemy at home and within 'kill boxes' it drew on battlefield maps."[39]

Again, this tension over the ATO process reflects fundamental differences between ground power and air power warfighting perspectives. From the perspective of the Air Force, the JFACC system "reflected its ethos," in that "air power would function as an independent combat arm that could be massed for attacks anywhere in the theater." In short, "Each service could 'nominate' targets, but Lt. Gen.

---

[34] Keaney and Cohen (1995), pp. 4–5.

[35] Keaney and Cohen (1995), p. 5. Keaney and Cohen also note that "[h]elicopters flying at less than five hundred feet above the ground were exempted from direct JFACC control, as were naval aircraft on overwater flights" (p. 5).

[36] Gordon and Trainor (1995), p. 472.

[37] Gordon and Trainor (1995), p. 472.

[38] Aspin and Dickinson (1992), p. 9.

[39] Gordon and Trainor (1995), p. 472.

Charles Horner and his fellow Air Force planners would be the men who would decide what, when, and how they would be hit."[40] The Army view, reflective of AirLand Battle doctrine and deep attack, was different:

> For the Army, the JFACC system was a beast to be tamed. New technology had expanded the Army corps commanders' capabilities to look deep into the battlefield and identify enemy targets, and an Army corps commander was not concerned with the entire theater. He looked at the battlefield like a giant bowling alley. To move down the lane, the corps needed to sweep the obstacles from its path, starting with those directly in front of it and then those a day or two away. For the corps commanders, air power was a form of flying artillery and should be on call immediately to support their attack.[41]

Despite these disputes, the "sheer abundance of assets such as aircraft, airfields, and tankers allowed the air campaign generally to accommodate all service points of view on the priorities of the air war." Nevertheless, the deputy commander in chief, Lieutenant General Calvin Waller, had to "step in and arbitrate" the disputes "among the Army, Marines, and Air Force over how best to prepare the battlefield."[42]

Notwithstanding the interservice bickering during and after Operation Desert Storm about the role of the JFACC and the ATO, it is

---

[40] Gordon and Trainor (1995), p. 310.

[41] Gordon and Trainor (1995), pp. 310–311. The authors go on to note that "[f]or the Marines, the JFACC system was first and foremost a drain on their resources. The Marines did not have heavy ground forces, but unlike the Army, they had their own air wing to make up the difference. Warplanes were an integral part of Marine Corps combat power, no different from artillery and tanks. They were all organized and trained to operate as parts of the whole." (p. 311).

See also Aspin and Dickinson (1992), p. 10, which notes that the Marines reacted to the ATO initially by "routinely and systematically diverting sorties from their preplanned [ATO] targets to 'more urgent' targets or stuffed the ATO with 'dummy' sorties to put extra aircraft in the air." Increasingly, as time went on, the Marines withheld more and more of their aircraft from the JFACC "pool of assets," and by the time the ground campaign commenced, they had taken back almost all of their aircraft.

[42] Aspin and Dickinson (1992), p. 12.

clear that General Schwarzkopf was comfortable with General Horner and the process and that Schwarzkopf, as the overall combatant commander for the theater, determined the overall apportionment of the air effort. An example of a meeting between General Schwarzkopf and his ground and air component commanders is instructive.

> A few days before the ground war commenced in February 1991 . . . he [General Schwarzkopf] met with his subordinate commanders to discuss the land offensive. General Horner explained his Push CAS modus of flowing airplanes to the battlefield twenty-four hours a day (rather than keeping them idle while sitting alert). When General [Frederick] Franks ignored what Horner had said and demanded that VII Corps be allotted hundreds of CAS sorties per day (whether needed or not), the airman angrily disputed the allocation of air power in that manner and reiterated his Push CAS procedures. Horner believed it important for unity of command to let his anger show as he vehemently rejected Franks's claim for so much unfocused air power. He remembered his outburst having no effect: "Everyone looked at me and said, 'Well, he fell on his sword; isn't that quaint.'" General [Walt] Boomer jumped in and requested as many dedicated sorties for his Marines, and General [Gary] Luck joined the "run on the bank" and demanded as many CAS flights for his XVIII Corps. The ground commanders argued for *their* sorties, but after a while Schwarzkopf called a halt to the debate, reminding all present, "You people don't understand. It's *all my air*, and I'll use it any way I please." "That ended the argument," Horner recalled, "and we maintained centralized command." The CINCCENT [commander in chief of Central Command] depended upon his JFACC to ensure that all the ground commanders received adequate air support.[43]

**Who Owns the Battlespace?** The tension between ground and air officers was largely about who would have authority over the theater battlespace. This tension was perhaps most apparent in the authorities vested in a specific fire support coordinating measure—the fire support

---

[43] Putney (2004), pp. 346–347. Emphasis in the original.

coordination line. In Army doctrine, the FSCL is a "permissive fire support coordinating measure" because it is employed "to facilitate the attack of targets."[44] The doctrine also notes the purpose of the FSCL: "to allow the corps and its subordinate and supporting units *(such as the Air Force)* to expeditiously attack targets of opportunity beyond the FSCL."[45] The manual goes on to note that the corps commander has the authority to establish FSCLs and that the "primary consideration for placement of an FSCL is that it should be located beyond the area in which the corps intends to shape its deep operations fight."[46] Targets short of the FSCL within a corps area required coordination with ground components. Attacking targets past the FSCL, however, imposed less restrictive requirements on the ground component, with FM 6-20-30 noting that "the attack of targets of opportunity beyond the FSCL by Army assets *should be coordinated with supporting tactical air . . .* defined as informing and/or consulting with the supporting tactical air component."[47] Nevertheless, "the inability to effect this coordination does not preclude attack of targets beyond the FSCL."[48]

---

[44] U.S. Department of the Army, "Annex F—Fire Support Coordinating Measures," in FM 6-20-30, *Tactics, Techniques, and Procedures for Fire Support for Corps and Division Operations*, October 18, 1989, p. F-2.

[45] U.S. Department of the Army, FM 6-20-30 (1989), p. F-3. Emphasis added.

[46] U.S. Department of the Army, FM 6-20-30 (1989), p. F-3. Terms and definitions continually evolve in U.S. military doctrine and concepts. Throughout this study, various terms appear—deep operations, deep strike operations, shaping operations, etc.—to describe the use of fires beyond the range of the indirect fire systems organic to U.S. Army divisions (and brigade combat teams). The purpose is not to advocate or debate specific terms and definitions but, rather, to assess which systems and capabilities are most effective in providing fires and effects for the overall joint force effort throughout a theater of operations.

[47] U.S. Department of the Army, FM 6-20-30 (1989), p. F-3. Emphasis added.

[48] U.S. Department of the Army, FM 6-20-30 (1989), p. F-3. See also Keaney and Cohen (1995), in which the authors point out that this issue of coordination played out differently in the Gulf War:

> The corps commanders were dismayed to find that until they launched their offensive, Schwarzkopf would not permit them to move the FSCL beyond the Saudi border. Since the JFACC had the principal responsibility for preparing the battlefield, the corps commanders were not given the air control they had come to expect during the years of preparing for a potential war in Europe with the Warsaw Pact. But visions of that war had never included an enemy army that would sit for weeks while bombing fatally weakened it. (p. 134)

For the Army, the FSCL facilitated control of its area of operations and the use of its organic weapons to execute deep battle. For the Air Force, the FSCL, placed deep in a corps area of operation, was a barrier to attacking targets short of the FSCL that the Army could not attack effectively. Additionally, the fact that the Army viewed the FSCL as a permissive fire support coordinating measure—that is, it could employ its weapons beyond the FSCL without coordination—ignored the fact that the FSCL restricted the employment of air power. Absent coordination or restrictive measures (e.g., airspace coordination areas or no-fire areas) to ensure that aircraft would not be flying into Army weapons effects, Air Force pilots could not operate freely beyond the FSCL. Thomas A. Keaney and Eliot A. Cohen explain this dichotomy in their book *Revolution in Warfare? Air Power in the Persian Gulf*:

> Ground forces used the FSCL to integrate fire support with their movement and to protect their troops from fratricide by "friendly" air attack. In the area between Coalition ground forces and the FSCL, Coalition aircraft could attack only under direction from ground or airborne controllers. This procedure could cost time to coordinate the actions and required suitable weather conditions and the presence of a controller to execute the attacks: far less weight of fixed-wing air power could be brought to bear under such circumstances. . . .
>
> Because the FSCL definition said little about coordination of weapons employment beyond the FSCL the corps commanders considered supporting fires beyond the line as "permissive," requiring no further coordination. That is, they resisted any restrictions on employing missiles or helicopters beyond the line and saw attempts to include such strikes in the ATO as efforts to put their organic firepower under JFACC control.[49]

To preserve its control of the battlespace during the ground campaign, the Army moved the FSCL far forward to facilitate the use of attack helicopters and prosecute the ground deep battle, but this made

---

[49] Keaney and Cohen (1995), pp. 133–134.

it difficult to employ air power against fleeing Iraqi forces.[50] A postwar study reflected the Army perspective: "Since the Air Force position was that anything beyond the FSCL was interdiction, and, interdiction was the domain of the JFACC, ground commanders were hampered from setting the conditions for the attack." Consequently, in the words of one ground officer,

> [b]ecause the Air Force absolutely would not fly short of the FSCL before G-Day, we kept the FSCL in close to facilitate air attack of division and corps high priority targets. This caused two problems. Every [artillery] fire mission or AH-64 [attack helicopter] attack beyond the FSCL had to be carefully and painstakingly cleared with the Air Force. Even counterfire required this lengthy process. Equally bad, air sorties beyond the FSCL were completely the domain of the Air Force. VII Corps could nominate targets beyond the FSCL, but could never be sure they would be attacked.[51]

This issue of controlling the battlespace, epitomized by the FSCL controversy in the Gulf War, would still not be resolved when U.S. armed forces returned to the region to fight Operation Iraqi Freedom in 2003. At stake was which service would ultimately have the lead on destroying the enemy at the operational level of war—a fundamental question in deciding the relative roles of ground and air power in American warfighting practice.

## The Institutionalization of "Lessons" from the Gulf War

The Gulf War was a seminal experience for the U.S. armed forces. The war, coming as it did near the collapse of the Soviet Union and the

---

[50]  Keaney and Cohen (1995), p. 134; Gordon and Trainor (1995), p. 472.

[51]  David H. Zook, *The Fire Support Coordination Line: Is It Time to Reconsider Our Doctrine?* thesis, Fort Leavenworth, Kan.: U.S. Army Command and General Staff College, 1992, quoted in Dwayne P. Hall, *Integrating Joint Operations Beyond the FSCL: Is Current Doctrine Adequate?* Maxwell Air Force Base, Ala.: Air University, Air War College, April 1997, p. 20.

intellectual framework that the Cold War provided for U.S. warfighting strategy, was the first font of "lessons" for the way forward in a post–Cold War world. Indeed, one author opined, "To varying extents, each service's vision of the future is based on conducting DESERT STORM faster and better."[52] Another author was more direct. Lieutenant Colonel Gordon M. Wells, U.S. Army, writing in the *Joint Force Quarterly*, believed that joint doctrine for command and control of deep operations was inadequate and that the ongoing interservice debate, based largely on "budget battles," was adversely affecting future joint capabilities. In Wells's view, "there are many doctrinal advocates firmly convinced of their views. As with any believers, they hold many opinions based on seemingly undeniable elements of truth." Wells went on to describe the post–Gulf War tensions between the Army and the Air Force. He noted that the Army believed that the JFACC "during Desert Storm and the Air Force as a whole reneged on prior agreements on battlefield air interdiction sortie allocation." Consequently, "the Army position has typically oriented on greater control of air sorties to shape the battlefield." According to Wells, the Air Force believed that air power required central planning "to ensure the use of available air power does not revert to a Vietnam–Tactical Air Command view when it was seen as little more than aerial artillery in support of the Army."[53]

The National Military Strategy evolved into one focused on two major regional contingencies and resulted essentially in a downsized military based on the doctrines and weapons of the Cold War. Indeed, the traditional paradigm of preparing for the worst case was embraced in the Chairman of the Joint Chiefs of Staff's *Joint Vision 2010*:

> Our forces have been largely organized, trained, and equipped to defeat military forces of our potential adversaries. Direct combat against an enemy's armed forces is the most demanding and complex set of requirements we have faced. Other operations from

---

[52] Earl H. Tilford, Jr., *Halt Phase Strategy: New Wine in Old Skins . . . With Powerpoint*, Carlisle, Pa.: Strategic Studies Institute, U.S. Army War College, 1998, p. 30.

[53] Gordon M. Wells, "Deep Operations, Command and Control, and Joint Doctrine: Time for a Change?" *Joint Force Quarterly*, Winter 1996–1997, pp. 102–103.

humanitarian assistance in peacetime through peace operations in a near hostile environment, have proved to be possible using forces optimized for wartime effectiveness.[54]

This narrow focus on winning the fight persisted, but, as Gordon Brown, General Schwarzkopf's foreign policy advisor, recalled, "We never did have a plan to terminate the war."[55] The Gulf War was also typical of past American wars in that there was an air campaign and a ground war.[56]

In the aftermath of the war, the services, although nodding in the direction of jointness, largely looked at the lessons of the war from individual perspectives. And the stakes were high. With the conclusion of the war, the implementation of the Base Force, and its attendant reductions in structure and resources, the so-called peace dividend, went into high gear. Furthermore, a small, but significant, shift occurred in the allocation of budget share: "the Army share of DoD budget authority fell from 26.8 percent in 1990 to 24.3 percent in 1993 . . .

---

[54] Chairman of the Joint Chiefs of Staff, *Joint Vision 2010*, U.S. Joint Chiefs of Staff, 1996, p. 17.

[55] Gordon and Trainor (1995), p. 461. See also Bobby R. Inman, Joseph S. Nye, and Roger K. Smith, "Lessons from the Gulf War," *The Washington Quarterly*, Winter 1992, p. 70, in which the authors note: "Whatever the success of the campaign, there has been far less evidence of careful preparation for war termination. The first lesson after the shooting stopped was that there was considerable ambiguity about objectives." As well, see Eliot A. Cohen, *Supreme Command: Soldiers, Statesmen, and Leadership in Wartime*, New York: The Free Press, 2002, pp. 189–198, for a critique of the failure to adequately plan for war termination. Cohen writes:

> The tale of the Gulf war and its aftermath is not one of usurpation of strategic control by the military but rather, in large part, one of abdication of authority by the civilian leadership. Like their military subordinates, they believed that civilian "micromanagement" had brought about the calamity in Vietnam; they confronted an extremely forceful, popular, and sophisticated chairman of the Joint Chiefs of Staff; they trusted the technical competence of the forces under their command; and they feared the consequences of a protracted commitment in a region that they viewed as culturally alien and of secondary importance as the Cold War ended. They yielded, finally, to the understandable temptation to bask in the admiration and approval that is the lot of successful warriors home from their wars. But war, like politics itself, almost never has a clear-cut terminus. (p. 198)

[56] Colin Powell (with Joseph E. Persico), *My American Journey*, New York: Random House, 1995, pp. 459–524.

the Air Force share rising from 31.7 percent in 1990 to 32.9 percent in 1993."[57] The 1993 Bottom-Up Review (BUR) forced further cuts in force structure and budgets, "leading to a total reduction in forces of roughly one-third—a level well beyond the base Force's planned 25 percent reduction . . . . Budgets would also fall beyond planned Base Force levels as a result of the BUR."[58]

## Immediate Ground-Centric Lessons

In the immediate aftermath of Operation Desert Storm, the Army's Chief of Staff, General Gordon R. Sullivan, identified five areas for change as a result of the Gulf War:

- Early or forced entry (since the Army would no longer be forward based in the most likely theater of operations).
- Mounted and dismounted maneuver.
- Fires across the depth of the battlespace.
- Battle command.
- Combat service support.[59]

In 1993, the Army published a new edition of FM 100-5, *Operations*. The manual, while recognizing the "greater ambiguity and uncertainty"

---

[57] Eric V. Larson, David T. Orletsky, and Kristin Leuschner, *Defense Planning in a Decade of Change: Lessons from the Base Force, Bottom-Up Review, and Quadrennial Defense Review*, Santa Monica, Calif.: RAND Corporation, MR-1387-AF, 2001, p. xvi. On the Base Force, see also Lorna Jaffe, *The Development of the Base Force, 1989–1992*, Washington, D.C.: Joint History Office, 1993.

[58] Larson, Orletsky, and Leuschner (2001), p. xviii. The authors also note that the Base Force, the Bottom-Up Review, and the 1997 Quadrennial Defense Review shared several features:

> First, each assumed that the most important (and taxing) mission for conventional forces was halting and reversing cross-border aggression by massed mechanized forces. . . . Second, each review in its own way treated presence and smaller-scale peace and other contingency operations as "lesser-included cases" that could be managed by a force structure designed primarily for warfighting—and assumed that these contingency operations would impose minimal costs and risks for warfighting. SSCs have not been lesser-included cases, however, and have instead represented competing claimants for increasingly scarce defense resources. (p. xxvii)

[59] Gregory Fontenot, E. J. Degen, and David Tohn, *On Point: The United States Army in Operation Iraqi Freedom*, 2004, p. 6.

and "wider variety of threats" in the post–Cold War and the reality of joint operations,[60] still took a traditional approach:

> In peace or war, the Army is the nation's historically proven decisive military force. A key member of the joint team, the Army serves alongside the Air Force, Navy, and Marine Corps to protect the nation's vital interests. The Army's primary mission is to organize, train, and equip forces to conduct prompt and sustained land combat operations. It is the Army's ability to react promptly and to conduct sustained land operations that make it *decisive*. The Army is competent in many areas, such as nation assistance, counterdrug operations, security assistance, deterrence, and stability operations that can combine with other elements of national power to achieve strategic effects favorable to US interests around the world. The Army's capabilities provide the nation a diverse, deployable, and sustainable set of options that include strategic and operational logistics and communications capabilities. Most of all, the Army represents the nation's only military force capable of prolonged land combat. Simply stated, the Army has strategic staying power.[61]

The manual also provided a definition of its charter going into the future:

> *The Army must be capable of achieving decisive victory.* The Army must maintain the capability to put overwhelming combat power on the battlefield to defeat all enemies through a total force effort. It produces forces of the highest quality, able to deploy rapidly, to fight, to sustain themselves, and to win quickly with minimum casualties. This is decisive victory.[62]

In the coming years, the Army would be called upon rather frequently to provide this "staying power" in ways it had perhaps not envisioned, in such places as Somalia, Haiti, Rwanda, Bosnia, Kosovo, Afghani-

---

[60] U.S. Department of the Army, FM 100-5, *Operations*, 1993, p. 1-1.

[61] U.S. Department of the Army, FM 100-5 (1993), p. 1-4. Emphasis in the original.

[62] U.S. Department of the Army, FM 100-5 (1993), p. 1-5. Emphasis in the original.

stan, and Iraq. Nevertheless, it did so from a doctrinal perspective that units trained for warfighting could handle lesser contingencies. Indeed, the 1994 doctrinal manual dealing with these operations, FM 100-23, *Peace Operations*, released after the failed October 1993 raid in Mogadishu, Somalia, by Task Force Ranger to capture warlord Mohammed Farah Aideed, was explicit in this regard:

> Training and preparation for peace operations should not detract from a unit's primary mission of training soldiers to fight and win in combat. *The first and foremost requirement for success in peace operations is the successful application of warfighting skills.*[63]

Thus, in many ways, the Gulf War affirmed senior Army leadership that the course the Army had pursued since the end of the Vietnam War in rebuilding the institution was correct. In the Army's view, it had the right doctrine, equipment, and formations, and still

---

[63] U.S. Department of the Army, FM 100-23, *Peace Operations*, 1994, p. C-1. Emphasis in the original. Quoted in David E. Johnson, "Preparing Potential Senior Army Leaders for the Future: An Assessment of Leader Development Efforts in the Post–Cold War Era," RAND Corporation, IP-224-A, 2002, pp. 15–16. See also Peter D. Feaver, *Armed Servants: Agency, Oversight, and Civil-Military Relations*, Cambridge, Mass.: Harvard University Press, 2003, p. 247. Feaver argues: "Somalia became synonymous with debacle, and civilian principals emerged from it weaker and from then on confronted stronger resistance from military agents to any involvement in similar operations." See also David E. Johnson, *Modern U.S. Civil-Military Relations: Wielding the Terrible Swift Sword*, Washington, D.C.: National Defense University Press, 1997. This essay argues that the deterioration in civil-military relations following Somalia was largely a continuation and reinforcement of the lessons learned by the U.S. military in Vietnam: "And the essential lesson of Vietnam was that only professional military officers can formulate the fundamental principles governing the application of American military power, or military doctrine" (p. vi). The Weinberger criteria (commit forces to combat only in defense of vital interests; go in to win; have clearly defined political and military objectives; must have the support of the American people and Congress; and combat should be the last resort) and the Powell doctrine of "overwhelming force" had their origins in the Vietnam experience and were strengthened after Somalia (pp. vi–vii). Finally, Frank Hoffman argues that the U.S. military exhibits "a distinct preference for limited civilian oversight and control, and cynical views about maintaining public support." He also notes the "historical resistance and institutional inadequacy of the U.S. military in limited or conventional conflict" and is troubled by "the U.S. military's separation of politics from military operations" (F. G. Hoffman, *Decisive Force: The New American Way of War*, Westport, Conn.: Praeger, 1996, p. 125).

maintained its preeminence as the nation's decisive, war-winning service. And, because the Army relied on the other services for strategic
mobility and air support, it came to "champion jointness" so long as its
"central role" was preserved.[64] The Army was, as always, the supported
service.

### Immediate Air-Centric Lessons

The Air Force also looked to the Gulf War for lessons for the future
and, not surprisingly, rendered a different assessment of the relative
roles of ground and air power. The Air Force had proven itself to be an
effective day or night force across the theater of operations. The *Gulf
War Air Power Survey Summary Report* noted this new reality:

> We may require a sterner test against a more capable adversary to
> come to a conclusive judgment. But if air power again exerts simi-
> lar dominance over opposing ground forces, the conclusion will
> be inescapable that some threshold in the relationship between
> air and ground forces was first crossed in Desert Storm.[65]

Not surprisingly, given its success in the Gulf War, the Air Force
focused increasingly on how to exploit the potential of air power in
warfare. General Fogleman, Air Force Chief of Staff, told an audi-
ence at the 1996 Air Force Air and Space Doctrine Symposium that
in Desert Storm "we discovered that conventional air operations could
not only support a ground scheme of maneuver but also could directly
achieve operational- and strategic-level objectives—independent of
ground forces, or even with ground forces in support."[66]

This shift in Air Force thinking had already made its way into
doctrine in the March 1992 version of AFM 1-1, *Basic Aerospace Doctrine of the United States Air Force*. The "The Nature of Aerospace
Power" chapter begins with a quote from Giulio Douhet, which sets
the tone for the manual: "Nowadays, anyone considering land and sea

---

[64] Gordon and Trainor (1995), p. 473.

[65] Keaney and Cohen (1995), pp. 246–247.

[66] Fogleman (1996), p. 41.

operations of any importance must of necessity remember that above the land and sea is the air."[67] The descriptive paragraphs concerning aerospace power contained several that noted the relative advantages of aerospace power, including:

- Elevation above the earth's surface provides relative advantages over surface-bound forces. . . . broader perspective, greater potential speed and range, and three-dimensional movement. The result is inherent flexibility and versatility.
- Aerospace power can quickly concentrate on or above any point on the earth's surface.
- Aerospace power can apply force against any facet of enemy power. Aerospace power can be brought to bear on an enemy's political, military, economic, and social structures simultaneously or separately. It can be employed in support of national, theater/joint, or other component objectives. It can be coordinated with surface power or employed independently.
- The inherent speed, range, and flexibility of aerospace power combine to make it the most versatile component of military power. . . . The versatility of aerospace power may easily be lost if aerospace forces are subordinated to surface elements of power.[68]

The discussion of aerospace roles and missions reinforced the importance of gaining and maintaining aerospace control, force enhancement for aerospace and surface forces (airlift, air refueling, spacelift, electronic combat, surveillance, and reconnaissance), and operational sustainment.[69] However, another role—force application—showed an expansion of airmen's views over the 1984 version of AFM 1-1, which had largely accepted the separate roles of land, naval, and aerospace forces in their domains:

---

[67] U.S. Department of the Air Force, AFM 1-1, *Basic Aerospace Doctrine of the United States Air Force*, 1992, p. 5.

[68] U.S. Department of the Air Force, AFM 1-1 (1992), pp. 5–6.

[69] U.S. Department of the Air Force, AFM 1-1 (1992), pp. 6–7.

**Force application brings aerospace power to bear directly against surface targets.** This role includes those missions that apply combat power against surface targets exclusive of missions whose objective is aerospace control. The objective of the strategic attack mission is to destroy or neutralize an enemy's war-sustaining capabilities or will to fight. Interdiction delays, disrupts, diverts, or destroys an enemy's military potential before it can be brought to bear against friendly forces. Close air support directly supports the surface commander by destroying or neutralizing enemy forces that are in proximity to friendly forces.[70]

The interdiction statement was expanded upon later in the manual and apparently staked out the Air Force's position on the ongoing debate about battlespace ownership:

**The depth at which interdiction is performed generally determines the freedom of action available to the attacking force.** Increasing the depth of operations reduces the danger of fratricide for friendly air and surface forces, reduces the coordination required between components, and allows increasingly flexible operations. The attacker's increased freedom of action compounds the defender's problem by leaving no location immune to attack.[71]

The potential effect of this statement was not lost on other observers. A 1998 RAND report noted: "Because interdiction encompasses attacks on forces operating in other mediums—namely, land and sea—it opens up a means within doctrine for air power to play some role in the 'land battle' and the 'naval battle.'"[72]

## The Failure to Create Joint Doctrinal Solutions

Given the fact that the Army and the Air Force each believed themselves to be the decisive component in war—and both wanted control

---

[70] U.S. Department of the Air Force, AFM 1-1 (1992), p. 6. Emphasis in the original.

[71] U.S. Department of the Air Force, AFM 1-1 (1992), p. 12. Emphasis in the original.

[72] Kent and Ochmanek (1998), p. 9.

of the deep battle—inevitable tension emerged between the two services.[73] Friction over this issue resurfaced following the release of JP 3-0, *Doctrine for Joint Operations*, in February 1995. Joint doctrine did not resolve service tensions; indeed, it may have exacerbated them.

### The Continuing Debate About Who Owns the Battlespace
JP 3-0 addressed the ownership of the battlespace issue in Chapter III, "Planning Joint Operations." Section 7 identified the control and coordinating measures that JFCs would employ to "**facilitate effective joint operations**." These included "boundaries, phase lines, objectives, coordinating altitudes to deconflict air operations, air defense areas, amphibious objective areas, submarine operating patrol areas, and minefields." The two measures that still generated ground-air tensions were boundaries and the FSCL.

JP 3-0 specified that "boundaries define surface areas to facilitate coordination and deconfliction of operations. **In land and sea warfare, a boundary is a line by which areas between adjacent units or formations are defined**." Boundaries were clearly focused on surface combat; the manual stated that "JFCs may use **lateral, rear, and forward boundaries** to define AOs [areas of operation] for land and naval forces." Furthermore, "[s]uch areas are sized, shaped, and positioned to enable land or naval force commanders to accomplish their mission while protecting deployed forces."[74]

JP 3-0 defined the FSCLs "as permissive fire support coordinating measures." Their placement was, however, still the prerogative of the ground commander:

> **FSCLs . . . are established and adjusted by appropriate land or amphibious force commanders. . . . The FSCL is not a boundary**—the synchronization of operations on either side of

---

[73] These service-centric perspectives were exacerbated by post–Gulf War (and post–Cold War) perceptions of a zero-sum budget environment in what was clearly a period of downsizing. Consequently, the service that "won" the debate over which form of operations was decisive was likely to garner a larger share of the DoD budget.

[74] U.S. Joint Chiefs of Staff, JP 3-0, *Doctrine for Joint Operations*, 1995, p. III-33. Emphasis in the original.

the FSCL is the responsibility of the establishing commander out to the limits of the land or amphibious force boundary.[75]

Both the Army and the Air Force understood the potential for tension posed by boundaries and FSCLs. In 1996, the Chief of Staff of the Army, General Dennis J. Reimer, and the Chief of Staff of the Air Force, General Ronald R. Fogleman, coauthored an article in *Joint Force Quarterly* titled "Joint Warfare and the Army–Air Force Team." In the piece, the authors clearly enunciated the issue of controlling the battlespace. Regarding boundaries, the chiefs agreed that "JFCs will normally establish forward AO [area of operation] boundaries and adjust as necessary to balance the needs of LCCs [land component commanders] to rapidly maneuver with the needs of ACCs [air component commanders] to rapidly mass and employ air power with minimal constraints."[76] Generals Reimer and Fogleman also discussed the placement of FSCLs:

> Whenever we discuss targeting the placement of the FSCL inevitably comes up. *Joint doctrine grants LCCs the authority to place this line anywhere within their AO.* To maximize the effectiveness of both land and air forces, LCCs should coordinate the placement of this line with ACCs to ensure maximum coverage of all enemy targets with available assets. It is incumbent on each component commander to establish a level of mutual trust with the other commanders to make this relationship work. ACCs must provide LCCs making FSCL decisions with relevant facts that will help them, but must trust LCCs to place FSCLs in the best location to support the objectives of JFCs.[77]

The article concluded with each chief challenging his service to understand the realities of war that are facing the other. Soldiers should realize "that airmen have theater-wide perspectives and responsibilities,"

---

[75] U.S. Joint Chiefs of Staff, JP 3-0 (1995), pp. III-33, III-34. Emphasis in the original.

[76] Dennis J. Reimer and Ronald R. Fogleman, "Joint Warfare and the Army–Air Force Team," *Joint Force Quarterly*, Spring 1996, p. 13.

[77] Reimer and Fogleman (1996), p. 13. Emphasis added.

while airmen "must appreciate the vital role of air power in land combat and understand that air flown in support of LCCs must complement the plans of LCCs."[78]

Despite the apparent public cordiality of Generals Reimer and Fogleman, some in the Air Force felt that joint doctrine, particularly that contained in JP 3-0, was wrongheaded and that the debate over battlespace control remained unresolved. A paper prepared by Air Force Lieutenant Colonel Carl R. Pivarsky, Jr.—"Airpower in the Context of a Dysfunctional Joint Doctrine"—at the Air War College brought into question the intellectual integrity of JP 3-0. In his foreword to the paper, Major General D. Bruce Smith, Commandant of the Air War College, wrote:

> This research focuses on that document [JP 3-0] and the impact it has on how we think about high-intensity, conventional combat operations. Specifically, it deals with the corruption of the definitions of maneuver and interdiction to serve parochial land force interests. The author shows in detail how definitions and terms have destroyed the joint force air component commander (JFACC) and relegated air component capabilities solely to the support of surface maneuver commanders. . . . A rewrite of Joint Pub 3-0 is required to reflect joint force capabilities for full-dimensional operations, not simply land force dominance of the entire battlespace. Sea, air, and space force dominance deserve equal discussion in this keystone joint operations doctrine.[79]

Colonel Pivarsky was even more scathing in his denunciation of JP 3-0 than General Smith: "[T]he emergence of a dominant land maneuver bias, fueled by parochial interest and sustained by its own internal logic, threatens to corrupt the intellectual foundations of the American profession of arms."[80] Pivarsky's principal concern centered on the language in JP 3-0 that defined maneuver as "the movement

---

[78] Reimer and Fogleman (1996), p. 15.

[79] Carl R. Pivarsky, Jr., "Airpower in the Context of a Dysfunctional Joint Doctrine," Air War College Maxwell Paper No. 7, 1997, p. iii.

[80] Pivarsky (1997), p. 2.

of forces in relation to the enemy to secure or retain positional advantage."[81] Thus, air power was not a maneuver force in the doctrine elaborated by JP 3-0; this role was restricted to land and naval forces.

Colonel Pivarsky's discussion of this exclusion of air power from being a maneuver force cut to the fundamental issue of battlespace control:

> The reason to keep Air Force air assets from being treated as maneuver forces is tied to the fact that the Air Force is a proponent of a theater-wide joint force air component commander (JFACC). If the JFACC was considered to be a maneuver commander, it would alter the command dynamics of the theater at the expense of surface maneuver commanders. This is because maneuver commanders are assigned an area of operations (AO) by the JFC. This is accomplished by the JFCs establishing boundaries for those forces within the theater. Boundaries are a control measure that define "surface areas to facilitate coordination and deconfliction of operations."[82]

Thus, the issue of boundaries was key:

> Inside a maneuver commander's boundary, he or she is the *supported commander for all operations* and can dictate what happens down to the "when, where, why, what, how, and by whom." This determination of who is in charge is no small matter and is a considerable source of friction within the surface component as well as between functional components.[83]

Aside from the continuing debate over battlespace control and the new air power as maneuver nuance, two further events only heightened the friction between the ground- and air-centric camps: the shooting war in Bosnia and the bureaucratic in-fighting within the Department of Defense (DoD) that resulted from the Air Force's development of the Halt Phase concept.

---

[81]   U.S. Joint Chiefs of Staff, JP 3-0 (1995), p. A-2, quoted in Pivarsky (1997), p. 5.

[82]   Pivarsky (1997), p. 7.

[83]   Pivarsky (1997). Emphasis in the original.

## The War in Bosnia

The war in Bosnia hardened the perspectives of the ground- and air-centric camps in the U.S. armed forces. It is beyond the scope of this study to discuss the tortured history of post–Cold War Yugoslavia. Suffice it to say that after four years of attempting to bring stability to the region with the United Nations, NATO decided to intervene in Bosnia to end the violence, ethnic cleansing, and instability. In the words of Richard Holbrooke, "The Western mistake over the previous four years had been to treat the Serbs as rational people with whom one could argue, negotiate, compromise and agree. In fact, they respected only force or an unambiguous and credible threat to use it."[84] The precipitating event was an August 28, 1995 mortar attack on the Sarajevo Markale marketplace by Bosnian Serb forces, which killed 37 people. The attack took place within a broader regional war in which the Bosnian Serbs were under attack by Croat and Bosnian Muslim forces.[85]

NATO intervened with an air campaign, Operation Deliberate Force, which lasted from August 30 to September 14. By Gulf War standards, the air campaign was modest: "U.S. air strikes delivered 1,026 bombs against 56 military targets in western Bosnia and near Sarajevo—less than half the munitions used per day against Saddam's army in the Persian Gulf War, but enough to debilitate the far smaller and less heavily armed Bosnian Serb Army."[86] In the end, the Bosnian Serbs agreed to the Dayton Accords, which ended the conflict and allowed the NATO-led Implementation Force (IFOR), whose U.S. contingent was drawn largely from the 1st Armored Division, into Bosnia "to oversee and enforce the implementation of the military

---

[84] Richard Holbrooke, *To End a War*, New York: Random House, 1998, p. 152.

[85] Robert A. Pape, "The True Worth of Air Power," *Foreign Affairs*, March/April 2004, pp. 122–123; Robert C. Owen, "The Balkans Air Campaign Study: Part 2," *Aerospace Power Journal*, Fall 1997b, pp. 6–7. For examinations of the events leading up to Operation Deliberate Force, see Karl Mueller, "The Demise of Yugoslavia and the Destruction of Bosnia: Strategic Causes, Effects, and Responses," in Robert C. Owen, ed., *Deliberate Force: A Case Study in Effective Air Campaigning* (final report of the Air University Balkans Air Campaign Study), Maxwell Air Force Base, Ala.: Air University Press, 2000, and Robert C. Owen, "The Balkans Air Campaign Study: Part 1," *Aerospace Power Journal*, Summer 1997a.

[86] Pape (2004), p. 123.

aspects of the peace agreement."[87] IFOR would be protected in its mission by NATO air power. In a harbinger of future contingency operations, Secretary of Defense William J. Perry stated that U.S. ground forces would be out of Bosnia within a year, an estimate that would prove highly optimistic.[88]

Postwar assessments ran the gamut from air-centric statements that argued "the 1995 air campaign was credited with having forced the Bosnian Serbs to the Dayton peace table,"[89] to ground-centric arguments focused on the decisive effect the Croatian ground offensive had on the outcome. The reality lies somewhere in between—that is, the twin dilemmas of the Croat-Bosnian Muslim ground offensives and the Deliberate Force air campaign put the Serbians in an untenable position.[90] Nevertheless, it is fair to say that absent the Deliberate Force air campaign, the war would have likely dragged on "for at least another campaign season or longer."[91]

The Air Force assessment of Deliberate Force—the Balkan Air Campaign Study (BACS)—while acknowledging the influence of ongoing ground operations in Bosnia, stated that "DELIBERATE FORCE 'broke' the Serbs and was the proximal cause for the cessation of large-scale fighting in Bosnia and of the Serb agreement to participate in future peace talks according to a timetable set by the intervention."[92] The BACS also stressed another dimension of the conflict that would repeat itself in the Balkans: "[A]ir power not only was the lead

---

[87] William J. Perry, "The Deployment of U.S. Troops to Bosnia: Prepared Statement of Secretary of Defense William J. Perry to the House International Relations and National Security Committees, Nov. 30, 1995," *Defense Issues*, Vol. 10, No. 102, quoted in Johnson (1997), p. iv.

[88] Johnson (1997), p. v.

[89] Hallion (1997–1998), p. 42.

[90] See Pape (2004), p. 123. Pape argues that it was this combination of ground and air that resolved the conflict. Nevertheless, this outcome seems to have been much more serendipitous than planned or coordinated.

[91] Owen (1997b), p. 24. This article is based on the Air Force's Balkan Air Campaign Study report, published as Owen (2000).

[92] Owen (1997b), p. 24.

arm of American involvement in the region but also was almost certainly the only politically viable offensive arm available for use by the United States and any of its partners."[93] In the estimation of the BACS, the Deliberate Force air campaign "did what three years of factional ground fighting, peacekeeping, and international diplomacy had yet to achieve," because it "drastically altered the military situation on the ground, and it gave the UN and NATO control of the pace and content of the peace process."[94]

The BACS, however, transcended a mere discussion of Deliberate Force. The report also discussed lessons from the operation that would inform the emerging Air Force Halt Phase concept, discussed below. First, the report noted the impact of precision weapons on achieving results and in limiting collateral damage "that would cause world opinion to rise against and terminate the operation."[95] Indeed, "69% of the weapons dropped during Deliberate Force were precision, compared to 8% during the Gulf War."[96] The report also stated that precision air power was a much better alternative in Bosnia than a "joint air and ground offensive," which would likely have resulted in a protracted war with more civilian and NATO casualties, because "the Serbs would have fought back, at least long enough to see if killing some number of interventionist troops would break the will of their political leaders."[97] In contrast, the air-only Deliberate Force campaign was virtually casualty free for NATO, because Serb antiaircraft missile batteries were suppressed and because NATO aircraft flew "generally above 15,000 feet" to avoid antiaircraft guns and man-portable missiles.[98] Thus, the report noted that

---

[93] Owen (1997b), p. 25.

[94] Owen (1997b), p. 24.

[95] Owen (1997b), p. 20.

[96] Robert C. Owen, "Operation Deliberate Force: A Case Study on Humanitarian Constraints in Aerospace Warfare," presented at Humanitarian Challenges in Military Intervention workshop, Washington, D.C., November 29–30, 2001, p. 62.

[97] Owen (1997b), p. 21.

[98] Owen (2001), p. 62. Owen notes that "only two allied aviators were shot down and captured, the crew of a French Mirage. None were killed. Casualties among the Serb military

airpower's role in the sphere of low intensity conflict (LIC) continues to expand as new strategies, weapons, and sensor systems improve the ability of airmen to find and destroy important targets of all types under varying conditions. To the extent that a given LIC or operation other than war requires military surveillance and attack (and most do), the DELIBERATE FORCE experience suggests that *air power is becoming an ever more equal partner with ground power.*[99]

Advocates of an air power–centric approach to warfare, however, did not limit their concepts to low-intensity conflict. They believed that air power—employed in a halt phase—offered a singularly decisive capability in addressing the "two major theater war" construct that formed the core of U.S. national military strategy after the Gulf War.

### The Halt Phase Concept

The Halt Phase concept had its origins in the post–Gulf War exchanges between the Army and the Air Force over which component could control the deep battle, particularly in mid- to large-scale wars. The Army's 1993 FM 100-5, *Operations*, continued to stress the decisiveness of ground forces and the close fight: "The enemy is best defeated by fighting him close and simultaneously." Deep operations contributed to the close fight by setting conditions for the close fight. Successful deep operations, however, required "the synchronization of supporting assets, including systems organic to Army echelons and those of other services or allied forces."[100]

The Army's position placed it at loggerheads with the post–Cold War Air Force assessment that the Gulf War "showed that the air component commander could take charge of the deep battle and interdict enemy forces to great effect. This marked a departure from AirLand

---

and non-combatant civilians are not precisely known, but the latter were less than thirty, or about one for every thirty of forty heavy weapons dropped" (p. 62).

[99] Owen (1997b), p. 23. Emphasis (italics) added.

[100] U.S. Department of the Army, FM 100-5 (1993), p. 6-14.

Battle because there was no simultaneous deep and close battle."[101]
A 1993 RAND study served as one of the earliest expositions of the
emerging air-centric view that would become the Halt Phase concept.
It noted:

> In posturing its forces to deal with short notice theater conflicts,
> the United States must rely heavily upon air power in the crucial
> initial stages of combat. Aircraft are highly responsive and mobile,
> capable with tanker and airlift support of deploying anywhere in
> the world in a matter of days. Such air forces can be supported,
> at least in the crucial initial stages of combat, by airlift and can
> outrange almost any opponent through use of the nation's tanker
> fleet. Though attrition cannot be ignored, judicious employment
> of electronic and lethal defense suppression systems can mini-
> mize losses. Moreover, air operations place at risk a much smaller
> number of U.S. personnel than large-scale ground operations.[102]

The report went on to state that "an air dominant" approach was not
appropriate to all scenarios (e.g., an insurgency) and that the United
States still needed robust land and sea forces to complement air
power in assuring U.S. national security.[103] Nevertheless, the report
emphasized:

> *But the results of our analysis do indicate that the calculus has changed*
> *and air power's ability to contribute to the joint battle has increased.*
> Not only can modern air power arrive quickly where needed, it
> has become far more lethal in conventional operations. Equipped
> with advanced munitions either in service or about to become
> operational and directed by modern $C^3I$ systems, air power has
> the potential to destroy enemy ground forces either on the move
> or in defensive positions at a high rate while concurrently destroy-
> ing vital elements of the enemy's war-fighting infrastructure. In

---

[101] Rebecca Grant, "Deep Strife," *Air Force Magazine*, June 2001a, p. 57.

[102] Christopher Bowie, Fred Frostic, Kevin Lewis, John Lund, David Ochmanek, and Philip
Propper, *The New Calculus: Analyzing Airpower's Changing Role in Joint Theater Campaigns*,
Santa Monica, Calif.: RAND Corporation, MR-149-AF, 1993, p. x.

[103] Bowie et al. (1993), pp. xx–xxi.

short, the mobility, lethality, and survivability of air power makes it well suited to the needs of rapidly developing regional conflicts. These factors taken together have changed—and will continue to change—the ways in which Americans think about military power and its application.[104]

This air-centric perspective first came to light during the 1993 BUR and continued to gain traction. Deliberate Force certainly reinforced the utility of an air-centric response in the minds of policymakers. In January 1996, Air Force Deputy Chief of Staff for Operations, Lieutenant General Ralph Eberhart, briefed Chief of Staff General Ronald Fogleman, noting "that a joint force commander could profitably use his air component to attack deep battle targets or at the start of an expeditionary operation *before ground forces were in place*."[105] Thus, the Air Force was positioning itself to play the central role in the U.S. national strategy of responding to two major theater wars, characterized by "a large-scale armored invasion of a friendly nation."[106]

In April 1996, General Fogleman, in a speech at the Air Force Air and Space Doctrine Symposium, showed that he had taken on Eberhart's ideas. Fogleman also demonstrated that he understood the perspective of the ground commander:

> [T]he essence of ground combat has been to synchronize the various contributions of the combined arms team to accumulate a series of tactical battlefield victories. Eventually, the sum of those tactical victories proves sufficient to defeat an adversary or occupy a geographically defined objective that makes the defeat of enemy forces unnecessary.

---

[104]Bowie et al. (1993), p. xxi. Emphasis in the original.

[105]Grant (2001a), p. 57. Emphasis in the original.

[106]James Riggins and David E. Snodgrass, "Halt Phase Plus Strategic Preclusion: Joint Solution for a Joint Problem," *Parameters*, Autumn 1999. For a discussion of how an air-centric approach would destroy and halt an adversary in a major theater war, see David A. Ochmanek, Edward R. Harshberger, David E. Thaler, and Glenn A. Kent, *To Find and Not to Yield: How Advances in Information and Firepower Can Transform Theater Warfare*, Santa Monica, Calif.: RAND Corporation, MR-958-AF, 1998.

Therefore, Fogleman explained, "the natural and the legitimate inclination of professional soldiers is to apply air power as simply another supporting combat arm to be synchronized by the respective land commander in support of his particular objective."[107] Nevertheless, Fogleman stressed that times had changed and air power had fully matured. Thus, Fogleman believed that air power could fundamentally change the way the United States fought wars in the future: "We don't need to occupy an enemy's country to defeat his strategy. We can reduce his combat capabilities and in many instances defeat his armed forces from the air."[108]

The September 1997 edition of AFDD 1, *Air Force Basic Doctrine*, reflected General Fogleman's vision. It advocated "A New View of Conflict," elaborating that "In this view of warfare, the halt phase may be planned as the conflict's decisive phase, not as a precursor necessarily to a build-up of ground forces." The manual went on: "*The point of the 'decisive halt' is to force the enemy beyond their culminating point through the early and sustained overwhelming application of air and space power.*"[109] Additionally, the "Air Force proposal led to revised programming and national security guidance in such documents as the Defense Planning Guidance, the National Security Strategy, The National Military Strategy, and the Joint Strategic Capabilities Plan."[110]

In July 1998, Earl H. Tilford, Jr., a member of the Strategic Studies Institute at the U.S. Army War College, published *Halt Phase Strategy: New Wine in Old Skins . . . With Powerpoint*, a monograph that succinctly captured the essence of the Halt Phase concept:

> Proponents of Halt advocate using joint air power as the primary or supported force in the first few days of a conflict. This strategy would be especially critical in a second major theater of war (MTW) when American ground forces are already heavily com-

---

[107] Fogleman (1996), p. 42.

[108] Fogleman (1996), p. 43.

[109] U.S. Department of the Air Force, AFDD 1, *Air Force Basic Doctrine*, 1997, p. 42. Emphasis in the original.

[110] Riggins and Snodgrass (1999), p. 2.

mitted to a first theater. It would also be viable as a response to the primary aggression if the aggressor attacked with mechanized forces across open terrain. Halt proponents claim that air power can stop enemy forces short of their objective in about 2 weeks. Once the enemy force has been stopped, the theater commander in-chief (CINC) can use air power to dominate the battlefield or, if appropriate, attack critical targets in the enemy's rear or homeland, while bringing additional forces into the theater for "countering action" (formerly known as the counteroffensive). If needed at all, a counterattack by land and air forces would be a kind of mopping up operation since the issue would have been decided in the Halt Phase. Halt proponents maintain that this strategy offers a more effective and efficient way of warfighting, one that will save not only American lives but also resources.[111]

Tilford went on to note that because the Halt Phase concept "calls for a significant reduction in the size of the Active Component of the U.S. Army, it has caused a great deal of consternation and internal discussion within the defense community." Tilford also signaled the Army's view of the concept: "Although Halt's primary proponents couch their rhetoric in terms of 'joint air power,' this is a service parochial, Air Force initiative."[112] Soon, the Halt Phase concept was firmly embedded in Air Force doctrine. The 1997 version of AFDD 1, *Air Force Basic Doctrine*, included the Halt Phase concept in its discussion of counterland:

> **Counterland involves those operations conducted to attain and maintain a desired degree of superiority over surface operations by the destruction or neutralization of enemy surface forces.** The main objectives of counterland operations are to *dominate the surface environment and prevent the opponent*

---

[111] Tilford (1998), pp. 1–2. Tilford provides a comprehensive discussion of the origins of the Halt Phase concept and notes that it was first officially unveiled in June 1997 by Major General Charles D. Link, Special Assistant to the Chief of Staff of the Air Force for the National Defense Review (p. 3). Tilford's study was written largely in response to a RAND study (Ochmanek et al., 1998).

[112] Tilford (1998), p. 2.

*from doing the same.* Although normally associated with support to friendly surface forces, *counterland* is a flexible term that can encompass the identical missions without friendly surface-force presence. *This independent or direct attack of adversary surface operations by air and space forces is the essence of asymmetric application and is a key to success during operations to decisively halt an adversary during initial phases of a conflict.* Specific traditional functions associated with air and space counterland operations are interdiction and close air support.[113]

The potential for an increased reliance by U.S. policymakers on air power to resolve wars, rather than ground power, clearly got the attention of the Army Chief of Staff, General Dennis J. Reimer. Writing in the *Joint Force Quarterly* in late 1996, General Reimer stressed, "Many believe that precision strike weapons can win all future wars. History has shown that the human dimension of warfare cannot be countered by technology alone."[114] Reimer then launched into a litany of the past failures of new technologies—most notably air power—to change the fundamental nature of war:

> The United States has relied on technological silver bullets in the past, sometimes with disastrous effects. In the 1930s strategic bombing promised to end war from a distance, pounding an enemy into submission before one soldier had to advance. World War II proved this wrong. By 1950 the atomic bomb was thought to make any invasion by large, massed land forces impossible. Korea proved this wrong. In the 1960s a high tech electronic barrier was intended to stop infiltration into South Vietnam as bombing critical targets in the north dissuaded Hanoi from pursuing the conflict. North Vietnam proved this wrong. In 1991 some believed that a month-long intensive precision bombardment of Iraqi troops would force them to withdraw from Kuwait without a land campaign. Hope proved wrong yet again.[115]

---

[113] U.S. Department of the Air Force, AFDD 1 (1997), p. 48. Emphasis in the original.

[114] Dennis J. Reimer, "Dominant Maneuver and Precision Engagement," *Joint Force Quarterly,* Winter 1996–1997, p. 13.

[115] Reimer (1996–1997), pp. 13–14.

General Reimer used the examples of Haiti and Bosnia to make his point: "In 1994 and 1995 President Clinton . . . had many options to deal with these crises—capabilities beyond silver bullets that would not work then and will not work tomorrow. It was forces on the ground with balanced full spectrum dominance that successfully secured U.S. interests."[116] What Reimer did not address adequately was the reality that in Bosnia, U.S. ground forces did not enter until the Serbs had agreed to the Dayton Accords, because of the political issues surrounding the use of ground forces before the agreement.

Clearly, as Rebecca Grant wrote, the Halt Phase concept "certainly didn't look much like AirLand Battle."[117] It also placed the Air Force in the position of being the lead and supported force: "If the halt phase attacks worked really well, the deep battle might create US battlefield dominance before enemy ground troops could ever reach the point of close contact with friendly forces."[118] The real rub for the Army, however, was the central implication of a successful air-centric halt phase if it ever became joint doctrine: "the fact that a successful halt strategy would point toward more air power and fewer ground forces."[119] Indeed, "as quickly as the 'Halt Phase' became an Air Force battle cry in the services' struggle over a shrinking budget, it became anathema to the Army."[120]

In 1999, the Army responded to the Halt Phase with its own concept, termed "Strategic Preclusion." This evolving doctrine sought to put the Army back in the supported role in ending a war:

> Contingency response operations will require joint maneuver and interdiction forces capable of moving with such speed . . . and with such overmatching lethality that a potential enemy cannot "set" his forces and operate at an advantage against our power projection forces. The ultimate objective of these operations is *Stra-*

---

[116] Reimer (1996–1997), p. 14.

[117] Grant (2001a), p. 58.

[118] Grant (2001a), p. 58.

[119] Grant (2001a), p. 58.

[120] Riggins and Snodgrass (1999), p. 1.

*tegic Preclusion*, where the adversary realizes he cannot achieve his objectives and ceases further escalation. These operations can resolve crises in their early stages, restore stability, and save lives and national treasure.[121]

To execute Strategic Preclusion, the Army envisioned a joint expeditionary force concept of Advanced Full Dimensional Operations (AFDO). AFDO would "exploit the effects of joint capabilities tailored from modular, adaptive early entry ground forces operating in conjunction with air, sea, space, and special operations forces," with the goal of exploiting "information superiority to establish superior capability in the critical place and time to achieve mastery at the decisive point of conflict." Key to the concept, from the Army's perspective, was the contention that AFDO would "require critical landpower contributions: the sustained exploitation of battlefield effects, the ability to overwhelmingly suppress and destroy an enemy, and the ability—through close, personal, and often brutal combat—to force the enemy to capitulate." And these were the timeless attributes of land power forces: "These landpower functions are essential today and will remain so in the future. The capability for sustained lethality, as well as the capability to control terrain and population, is the cornerstone of deterrence and the guarantors of victory."[122] In essence, the Army was arguing that robust, early-arriving ground forces were required to win wars, and that the nation had to resource this ground power capability.

Other advocates of air power went beyond the Halt Phase concept and put forward a more expansive vision of the future role of air power. Richard Hallion, the Air Force historian, discussed air power as a maneuver force and also laid out the institutional stakes for ground and air forces: "[W]hen airpower—an inherently maneuver-oriented force—is applied, the land effort is not only increasingly reduced in

---

[121] U.S. Department of the Army, *Army Strategic Planning Guidance '99*, draft, February 5, 1999, pp. 14–15, cited in Riggins and Snodgrass (1999), pp. 1–2. Emphasis in the original.

[122] William S. Cohen, *Annual Report to the President and the Congress*, U.S. Department of Defense, 1999, p. 5.

cost and complexity but often deflated in importance."[123] Consequently, he opined:

> In the wars of tomorrow, a new air power and artillery paradigm for military force will predominate, not the old infantry-armor team. Except for a few scenarios, the need (as opposed to the ability or the desire) to commit friendly ground forces to close combat with an enemy simply will not exist.[124]

He further elaborated that using ground forces could in fact unhinge national strategic objectives:

> Inserting ground forces in a region today may create more problems than it resolves. For example, in Bosnia U.N. peacekeepers became hostages to hostile forces who used them as cheap air defense systems to guard against NATO air power. . . . Before the fighting ended in Bosnia after a swift air campaign, a major concern of both American and European staff was what to do if it became necessary to extract the large numbers of ground forces who were supporting the U.N. effort. . . . In short, strategists must realize that if land forces are deployed, the "unequivocal message" may not be one of "U.S. resolve," but rather one of how the U.S. military is trapped in an operational morass. The penalty, as in Somalia, may be an embarrassing withdrawal.[125]

The ability of air power to take the lead in defeating an adversary's strategy was about to be tested. This new war, once more in the Balkans, would again ignite the controversy over the relative roles of ground and air power.

---

[123] Hallion (1997–1998), p. 44.

[124] Hallion (1997–1998), p. 46.

[125] Hallion (1997–1998), pp. 44–45.

# CHAPTER FOUR

# Kosovo, 1999

## Background

On March 24, 1999, NATO began Operation Allied Force to compel Slobodan Milosevic, president of Yugoslavia, to end the human rights abuses Serbs were committing against ethnic Albanians in the Serbian province of Kosovo. Following a 78-day campaign, Operation Allied Force ended on June 9, when Milosevic met NATO's demands and Serbian forces began withdrawing from Kosovo.[1]

Real difficulties, however, came about in prosecuting Allied Force. To begin with, the initial NATO plan assumed that Milosevic would accede to NATO demands with a two- to three-day air power demonstration focused on military targets. Essentially, NATO planners expected "a reprise of Deliberate Force" and that Milosevic would "fold quickly, as he had in 1995."[2] This was a serious strategic miscalculation that failed to recognize the political and psychological importance of Kosovo to Milosevic and the Serbs. In short, "it was all but inconceivable that Milosevic would be talked out of Kosovo by allied diplomacy, even if supported by a threat of NATO bombing."[3]

The application of military power in Allied Force was also constrained by a number of political factors. First, because Allied Force was a NATO operation (as Deliberate Force had been), all 19 mem-

---

[1] Benjamin S. Lambeth, *NATO's Air War for Kosovo: A Strategic and Operational Assessment*, Santa Monica, Calif.: RAND Corporation, MR-1365-AF, 2001, p. v.

[2] Owen (2001), pp. 68–69.

[3] Lambeth (2001), p. 183.

bers of the alliance had to agree on the war's strategic and operational parameters. This political reality affected the air campaign across the board—from what targets could be attacked to the aggressiveness of the campaign itself. As one author wrote, "the conduct of the air war as an allied effort came at the cost of a flawed strategy that was hobbled by the manifold inefficiencies that were part and parcel of conducting combat operations by consensus."[4] Second, a ground invasion was ruled out as an option at the beginning of Allied Force. Again, this was a political decision whose purpose was keeping the alliance together.

As the short air war option floundered, the absence of a ground option caused some to doubt that NATO could conclude Allied Force successfully. In a March 25, 1999, *New York Times* article, Senator John McCain compared Allied Force to Vietnam:

> These bombs are not going to do the job. . . . It's almost pathetic. . . . You'd have to drop the bridges and turn off the lights in Belgrade to have even a remote chance of changing Milosevic's mind. What you'll get is all the old Vietnam stuff—bombing pauses, escalation, negotiations, trouble.[5]

Mackubin Owens, a professor at the Naval War College, wrote in May 1999 that, in addition to making "it possible for Milosevic to redeploy his ground forces in order more efficiently and quickly to pursue his bloody campaign against the Albanian Kosovars without threat of interference," not having a ground option left NATO with two bad choices: "continue with a flawed air campaign that is unlikely to achieve the desired outcome; or return to the negotiating table with a strengthened Milosevic."[6]

---

[4]  Lambeth (2001), p. xviii.

[5]  R. W. Apple, Jr., "Conflict in the Balkans: News Analysis, A Fresh Set of U.S. Goals," *New York Times*, March 25, 1999, p. A1. This article was cited in William M. Arkin, "Operation Allied Force: The Most Precise Application of Air Power in History," in Andrew J. Bacevich and Eliot A. Cohen, eds., *War Over Kosovo: Politics and Strategy in a Global Age*, New York: Columbia University Press, 2001, pp. 9–10.

[6]  Mackubin T. Owens, "Vietnam, Kosovo, and Strategic Failure," editorial, Ashbrook Center for Public Affairs at Ashland University, May 1999, p. 3.

NATO found itself in a particularly unenviable military situation, confronted as it was with "the unwelcome prospect of conducting a military campaign of indeterminate length, with political restrictions on their use of air power, and a seeming irrevocable prohibition on the use of ground forces."[7] Figuring out what to do next brought General Wesley K. Clark, the Supreme Allied Commander (SACEUR), and his air component commander, Lieutenant General Michael Short, into conflict. On May 27, NATO—in the face of Milosevic's recalcitrance and a massive exodus of Kosovar Albanians—voted "to escalate the air campaign to Phase 2." General Clark wanted to use air power to attack Serb ground forces in Kosovo, thereby attacking "the Serb ethnic cleansing machine." The Serb ground forces became Clark's "top priority of the campaign. . . . It was a political, legal, and moral necessity." Furthermore, from Clark's ground-centric perspective, this "made excellent military sense. We wanted to go after Milosevic's 'centers of gravity,' the sources of his power and strength."[8] General Short was equally convinced that the appropriate use of

> air power would be to pay little heed to dispersed Serbian forces in Kosovo and to concentrate instead on infrastructure targets in and around Belgrade, including key electrical power plants and government ministries.[9]

Ironically, General Clark understood the differences between his and Short's perspectives:

> This was also the classic struggle between Army leaders, who want the Air Force to make a difference in the fight on the ground, and some adherents of air power, who saw air power as strategically decisive without recourse to the dirty business of ground combat.[10]

---

[7]  Arkin (2001), p. 9.

[8]  Wesley K. Clark, *Waging Modern War*, New York: PublicAffairs, 2001, p. 241.

[9]  Lambeth (2001), p. xix.

[10]  Clark (2001), pp. 243–244.

In the end, NATO continued to escalate the air campaign and did eventually hit targets in Belgrade. Milosevic acceded to NATO demands. The shooting war was over, but the "who won the war" debate was just beginning.

## Ground-Centric View

General Clark, writing in his postretirement memoirs, captured the essence of the ground perspective on why Milosevic quit when he did: "Planning and preparations for ground intervention were well under way by the end of the campaign, and I am convinced that this, in particular, pushed Milosevic to concede."[11] Part of Clark's preparations included deploying Task Force Hawk, consisting of 24 AH-64 Apache attack helicopters, a corps headquarters, and a ground brigade combat team. Additionally, Clark had briefed the NATO Secretary General, Javier Solana, saying that he believed he "had a feasible military option to secure Kosovo with ground forces, and that we would need between 175,000 and 200,000 troops to succeed."[12]

Many in the Army echoed General Clark's conviction that the threat of a future ground invasion was the key threat that caused Milosevic's capitulation. Earl Tilford wrote in *Parameters*:

> The Serbs seemed to have understood that they could not possibly endure a NATO ground attack. They caved in when it became apparent that one might be in the offing, and they might well have done so sooner had they not been assured that this was the last thing NATO would do.[13]

---

[11]  Clark (2001), p. 425.

[12]  Clark (2001), p. 339. See also "UK: 'No Plans' for Kosovo Call-Up," *BBC News* (online), May 30, 1999, which reports on the rumor that the British "Ministry of Defence had offered to supply 50,000 British troops towards a 150,000-strong Kosovo invasion force."

[13]  Earl H. Tilford, "Operation Allied Force and the Role of Air Power," *Parameters*, Winter 1999–2000, p. 11.

Tilford continued, offering his view of the utility of air power in Allied Force:

> Air power, despite valid reservations concerning its performance in Yugoslavia and the high cost to low benefit ratio resulting from its employment there, still has a role to play in the future of US national security.[14]

He then concluded on a cautionary note:

> Currently, many air power enthusiasts, defense analysts, policymakers, and politicians have been seduced by the promise of bloodless, low-cost victory through precision strike. The sooner they discard this discredited notion, the sooner they will discover the means for waging war that are truly effective and decisive. To be effective, the forces we commit to combat must be balanced and flexible, thus capable of meeting whatever challenges may arise.[15]

The threat of a ground invasion argument as an explanation for Milosevic's ending the war is one that persists, as shown in a 2004 *Foreign Affairs* article by Robert Pape. Pape argues, "Milosevic surrendered from fear that NATO would invade Kosovo, with the devastating help of precision air power."[16]

Perhaps the least plausible ground-centric theory for the success of Allied Force was that Milosevic feared that the Kosovo Liberation Army (KLA) "might seize Kosovo with the support of NATO tactical air power."[17] Retired Army General Theodore G. Stroup, Jr., a senior staff member at the Association of the United States Army, wrote in *Army Magazine,*

---

[14] Tilford (1999–2000), p. 13.

[15] Tilford (1999–2000), p. 13.

[16] Pape (2004), p. 125.

[17] Pape (2004), p. 124.

> Milosevic lost his nerve when ground power—in the form of the Kosovar offensive and the capability of Task Force Hawk to take advantage of the offensive to illuminate the battle with its intelligence, surveillance, and reconnaissance assets—first unlocked the full capability of air power.[18]

Consequently,

> NATO air power was finally able to target precisely and hit the Serb Army in the field. The Kosovars acted as the anvil and TF [Task Force] Hawk as the eyes and ears of the blacksmith so that the hammer of air power could be effective.[19]

Indeed, Task Force Hawk did provide critical intelligence, surveillance, reconnaissance (ISR) support through its counterbattery radars, EH-60 helicopters, and RC-12 Guardrail electronic intelligence aircraft during the KLA offensive against Serb forces near Mount Pastrik.[20] Nevertheless, the effect of Army assets was marginal in the overall context of Allied Force, given the reality that "Yugoslav forces still controlled Kosovo and continued their attacks on the KLA and civilian population there."[21]

The ground-centric community also used the Allied Force experience to attack the Halt Phase concept. Major General Robert H. Scales, Jr., the U.S. Army War College Commandant, wrote that Allied Force disproved the Halt Phase concept, because air power could not stop the Serbs from executing Operation Horseshoe, their ethnic cleansing campaign. Scales stressed, "The example of the Serbian dash into Kosovo demonstrates the particular futility of attempting to preempt

---

[18] Rebecca Grant, "Nine Myths About Kosovo," *Air Force Magazine*, June 2000. The Stroup quote is from Theodore G. Stroup, Jr., "Task Force Hawk: Beyond Expectations," *Army Magazine*, August 1999.

[19] Stroup (1999), cited in Lambeth (2001), p. 157.

[20] Lambeth (2001), p. 157; Clark (2001), pp. 327–337.

[21] Bruce R. Nardulli, Walter L. Perry, Bruce Pirnie, John Gordon IV, and John G. McGinn, *Disjointed War: Military Operations in Kosovo, 1999*, Santa Monica, Calif.: RAND Corporation, MR-1406-A, 2002, p. 49.

an enemy force using air power alone."[22] Scales went on to catalog lessons from past conflicts to make a point whose importance would be verified in Operations Enduring Freedom in Afghanistan in 2001:

> Similar experiences with strategic intervention by air in previous limited wars suggests that such an effort can be made orders of magnitude more effective if aerial platforms are guided to their targets by eyes on the ground. Special operations forces planted deep inside North Korean, North Vietnamese, and Iraqi territory have proven their ability repeatedly both to survive and to take away the enemy's ability to hide from or spoof attacking aircraft.[23]

The most important lesson the Army learned from Allied Force was that it had to change. Task Force Hawk demonstrated

> how little the U.S. Army, by its own leadership's candid admission, had done since Desert Storm to get to an emergent theater of operations rapidly and with sufficient forces to offer a credible combat presence.[24]

Task Force Hawk was built around 24 AH-64 attack helicopters, but the Army deployed a significant support package that included

> 6,200 troops . . . more than a dozen 70-ton M1A1 tanks—too heavy to use on most Albanian roads—42 Bradley fighting vehicles, and 24 Multiple Launch Rocket Systems [MLRSs] with extended-range Army Tactical Missile System missiles . . . [and t]hirty-seven other utility helicopters.[25]

---

[22] Robert H. Scales, Jr., "From Korea to Kosovo: How America's Army Has Learned to Fight Limited Wars in the Precision Age," in Robert H. Scales, ed., *Future Warfare Anthology*, Carlisle, Pa.: Strategic Studies Institute, U.S. Army War College, 2000, pp. 102–103. This anthology chapter originally appeared as an article in *Armed Forces Journal* (December 1999).

[23] Scales (2003), p. 103.

[24] Lambeth (2001), p. 156.

[25] Michael G. Vickers, "Revolution Deferred: Kosovo and the Transformation of War," in Bacevich and Cohen (2001), p. 198.

To command the unit, a corps headquarters deployed from Germany. To move Task Force Hawk to its location at an airfield in Rinas, Albania, required 550 C-17 sorties.[26]

Soon after taking office, the Army's new chief of staff, General Eric K. Shinseki, hinted that changes were in store for the Army. He admitted:

> [O]ur heavy forces are too heavy and our light forces lack staying power . . . . Heavy forces must be more strategically deployable and more agile with a smaller logistical footprint, and light forces must be more lethal, survivable, and tactically mobile. Achieving this paradigm will require innovative thinking about structure, modernization efforts, and spending.[27]

Others were more direct. Deputy Secretary of Defense John Hamre stated in an August 4, 1999, speech,

> If the Army holds on to nostalgic versions of its grand past, it is going to atrophy and die. . . . It cannot simply be what it was, and think it is going to be relevant for this new, complex world that is emerging.[28]

On October 12, 1999, the Army leadership announced a vision to transform the Army "into a force strategically responsive and dominant at every point on the spectrum of conflict."[29] Rapid deployment of highly capable Objective Force units, using medium-weight Future Combat Systems (FCS), was central to the new Army vision. Survivability and lethality for the FCS-equipped units would come from vastly improved situational awareness, which would give Objective

---

[26] Vickers (2001).

[27] "Shinseki Hints at Restructuring, Aggressive Changes for the Army," *Inside the Army,* June 28, 1999, p. 1.

[28] Anthony H. Cordesman, *The Lessons and Non-Lessons of the Air and Missile Campaign in Kosovo,* Washington, D.C.: Center for Strategic and International Studies, 1999 (September 29, 1999 revision), p. 192.

[29] U.S. Department of the Army, *Concepts for the Objective Force,* 2001, p. ii.

Force units the capability to "see first, understand first, act first and finish decisively as the means to tactical success."[30] And the Army's deployment goals were ambitious: "a brigade combat team anywhere in the world in 96 hours after liftoff, a division on the ground in 120 hours, and five divisions in theater in 30 days."[31] To plug the capability gap pending the procurement of the FCS, the Army began fielding what became known as Stryker Brigade Combat Teams, using off-the-shelf medium-weight wheeled armored vehicles.[32]

It would appear that the Army's reaction to Allied Force and its experience with Task Force Hawk was to respond to the lesson of how to get Army forces to future contingencies, rather than to address why the Apaches of Task Force Hawk were not used—even though General Clark frequently requested the authority to use its Apaches and indirect fire systems in Kosovo.[33] A 2002 RAND report, *Disjointed War: Military Operations in Kosovo, 1999,* specifically addressed the question of "Why wasn't Task Force Hawk employed in Kosovo?" It stated the following:

> Having gone to great effort to deploy TF Hawk, why did the United States decline to employ it? Ultimately, it was because decision makers perceived the risks to outweigh the potential benefits. This cost-benefit imbalance was the result of several interrelated factors: vulnerability of the attack helicopters to low-altitude air defenses; restrictive rules of engagement that did not permit those air defenses to be suppressed by area fires; the large number of hard-to-locate low-altitude air defense systems; the dearth of lucrative targets to justify high-risk helicopter operations; and the sensitivity to crew and helicopter losses, magnified after two training accidents. Furthermore, by the time TF Hawk

---

[30] U.S. Department of the Army, *Concepts for the Objective Force*, 2001, p. 6.

[31] U.S. Department of the Army, *Concepts for the Objective Force*, 2001, p. 9.

[32] Alan Vick, David Orletsky, Bruce Pirnie, and Seth Jones, *The Stryker Brigade Combat Team: Rethinking Strategic Responsiveness and Assessing Deployment Options*, Santa Monica, Calif.: RAND Corporation, MR-1606-AF, 2002, pp. 6–8.

[33] Clark (2001), pp. 332, 336–337, 425.

was operational, NATO fixed-wing aircraft were flying many sorties and suffering no casualties at medium altitude.[34]

The employment of Task Force Hawk could have been problematic, particularly if its Apache helicopters were going to rely on air and space systems to provide suppression of enemy air defenses (SEAD), targeting, and intelligence support. As the General Accounting Office observed, significant interoperability problems existed between "the two services' command control, communications, computer, and intelligence equipment."[35]

In the aftermath of Allied Force, the United States deployed Army and Marine Corps ground forces into Kosovo as part of the multinational Kosovo Force.[36] American ground forces remain in Kosovo to this day, still trying to consolidate the victory achieved in Allied Force.

---

[34] Narduli et al. (2002), p. 94.

[35] U.S. General Accounting Office, *Kosovo Air Operations: Army Resolving Lessons Learned Regarding the Apache Helicopter*, GAO-01-401, 2001a, p. 12. This report notes that

> The Task Force Hawk experience highlighted difficulties in several areas pertaining to how the Army operates in a joint environment. One area was determining the most appropriate structure for integrating Army elements into a joint task force. Doctrine typically calls for a Joint Force Land Component Commander or an Army Force Commander to be a part of a joint task force with responsibility for overseeing ground elements during an operation. The command structure for the U.S. component of Operation Allied Force did not have a Joint Force Land Component Commander. Both Army officials and the Joint Task Force Commander in retrospect believe that this may have initially made it more difficult to integrate the Army into the existing joint task force structure. The lack of an Army Force Commander and his associated staff created difficulties in campaign planning because the traditional links with other joint task force elements were initially missing. These links would normally function as a liaison between service elements and coordinate planning efforts. Over time, an ad hoc structure had to be developed and links established. The Army has conducted a study to develop a higher headquarters design that would enable it to provide for a senior Army commander in a future Joint Task Force involving a relatively small Army force. This senior commander would be responsible for providing command, control, communications, computers, and intelligence capability to the joint task force.

[36] Following its large-scale role in the 2003 war in Iraq, the Army perspective on Kosovo changed, as reported in *On Point: The United States Army in Operation Iraqi Freedom*, and was more willing to accept the role of air power in the outcome: "The first lesson was that the air component produced the combat victory, but the Kosovars did not return until the combined ground forces secured the province—achieving the US strategic objective. In every way that mattered, air power won the fighting in Kosovo, while ground units served to consolidate that victory" (Fontenot, Degen, and Tohn, 2004, p. 13).

With General Shinseki's arrival as chief of staff, the Army embarked on the ambitious transformation strategy, whose fundamental premise was the conviction that ground combat remained the decisive element in war:

> Winning decisively means dominating our enemies. Potential opponents must be convinced that we are able to break them physically and psychologically and that we are willing to bear the cost of doing so.

The Army also took on the notion that Kosovo heralded an emerging air-centric American way of war:

> For some opponents, mere punishment from afar is not enough. With these adversaries, the only way to guarantee victory is to put our boots on his ground, impose ourselves on his territory, and destroy him in his sanctuaries. . . . This is the foundation of decisiveness.[37]

The 2001 version of the Army's *Operations* field manual reflected General Shinseki's conviction that the Army was still central to winning America's wars:

> In war, Army forces form the nucleus of the joint force land component—imposing the nation's will on the enemy and causing his collapse. . . . Army forces defeat the enemy, end the conflict on terms that achieve national objectives, and establish self-sustaining postconflict stability.[38]

---

[37] U.S. Department of the Army, *Concepts for the Objective Force* (2001), p. v. See also Huba Wass de Czege, "The Continuing Necessity of Ground Combat in Modern War," *Army Magazine*, September 2000. In this article, the author asserted that if the Army had been transformed to the Objective Force before Allied Force, "*The incursion of the Serb Army into Kosovo could have been preempted before the genocide began*. . . . One or two objective force divisions could have been flown into Kosovo to block the entry of most of the Serbian forces. They would have used organic aircraft with enough range to fly into Kosovo from at least beyond the Adriatic Sea" (p. 11). Emphasis in the original.

[38] U.S. Department of the Army, FM 3-0 (2001), p. 1-3.

Future contingencies would soon test the Army's emerging concepts and its views about its role in winning the nation's wars.

## Air-Centric View

At a post–Allied Force colloquy at the Air Force Association's Eaker Institute to examine the operation, Retired General Michael J. Dugan, a former Air Force Chief of Staff, captured the essence of the air-centric view of what Allied Force had accomplished:

> For the first time in some 5,000 years of military history—5,000 years of history of man taking organized forces into combat—we saw an independent air operation produce a political result. What that means for the future we will still have to divine. . . . This kind of utility can do nothing but place greater demands on air and space forces for the future.[39]

For the Air Force as an institution, the lessons were focused in the main on understanding how Allied Force could have been better executed. Thus, Air Force lessons were generally in two categories: lessons about the appropriate use of air power, and technical and procedural lessons for improving performance.

---

[39] James A. Kitfield, "Another Look at the Air War That Was," *Air Force Magazine*, Vol. 82, No. 10, October 1999, p. 2. See also John Keegan, "Please, Mr. Blair, Never Take Such a Risk Again," *London Daily Telegraph*, June 6, 1999. Noted British historian John Keegan was also convinced that air power had forced the solution in Kosovo, writing: "[T]he air forces have won a triumph, are entitled to every plaudit they will receive and can look forward to enjoying a transformed status in the strategic community, one they have earned by their single-handed efforts." He was also dismissive of ground-centric arguments that Milosevic capitulated because of the threat of a ground invasion:

> Already some of the critics of the war are indulging in ungracious revisionism, suggesting that we have not witnessed a strategic revolution and that Milosevic was humbled by the threat to deploy ground troops or by the processes of traditional diplomacy, in this case exercised—we should be grateful for their skills—by the Russians and the Finns. All to be said to that is that diplomacy had not worked before March 24, when the bombing started, while the deployment of a large ground force, though clearly a growing threat, would still have taken weeks to accomplish at the moment Milosevic caved in. The revisionists are wrong. This was a victory through air power.

## The Appropriate Use of Air Power

A broad conviction existed among airmen that the air war was not properly conducted. Lieutenant General Michael C. Short, the combined forces air component commander (CFACC) during Allied Force, thought that the initial bombing demonstration was doomed to failure. Instead, he believed that a punishment campaign was the correct approach and

> that the most effective tactic for the first night of the war would be a knockout punch to Belgrade's power stations and government ministries. Such a strike had worked in Iraq in 1991, and it was the foundation of air power theory, which advocates heavy blows to targets with high military, economic, or psychological value as a way to collapse the enemy's will.[40]

In more graphic terms, General Short later told the U.S. Senate Armed Services Committee:

> I'd have gone for the head of the snake on the first night. . . . I'd have turned the lights out. . . . I'd have dropped the bridges across the Danube. I'd have hit five or six political-military headquarters in downtown Belgrade. Milosevic and his cronies would have woken up the first morning asking what the hell was going on. . . . If you hit that man [Milosevic] hard—slapped him up side the head—he'd pay attention.[41]

General Short did, however, understand the political constraints that General Clark faced, saying he was "not so naïve as to believe that politicians are ever just going to turn soldiers loose to do the job they think ought to be done." Nonetheless, in the case of Allied Force, General

---

[40] Paul C. Strickland, "USAF Aerospace-Power Doctrine: Decisive or Coercive?" *Aerospace Power Journal*, Fall 2000.

[41] Linda D. Kozaryn, "Air Chief's Lesson: Go for Snake's Head First," American Forces Information Service, June 18, 2004.

Short believed that "we were constrained from conducting an air campaign as professional airmen would have wanted to conduct it."[42]

In the extended phase of Allied Force, when General Clark designated Serbian fielded forces in Kosovo as Milosevic's center of gravity, General Short continued to advocate attacking strategic targets in Serbia. As the air war gradually escalated in the face of Milosevic's intransigence, General Short was able to attack these targets. In the opinion of General Michael E. Ryan, Air Force Chief of Staff, Milosevic quit because air power had brought the war home to Serbia:

> The lights went out, the water went off, the petroleum production ceased, the bridges were down, communications were down, the economics of the country were slowly falling apart, and I think he came to the realization that in a strategic sense, he wasn't prepared to continue this. . . . [Milosevic's] strategic center of gravity was in and around Belgrade[, the focus of] . . . support for Milosevic and his repressive regime.[43]

General Ryan also stressed that he did not believe air power could have stopped the atrocities in Kosovo.[44] Colonel William L. Holland, Air Force Chief of Staff of the Combined Air Operations Center (CAOC) during Allied Force, captured this view quite well:

> There was a lack of understanding about what air power should do, not what it can or can't do, but what it should do. Our desired air strategy was to take it to the people who had an effect on fighting. Not the people who were just carrying out the orders.[45]

### Improving Air Power Performance

Allied Force demonstrated that air power had made significant strides since the Gulf War. The DoD after-action report to Congress noted

---

[42] Strickland (2000), p. 3.

[43] Arkin, "Operation Allied Force," in Bacevich and Cohen (2001), p. 27.

[44] Arkin, "Operation Allied Force," in Bacevich and Cohen (2001), p. 27.

[45] Strickland (2000), p. 5.

that during Allied Force, 35 percent of the bombs delivered were precision munitions, compared with 8 percent in the Gulf War.[46] The Joint Direct Attack Munition (JDAM), employed for the first time during Allied Force, gave American air power a truly all-weather, day-or-night precision attack capability.[47] In the aftermath of the conflict, DoD moved quickly to improve its capability in precision attack by procuring additional standoff and GPS weapons; converting Tomahawk missiles to the latest land-attack configuration; procuring approximately 11,000 additional JDAM kits; converting 322 air-launched cruise missiles to a conventional configuration; buying substantial additional numbers of expanded response standoff land attack missiles and high-speed antiradiation missiles, Maverick air-to-surface missiles, and laser-guided bombs; and investing in various precision strike systems, including targeting pods.[48]

Other technical lessons included the importance of, and need for, improvements and more capacity in electronic warfare, particularly in SEAD.[49] In the realm of ISR, Allied Force witnessed the first large-scale use of unmanned aerial vehicles (UAVs) with near real-time sensors, which provided persistent surveillance in defended areas without putting air crews at risk:

> Furthermore, JSTARS [Joint Surveillance Target Attack Radar System], the ABCCC [airborne battlefield command and control center], U-2 . . . and better satellite and reconnaissance coverage—plus target analysis—proved critical in giving attack sorties more lethality.[50]

---

[46] Anthony H. Cordesman, *The Lessons of Afghanistan: War Fighting, Intelligence, and Force Transformation*, Washington, D.C.: Center for Strategic and International Studies, 2002, p. 11.

[47] U.S. Department of Defense, "Joint Statement on the Kosovo After Action Review," news release, October 14, 1999.

[48] "Message from Secretary of Defense William S. Cohen and Chairman of the Joint Chiefs of Staff Henry H. Shelton," in U.S. Department of Defense, *Report to Congress: Kosovo/Operation Allied Force After-Action Report*, 2000, p. 3; Cordesman (1999), pp. 195–199.

[49] Cordesman (1999), p. 189.

[50] Cordesman (1999), p. 201.

Consequently, Allied Force showed that "[t]he basic systems now seem to be in place to use air and missile power far more synergistically, but questions exist as to the adequacy of the current fleet, and as to the integration of national intelligence assets in supporting theater operations."[51] Nevertheless, ISR integration shortcomings needed addressing in the areas of "tasking, production, exploitation, and dissemination (TPED) of intelligence assets"[52] and in the "pass[ing] on real-time command and targeting data efficiently."[53]

Despite the improvements made in the effectiveness and efficiency of air power—and the promise of still greater enhancements—significant issues still lingered. Allied Force showed how far apart U.S. and coalition partners had grown since the end of the Cold War in capabilities and interoperability. Most NATO aircraft could not employ laser-guided munitions; there was a lack of interoperable field equipment; and training was not adequate in many allied air forces. Admiral Guido Venturoni, chairman of NATO's military committee, later admitted,

> Indeed, without the United States's [sic] assets, the European Alliance members and Canada could never have mounted a successful air campaign such as this. Quite frankly, they simply do not have the capacity.[54]

Furthermore, Allied Force showed that attacking land targets in complex terrain, bad weather, and with restrictive rules of engagement and no ground observers to direct air strikes posed significant problems:

---

[51] Cordesman (1999), p. 201.

[52] "Message from Secretary of Defense William S. Cohen and Chairman of the Joint Chiefs of Staff Henry H. Shelton," in U.S. Department of Defense (2000), p. 3.

[53] Cordesman (1999), p. 201.

[54] Cordesman (1999), p. 182. See also U.S. General Accounting Office, *Kosovo Air Operations: Need to Maintain Alliance Cohesion Resulted in Doctrinal Departures*, GAO-01-784, 2001b.

The targeting of ground forces remains a major problem, and the difficulties posed by weather, the need to operate at stand-off ranges, decoys, Serbian ability to shelter in civilian areas or disperse and hide in rough terrain, are likely to be far more typical of most air operations than the static, exposed target arrays that Iraq presented during the Gulf War.

The battle damage assessment of strikes against individual ground weapons remains as much an uncertain art form as during the Gulf War in spite of advances in UAVs, reconnaissance and intelligences systems, and analysis. NATO and the US lack the capability to "close the loop" in terms of reliable, real-time battle damage assessment that can be used for effective tactical decision making.[55]

General John P. Jumper, Commander, U.S. Air Forces in Europe during Allied Force, later recalled that the difficulty

of attacking fielded enemy forces without the shaping presence of a NATO ground threat had produced "major challenges," including creating a faster flexible targeting cycle; putting a laser designator on Predator [a UAV]; creating new target development processes within the CAOC; creating real-time communications links between finders, assessors, and shooters; and developing more real-time retargeting procedures.[56]

The Air Force's leadership emerged from the experience of Operation Allied Force with a determination to improve the service's performance in two major areas: First, they were determined that future air operations centers would be staffed by airmen who were better trained and better prepared than their predecessors to develop and execute a large-scale, complex air operation. Second, they were determined to streamline and improve the integration of sensors, controllers, and

---

[55] Cordesman (1999), p. 152. See also Nardulli et al (2002), pp. 48–49.

[56] Lambeth (2001), p. 242. Army AH-64 Apache helicopters would have faced similar challenges. Thus, the Kosovo experience suggests that deep operations, by any service, may have difficulty targeting a dispersed adversary, particularly in complex terrain.

shooters so that air forces could become more effective in prosecuting attacks on small but high-value mobile targets.[57]

## Areas of Ground-Air Tension

Allied Force showed the clear differences between ground- and air-centric perspectives on warfighting. Nowhere was this more clear than from the perspectives of the Generals Clark and Short. General Clark believed that Milosevic's forces in the field, particularly the Serbian Third Army, was the top priority. Clark wrote in his memoirs:

> I found myself reiterating our priorities again and again. "You must impact the Serb Forces on the ground." "Do you understand that attacking the Serb forces on the ground is my top priority?" "We're going to win or lose this campaign based on how well we go after the ground targets."[58]

Consequently, as Air Force General Joseph Ralston, Vice Chairman of the Joint Chiefs of Staff during Allied Force, recalled, "The tank, which was an irrelevant item in the context of ethnic cleansing, became the symbol of Serbian ground forces. How many tanks did you kill today: All of a sudden, this became the measure of merit although it had nothing to do with reality."[59]

General Short, as already noted, favored a punishment campaign inside Serbia that would be "focused on the positive military objective of defeating Serbia's will and ability to fight." General Short noted:

---

[57] Interview by RAND research team with General John P. Jumper (Commander, U.S. Air Force's Europe during Operation Allied Force), at Ramstein AB, Germany, June 1999. For more on General Jumper's views regarding attacks on fleeting targets see John Jumper, Testimony to the Military Readiness Subcommittee, House Armed Services Committee, Washington, DC, October 26, 1999.

[58] Clark (2001), p. 245.

[59] Arkin, "Operation Allied Force," in Bacevich and Cohen (2001), p. 27.

I felt I did everything I could to get SACEUR to understand air power. I did everything I could to oppose what I thought was bad guidance . . . I don't know what more I could've done to get SACEUR to understand the process.[60]

General Short was advocating an evolving concept known as "effects-based targeting," which he described after Allied Force:

Effects-based is when you take down the electrical grid and to do that a sophisticated target analysis tells us to get the desired effects measured in days, hours, weeks or months, we have to hit these critical nodes in his network. You go after that effect.[61]

In the end, Vice Admiral Daniel J. Murphy, commander of NATO naval forces during Allied Force, probably has the best explanation for the fundamental differences in warfighting perspectives of Generals Clark and Short: "There was a fundamental difference of opinion at the outset between General Clark, who was applying a ground commander's perspective . . . and General Short as to the value of going after fielded forces."[62]

In the aftermath of Allied Force, the debate over why Milosevic capitulated to NATO's demands was all over the map. In general, the arguments were centered on whether ground attack (in the form of the KLA offensive or a potential NATO invasion) or strategic air attack was the war-winning factor. Perhaps the most cogent argument is that offered by Stephen T. Hosmer in his RAND study *The Conflict Over Kosovo: Why Milosevic Decided to Settle When He Did*. Hosmer writes,

According to Milosevic's own testimony and the contemporary statements of senior FRY [Former Republic of Yugoslavia] officials and close Milosevic associates, the key reason Milosevic

---

[60] Strickland (2000), p. 7.

[61] "An Eaker Colloquy on Aerospace Strategy, Requirements, and Forces," transcript, August 16, 1999.

[62] Cordesman (1999), p. 205.

agreed to accept NATO's terms was his fear of the bombing that would follow if he refused.[63]

Milosevic was isolated diplomatically and facing what he believed to be vastly more destructive bombing in Serbia. It was also a campaign against which he had no defenses. The alliance had held together, and Milosevic realized that he had been unable to outlast NATO. Hosmer also notes that the threat of a NATO ground invasion was a lesser factor in Milosevic's decision, because a ground invasion was clearly months away. Hosmer concludes,

> As of 2 June, however, Milosevic appeared clearly more con-cerned about the threat to his power from an intensified NATO bombing campaign than about the possible consequence of a still-distant invasion.[64]

This reading of the Kosovo outcome is buttressed by Ivo Daalder and Michael O'Hanlon. They argue that Milosevic capitulated because

> the combination of NATO airpower and a possible ground inva-sion confronted Serbia with certain defeat, a defeat that neither Russia nor anyone else would save him from. As soon as that became apparent to him, Milosevic accepted the loss of Kosovo and concentrated on strengthening his power base at home. . . . NATO's bombardment of civilian and economic assets through-out Belgrade and other parts of Serbia was undoubtedly an important factor in forcing Milosevic's ultimate capitulation. . . . Airpower did not by itself produce victory, but it does, in our judgment deserve principal military credit for the outcome.[65]

---

[63] Stephen T. Hosmer, *The Conflict Over Kosovo: Why Milosevic Decided to Settle When He Did*, Santa Monica, Calif.: RAND Corporation, MR-1351-AF, 2001, p. xvii.

[64] Hosmer (2001), p. xix.

[65] Ivo H. Daalder and Michael E. O'Hanlon, *Winning Ugly: NATO's War to Save Kosovo*, Washington, D.C.: Brookings Institution Press, 2000, pp. 199–202.

Regarding Milosevic's concerns about a ground war, the authors note that

> [W]ere the possibility of invasion Milosevic's main fear, he prob-
> ably would have tested NATO further to make sure it had the
> gumption to undertake a ground war before relenting. Given Bill
> Clinton's frequent wavering on the subject, his general reluctance
> to use ground forces throughout his presidency (continuing an
> American aversion to casualties that had been recognized even
> if often exaggerated, since Vietnam), the possibility that NATO
> would not approve such a mission, and the challenging terrain
> in Kosovo that would have required as many as three months to
> prepare for the type of ground war NATO was contemplating,
> Milosevic had ample reason to doubt whether he should worry
> about a ground war—or at least whether he had to worry about
> it right away. Still, a ground war had become a decided likeli-
> hood, even if not a certainty by June 1999. Given the punishment
> of airpower, and the closing of the diplomatic noose around his
> neck, Milosevic made what was undoubtedly a wise decision not
> to push his luck any further.[66]

Attempting to determine the specific causal factors for the final results in Kosovo remains a speculative exercise. Nevertheless, these assessments of the outcome in Kosovo by Hosmer and by Daalder and O'Hanlon—as well as the nuances of the earlier discussed Bosnia case—also point to the importance of the nonmilitary dimensions of coercive diplomacy, particularly when the goal is to compel an adver-sary to undo an action.[67] At the strategic level, ground power (Croatian ground forces in Bosnia; the potential of Allied ground operations in

---

[66] Daalder and O'Hanlon (2000), p. 204.

[67] See Johnson, Mueller, and Taft (2002). Coercion has two dimensions—deterrence and compellence: "Whereas deterrence seeks to dissuade the target from doing something the coercer wishes to avoid, compellence attempts to make the target change its behavior in accordance with the coercer's demands—for example, to halt an invasion, to withdraw from disputed territory, or to surrender" (p. 13). See also Daniel Byman and Matthew W. Waxman, *The Dynamics of Coercion: American Foreign Policy and the Limits of Military Might*, Cambridge, UK: Cambridge University Press, 2002.

Kosovo) and air power complemented the NATO strategy, which relied heavily on a broad usage of the diplomatic, informational, and economic instruments of coercive power. Arguably, in both of these cases, particularly Kosovo, the alliance would not have achieved its strategic ends absent the application of other than military means. Thus, the cases of Bosnia and Kosovo still have much to offer in understanding coercion at the strategic level in that they both worked toward clearly articulated and achievable end states that transcended military victory and which leveraged all the instruments of power.

After Allied Force, the services once more turned their attention to the bureaucratic battlefields of Washington, using the "lessons" of Kosovo to buttress their arguments. As Daniel Byman and Matthew Waxman noted in spring 2000,

> The importance of this debate [over why Milosevic settled] goes beyond bragging rights. Already, some military planners are using their interpretations of the air war in Kosovo, Operation Allied Force, to design future campaigns. All the services are drawing on Kosovo's supposed lessons in their procurement requests.[68]

Once again, the Halt Phase concept became a point of contention between the Air Force and the Army. As already noted, the Halt Phase had been integrated into a number of DoD publications and plans. In

---

[68] Daniel L. Byman and Matthew C. Waxman, "Kosovo and the Great Air Power Debate," *International Security*, Vol. 24, No. 4, Spring 2000, p. 6. This article contains a very lucid discussion about Operation Allied Force and its implications for air power as a coercive instrument, noting that

> Despite a partial shift in the air force's own thinking, the most prominent work on air power theory remains focused on air power–centric or air power–only strategies. . . . This article argues that the current air power debate is fundamentally flawed. The classic question—can air power alone coerce?—caricatures air power's true contributions and limits, leading to confusion over its effectiveness. In Kosovo the use of air power was a key factor in Belgrade's decision to surrender, but even here it was only one of many. U.S. and coalition experience in Kosovo and in other conflicts suggests that air power can make a range of contributions to the success of coercion, including: raising concern within an adversary regime over internal stability by striking strategic targets, including infrastructure; neutralizing an adversary's strategy for victory by attacking its fielded forces and the logistics upon which they depend; bolstering the credibility of other threats, such as a ground invasion; magnifying third-party threats from regional foes or local insurgents; and preventing an adversary from inflicting costs back on the coercing power by undermining domestic support or by shattering the coercing coalition.

February 2001, a draft of the new JP 3-0, *Doctrine for Joint Operations*, included the phrase: "A possible halt phase is necessary when decisive combat operations are required to terminate aggression and achieve US objectives."[69] The importance of the phrase, however, was more than operational; it had the potential to affect budgets. The Army went on record to say that "it would protest any reference to the halt phase in joint publications."[70] The Army took this position regarding a draft of the *Joint Strategy Review* (JSR), which would

> serve as part of the analytical foundation for the 2001 Quadrennial Defense Review. Army officers were particularly concerned by the JSR's reference to a "rapid halt" . . . . The adjective only adds to the impression that heavy ground forces could not deploy in time to execute such a phase.[71]

Chairman of the Joint Chiefs of Staff General Shelton "personally ordered that the halt-phase language be excised from the JSR" because he

> thought it inappropriate to send the Joint Strategy Review to Donald H. Rumsfeld, the Defense Secretary, before the services had a chance to sort out pending disagreements over the halt approach in the doctrine document [Joint Pub 3-0].[72]

The Army seemed to be relying on the lessons learned in Kosovo to justify including robust joint, particularly ground force, capabilities early in a campaign. As one "senior Army officer" explained to reporter Elaine Grossman, there were

> low-tech solutions that the enemy can use against high-tech capabilities. . . . If you've got an enemy that's presenting a great target,

---

[69] Elaine M. Grossman, "The Halt Phase Hits a Bump," *Air Force Magazine*, April 2001, p. 35.

[70] Grossman (2001), p. 35.

[71] Grossman (2001), p. 35.

[72] Grossman (2001), p. 35.

you can do some pretty good damage against him [from the air]. [But] if he's rooting himself down into some tough terrain, or he's in an urban area, or you've got somebody that wants to use human shields, that is potentially a much greater challenge for attack from the air.[73]

This ground-centric argument, however, would seem relevant only in the aftermath of a successful cross-border attack but not particularly relevant in the major theater war scenarios (e.g., Korea, Iraq), which served as the basis for defense planning.[74] Enemy forces would probably not "go to ground" until either the operational objectives supporting the invasion had been achieved or they were forced to stop their offensive. One air power supporter responded to Army officials who were blocking the incorporation of the Halt Phase concept in joint doctrine, saying, "What they can't win in real life, they try to win in doctrine."[75]

In the end, the word "halt" was mentioned one time in the nearly 200 pages of the September 10, 2001 version of JP 3-0. There was no mention of a Halt Phase. Rather, the manual recommended four phases for a joint campaign: Deter/Engage, Seize Initiative, Decisive Operations, and Transition.[76] "Halt" was included in the Seize Initiative phase, when "JFCs seek to seize the initiative in combat and noncombat situations through the application of appropriate joint force capabilities."[77] Specifically,

---

[73] Grossman (2001), p. 36.

[74] U.S. Joint Chiefs of Staff, *The National Military Strategy: Shape, Respond, Prepare Now—A Military Strategy for a New Era*, 1997; U.S. Department of Defense, *Quadrennial Defense Review Report*, 2001). The *National Military Strategy* promulgated during the Clinton administration (in the Chairman's cover letter) called for "fighting and winning two nearly simultaneous wars." The *Quadrennial Defense Review* noted, "For planning purposes, U.S. forces will remain capable of swiftly defeating attacks against U.S. allies and friends in any two theaters of operation in overlapping timeframes" (p. 21).

[75] Grossman (2001), p. 36.

[76] U.S. Joint Chiefs of Staff, JP 3-0 (2001), pp. III-18, III-19.

[77] U.S. Joint Chiefs of Staff, JP 3-0 (2001), p. III-20.

[I]n combat operations this involves executing offensive operations at the earliest possible time, forcing the adversary to offensive culmination and setting the conditions for decisive operations. Rapid application of joint combat power may be required
to delay, impede, or *halt* the adversary's initial aggression and to
deny the initial objectives. If an adversary has achieved its initial objectives, the early and rapid application of offensive combat
power can dislodge adversary forces from their position, creating
conditions for the exploitation, pursuit, and ultimate destruction
of both those forces and their will to fight during the decisive
operations phase. During this phase, operations to gain access to
theater infrastructure and to expand friendly freedom of action
continue while the JFC seeks to degrade adversary capabilities with
the intent of resolving the crisis at the earliest opportunity.[78]

Despite the contentiousness of the Halt Phase concept, it did
have a significant indirect effect on Air Force conceptual thinking. The
phase broadened the intellectual construct and internal debate within
the Air Force, from one that viewed strategic attack against an enemy's
means of making and controlling war as the most efficacious use of
air power (as advocated by General Short and General Ryan in Allied
Force) to one that accepted "an application of air power to directly
defeat an enemy by defeating/destroying its fielded forces."[79] The war
in Afghanistan provided the context for using air power as a strategic
instrument against an enemy's fielded forces.

---

[78] U.S. Joint Chiefs of Staff, JP 3-0 (2001), pp. III-20, III-21. Emphasis added.

[79] Phil M. Haun, *Air Power Versus a Fielded Army: A Construct for Air Operations in the 21st Century*, Maxwell Air Force Base, Ala.: Air University, Air Command and Staff College, AU/ACSC/054/2001-04, 2001, p. 2.

# CHAPTER FIVE

# Afghanistan, 2001

## Background

On October 7, 2001, President George W. Bush announced that the United States and its coalition partners had begun operations in Afghanistan.[1] The campaign was in direct response to the September 11, 2001 terrorist attacks on the U.S. homeland by al Qaeda, which had found sanctuary and state support in a Taliban-ruled Afghanistan. That same day, Secretary of Defense Donald Rumsfeld and Chairman of the Joint Chiefs of Staff General Richard B. Myers gave a briefing on Operation Enduring Freedom (OEF), the name given to military operations in Afghanistan. OEF had six objectives:

- To make clear to the Taliban leaders and their supporters that harboring terrorists is unacceptable and carries a price.
- To acquire intelligence to facilitate future operations against al Qaeda and the Taliban regime that harbors the terrorists.
- To develop relationships with groups in Afghanistan that oppose the Taliban regime and the foreign terrorists that they support.
- To make it increasingly difficult for the terrorists to use Afghanistan freely as a base of operation.

---

[1]  U.S. Department of State, "Text: President Bush Announces Military Strikes in Afghanistan," Office of International Information Programs, October 7, 2001.

- And to alter the military balance over time by denying to the Taliban the offensive systems that hamper the progress of the various opposition forces.
- And to provide humanitarian relief to Afghans suffering truly oppressive living conditions under the Taliban regime.[2]

General Tommy R. Franks, Combatant Commander of CENTCOM, directed the planning for and execution of OEF. From the beginning, General Franks had to deal with competing service views, as seen in his recollection of the meeting at which he briefed the operational plan OEF to the leadership of DoD and the Joint Chiefs of Staff:

> One after the other the [service] Chiefs offered their views of the concept. The Army argued the efficacy of Land Power, and described the difficulties of sustaining Army forces. The Marine view suggested "From the Sea" as the most effective approach to war-fighting—even in a landlocked country. Airpower was offered by the Air Force Chief as the most powerful of the contributing arms. None of which, of course, meshed totally with CENTCOM's operational concept—or my view of joint warfare.[3]

The day after the briefing, General Franks met with Secretary Rumsfeld and shared his concerns about unity of command: "I work for you and for the President, not for the Service Chiefs. They were fighting for turf yesterday. If this continues, our troops—and the country—will suffer. We should not allow narrow-minded four-stars to advance their

---

[2]   U.S. Department of State, "Transcript: Rumsfeld, Myers Brief on Military Operation in Afghanistan," Office of International Information Programs, October 7, 2001.

[3]   Tommy Franks, *American Soldier*, New York: ReganBooks, 2004, p. 275. Attendees at the briefing included Secretary Rumsfeld; Deputy Secretary of Defense Paul Wolfowitz; Chairman of the Joint Chiefs of Staff Hugh Shelton; Vice Chairman of the Joint Chiefs of Staff (soon to be Chairman) Richard B. Myers; Army Chief of Staff General Eric Shinseki; Air Force Chief of Staff Michael Ryan and his successor, General John Jumper; Chief of Naval Operations Admiral Vernon Clark; and Commandant of the Marine Corps General Jim Jones.

share of the budget at the expense of the mission." Secretary Rumsfeld assured General Franks that Franks was the commander.[4]

Operation Enduring Freedom was a four-phase operation. During Phase I, "Set conditions and build forces to provide the National Command Authority credible military operations," CENTCOM laid the groundwork for the operation. Basing and staging agreements were reached with countries bordering Afghanistan, and Central Intelligence Agency (CIA) and special operations forces infiltrated Afghanistan to support Afghan opposition forces.[5] In Phase II, "Conduct initial combat operations and continue to set conditions for follow-on operations," CENTCOM directed missile and air attacks against "Taliban and al Qaeda Command and Control targets, early warning radars, and major air defense systems—principally Soviet-built SA-3 missiles."[6] Following these strikes, special forces teams linked up with the Northern Alliance and opposition forces to support offensives with air strikes against the Taliban and al Qaeda forces. In Phase III, "Conduct decisive combat operations in Afghanistan, continue to build coalition, and conduct operations AOR [area of responsibility] wide," coalition troops, deployed into Afghanistan "to seek out and eliminate pockets of resistance" after "indigenous allies, augmented by about 200 SOF (Special Operations Forces), had routed the enemy."[7] General Franks estimated that 10,000 to 12,000 U.S. ground forces would be required for this phase.[8] Finally, Phase IV, "Establish capability of coalition partners to prevent the re-emergence of terrorism and provide support for humanitarian assistance efforts," envisioned a three- to five-year effort to stabilize and rebuild Afghanistan.[9]

From a military perspective, the first three phases of OEF were wildly successful. The Taliban air defense "system" was rapidly

---

[4]  Franks (2004), pp. 277–278.

[5]  Franks (2004), pp. 269–270.

[6]  Franks (2004), p. 270.

[7]  Franks (2004), pp. 270–271.

[8]  Franks (2004), p. 271.

[9]  Franks (2004), pp. 271–272.

destroyed and the coalition maintained total air supremacy throughout the operation.[10] Furthermore, the addition of precision air power quickly tilted the scales in the favor of the Afghan opposition forces, and Taliban and al Qaeda forces were shattered as a large fighting force and dispersed. Unfortunately, the Afghan opposition forces were less than reliable in pursuing the remnants of the Taliban and al Qaeda. This allowed them to disperse, thus hindering success in Phase IV and requiring U.S. ground forces to root out remaining pockets of resistance in the difficult mountainous Afghan terrain and to conduct an ongoing counterinsurgency campaign.[11]

## Ground-Centric View: Strategic and Operational Lessons

OEF was a unique war. Although there was an overall U.S. strategy, delineated in the CENTCOM operational plan, the "operational" phase of the war was a series of engagements by "surrogate" Afghan opposition forces, buttressed by U.S. air power and special forces, against Taliban and al Qaeda forces. Conventional U.S. ground forces played little, if any, role in the regime-toppling phase of the war.

The perspective of ground advocates concerning the lessons of Afghanistan are perhaps best summarized by Stephen Biddle, an associate research professor at the U.S. Army War College Strategic Studies Institute. In his book *Afghanistan and the Future of Warfare: Implications for the Army and Defense Policy*, Biddle surveys the various lessons emerging from the war, which ranged from those advocating the "Afghan model" of "special forces (SOF) plus precision munitions plus an indigenous ally is a widely applicable template for American

---

[10] Indeed, one could argue that Phase III was not necessary, given the fact that U.S. ground forces never had to conduct "decisive operations" and given the success of air power and indigenous forces in Phase II. Instead, U.S. ground forces conducted largely tactical operations to kill or capture al Qaeda and Taliban fighters the Afghan opposition forces refused to pursue.

[11] Franks (2004), pp. 283–381. See also Stephen Biddle, *Afghanistan and the Future of Warfare: Implications for Army and Defense Policy*, Carlisle, Pa.: Strategic Studies Institute, U.S. Army War College, 2002, p. vii, and Cordesman (2002), pp. 3–25.

defense planning" to those that declared the war "a nonreplicable product of local idiosyncrasies."[12] Instead, Biddle argues that Phase II of the campaign in Afghanistan, when the Afghan opposition defeated the Taliban and al Qaeda, was "a typical 20th century mid-intensity conflict."[13]

The essence of Biddle's argument is that air power was able to tip the scales in Afghanistan because both the Taliban/al Qaeda forces and the opposition forces were fairly evenly matched in training and motivation. Absent this equivalence of competence and zeal, as Biddle believes was the case in the battle of Tora Bora, the "failure to commit properly trained and motivated troops to traditional close combat probably allowed the al Qaeda quarry to escape."[14]

This is not an unimportant argument for ground-centric proponents. In essence, it contends with those who, in Biddle's view,

> now see the Afghan campaign as evidence that the American military can be redesigned to emphasize long-range precision strike at the expense of close combat capability. If the Afghan Model can do everywhere what it did in Afghanistan, it would make sense to restructure our forces to reduce dramatically the ground forces that make up such a large fraction of today's military, and shift toward a much greater reliance on standoff precision engagement forces and the SOF teams needed to direct their fires.[15]

Regarding the implications for American foreign policy, Biddle's principal concern was that a misreading of the Afghan campaign "would underestimate the costs of future American military action" if it were taken as "evidence of a new American way of war that could defeat enemies quickly and cheaply, with little U.S. casualty exposure and limited U.S. political footprint," thus heightening the attraction of a

---

[12] Biddle (2002). For various views of the "Afghan model" and a new "American way of war," see Biddle's footnotes on pp. 1–5.

[13] Biddle (2002), p. vii.

[14] Biddle (2002), pp. vii–viii.

[15] Biddle (2002), p. 50.

"neo-imperial foreign policy underwritten by frequent American military intervention."[16]

U.S. conventional ground forces played no direct offensive combat role in the first two phases of OEF. Their introduction to close combat would come in March 2002 in Operation Anaconda, which would reveal several lessons for ground power and interservice relations between the Army and the Air Force. The lessons of Anaconda are discussed later in this monograph.

## Air-Centric View

From the perspective of its advocates, air power had truly come of age in OEF. As Rebecca Grant wrote in April 2002, "The nation's air component passed a major test in Afghanistan."[17] Clearly, air power provided the scale-tipping support that the Northern Alliance and Afghan opposition forces needed to topple the Taliban and al Qaeda. OEF also yielded a number of battlefield "firsts" in the employment of air power, including

> [f]irst combat deployment of the Global Hawk Unmanned Aerial Vehicle, first operational use of an armed version of the Predator UAV, and the widespread use of the satellite-guided Joint Direct Attack Munition, which previously had been used in combat only by the stealth B-2 bomber. The operation also saw the first combat use of the Wind-Corrected Munitions Dispenser, a vastly refined use of the Combined Air Operations Center as a weapon system itself, and a sharp reduction in the time required to identify targets and strike them.[18]

---

[16] Biddle (2002), p. 53. Biddle also noted the implications of the Afghan model for what, at the time he wrote his monograph, was a looming crisis in Iraq: "To invade [Iraq] without sufficient ground forces on the assumption that there will be no fighting to be done would thus be a major gamble" (p. 55).

[17] Rebecca Grant, "The War Nobody Expected," *Air Force Magazine*, April 2002, p. 34.

[18] John A. Tirpak, "Enduring Freedom," *Air Force Magazine*, February 2002, p. 32.

Furthermore, given the fact that the coalition enjoyed total air supremacy, or "air dominance" (to use the new term of art), aircraft such as the B-52 bomber loitered on station with near impunity. Indeed, B-52s were used to provide CAS to ground forces.[19] Precision, coupled with the capability to provide in-flight targeting to aircrews, improved the flexibility of air power and its ability to hit not only preplanned targets but also emerging targets. Vice Admiral John B. Nathman, commander of the Naval air forces in OEF, later recalled, "After the first week, the pilots didn't know what targets they'd be striking when they launched."[20]

Nevertheless, one notable instance of interservice tension arose during OEF after an Army general made critical comments over the ability of the Air Force to provide adequate support to his forces during Operation Anaconda.

## Ground-Air Tensions and the Tactical Ground-Centric Lessons of Operation Anaconda

The first major combat operation of U.S. ground forces during OEF was Operation Anaconda in March 2002. Anaconda's purpose was the encirclement and annihilation of Taliban and al Qaeda fighters in the Shah-I-Kot Valley who had escaped the Afghan opposition offensives, most notably at Tora Bora.[21] Anaconda showed the significant shortfalls in the ability of U.S. forces to achieve "battlespace awareness" in complex terrain, significant problems with integrating cross-service capabilities, and the vulnerability of attack helicopters to ground fire.

Major General Franklin L. "Buster" Hagenbeck, commander of the Army's 10th Mountain Division, led the force that executed Oper-

---

[19] Tirpak (2002), pp. 32–33. AC-130s were also used to great effect but were operated at night because of their vulnerability to surface fires.

[20] Grant (2002a), p. 37.

[21] Franks (2004), p. 377. See also Sean D. Naylor, *Not a Good Day to Die: The Untold Story of Operation Anaconda*, New York: Berkley Books, 2005, for a detailed description of Operation Anaconda.

ation Anaconda, CJTF (combined joint task force) Mountain. CJTF Mountain had some 200 special forces soldiers, 1,400 U.S. conventional troops (from the 10th Mountain Division and the 101st Airborne Division), and 800 to 1,000 Afghans, supported by 24 lift helicopters and 8 AH-64 Apache attack helicopters. Although CENTCOM had estimated that some 1,500 to 2,000 Taliban and al Qaeda fighters were in the Anaconda operational area, CJTF Mountain revised that estimate to between 125 and 200 enemy fighters, based on an additional month of satellite, UAV, and human intelligence.[22] This latter estimate was woefully too low and provides insight into how a determined enemy can escape detection from U.S. ISR systems. Lieutenant Colonel Christopher F. Bentley, Deputy Fire Support Coordinator for the 10th Mountain Division, explained:

> We have an exceptional suite of ISR platforms. But what was clear early on was the immutable importance of terrain to an enemy who didn't want to be found. Afghanistan's rugged terrain is, in and of itself, a combat multiplier. It provided the enemy sanctuary, especially as he studied how we employed our systems. . . . [I]t was apparent that imagery intelligence (IMINT) and the Predator [UAV] were not going to identify robust target sets to engage when facing an enemy employing asymmetrical operations.[23]

The inaccurate intelligence estimate led to a plan for Anaconda that envisioned the Taliban and al Qaeda leadership attempting to escape, with some forces remaining in defensive positions to support their withdrawal. The scheme of maneuver for Anaconda was essentially a "hammer and anvil" operation, with SOF and Afghan forces serving as the hammer to push enemy forces against the anvil provided by U.S. conventional ground forces. Additional U.S. and Afghan forces would cordon off the area to catch fleeing Taliban and al Qaeda

---

[22] Mark G. Davis, *Operation Anaconda: Command and Confusion in Joint Warfare*, thesis, School of Advanced Air and Space Studies, Air University, 2004, pp. 95–100.

[23] Christopher F. Bentley, "Afghanistan: Joint and Coalition Fire Support in Operation Anaconda," *Field Artillery*, September–October 2002, pp. 11–12.

fighters.[24] Although a more difficult course of action, "al Qaeda forces would conduct a defense in depth, ambush the AMF [Afghan Military Force], and have prepared positions," was considered by Anaconda planners, it "was not considered likely because it created a massed target for US air and ground power and offered fleeing al Qaeda forces little in the way of mobility along the highly restricted trail network."[25] Because a strong enemy defense was not expected, "no formal requests were submitted for airlift or alerting forces."[26]

The assault phase of Anaconda began on March 2. The main-effort Afghan force ran into "heavy enemy fire, including 122mm howitzers and mortars." Additionally, an Air Force AC-130 mistakenly engaged the Afghanis, and they quickly withdrew.[27] After "the AMF 'hammer' disintegrated, the enemy forces then focused on the 'anvil,'" and "within a matter of hours, CJTF Mountain was fighting for its life."[28] General Hagenbeck—who was "initially convinced he could wrap up the fight in just a few days using ground forces with little external support—was forced to issue an emergency appeal for air and naval fires and logistical assistance."[29] This was necessary, because the 10th Mountain Division had not brought its organic 105mm howitzers to Afghanistan, and only one of the two U.S. infantry battalions employed in Anaconda brought any of its 81mm and 120mm mortars with it on the first day of Anaconda. And these mortars were initially unavailable because they were under fire and could not provide support. As Major Dennis Yates, fire support officer for the 101st Airborne Division's 3rd Brigade, later recalled, "we were forced to use the close air support . . . to provide suppressive fires for our ground forces because we were unable to get

---

[24] Davis (2004), pp. 104–105.

[25] Davis (2004), pp. 98–99.

[26] Davis (2004), pp. 104–105, footnote 21.

[27] Davis (2004), pp. 110–111.

[28] Davis (2004), p. 113.

[29] Elaine M. Grossman, "Was Operation Anaconda Ill-Fated from Start? Army Analyst Blames Afghan Battle Failing on Bad Command Set-Up," *Inside the Pentagon*, July 29, 2004a.

our mortars into action, on that first day at least."[30] Unfortunately, this critical CAS had not been planned for adequately, because General Hagenbeck had not directly involved the CENTCOM air component in his preparations for Operation Anaconda.[31]

In the aftermath of Anaconda, General Hagenbeck conducted an interview with *Field Artillery* in which he was critical of the CAS he received from the U.S. Air Force. He implied that Air Force pilots would not fly low enough to the ground to be effective and that they were not responsive.[32] Understandably, these claims ignited a debate between the two services.

At the end of the day, most of General Hagenbeck's complaints about air support proved unfounded.[33] Nevertheless, there was a clear lesson for both services:

> The message that needs to come of this issue is that to optimize air-ground synergy, the air component must be included in all phases of planning surface operations and vice versa. That is what went awry in Anaconda, not CAS.[34]

A thesis by Army Major Mark G. Davis is probably the best publicly available analysis of what happened during Anaconda, particularly from the perspective of understanding command and control and

---

[30] Elaine M. Grossman, "Anaconda: Object Lesson in Ill Planning or Triumph of Improvisation?" *Inside the Pentagon*, August 19, 2004b. On the absence of mortars because a perceived lack of need by Army planners, see also Elaine M. Grossman, "Left in Dark for Most Anaconda Planning, Air Force Opens New Probe," *Inside the Pentagon*, October 3, 2002.

[31] Davis (2004), pp. 94–125.

[32] Robert H. McElroy and Patrecia Slayden Hollis, "Afghanistan: Fire Support for Operation Anaconda, Interview with Major General Franklin L. Hagenbeck," *Field Artillery,* September-October 2002, pp. 7-8.

[33] Benjamin S. Lambeth, *Air Power Against Terror: America's Conduct of Enduring Freedom* (Santa Monica: RAND, MG-166-CENTAF). See pp. 163-231 for a discussion of Operation Anaconda. General Hagenbeck's criticisms and an assessment of their validity are on pp. 204-221.

[34] Major General David Deptula, USAF, quoted in Lambeth, *Air Power Against Terror,* p. 231.

planning issues. Davis is surprisingly candid for a serving officer, writing that

> Instead of pinpointing the defects in command and control and exposing how they degraded the planning and execution of Anaconda, the senior military leadership in both the Army and Air Force have found it more comfortable to blame intelligence for underestimating the enemy and civilian authorities for imposing troop limits.[35]

In Davis's estimation, the difficulties experienced during Anaconda were traceable to the fact that "Joint operations today are characterized by stovepipe planning at component level and de-confliction during execution." Consequently, in his view, "[t]he most contentious issue surrounding Anaconda is *the lack of integration between the Army and Air Force.* The component stovepipe command structure is the source of these problems. Indeed, stovepiping has the unintended effect of promoting service parochialism and a single service mentality in planning and executing operations."[36]

Aside from the ground-air issues, largely between the Army and the Air Force, Operation Enduring Freedom offered several other lessons about Army operations that went largely unlearned and would manifest themselves again during 2003 war in Iraq and its aftermath. One concerned the vulnerability of attack helicopters; another involved the nature of the kinds of war the Army could expect to fight in the future.

Operation Anaconda witnessed the use of AH-64 Apache attack helicopters in a ground support role (CAS). General Hagenbeck, in his interview with *Field Artillery*, emphasized that "[t]he most effective close air support asset we had was the Apache . . . *hands down.* They are extraordinary—they were lethal and survivable."[37] Nevertheless, in his next breath, Hagenbeck casts doubt on the survivability of the Apache

---

[35] Davis (2004), p. 126.

[36] Davis (2004), p. 132. Emphasis added.

[37] McElroy and Hollis (2002), p. 7. Emphasis in the original.

in a low-altitude environment with a significant small-arms threat: "We had six in the fight with two left flying at the end of the first day. They were so full of holes—hit all over, one took an RPG [rocket-propelled grenade] in the nose—I don't know how they flew."[38]

The Apache survivability issue is of importance beyond the context of Afghanistan, because the Apache was (and is) a key system in the Army's concept of executing deep battle operations. Thus, to employ the Apache effectively in deep battle at operational depths, the Army doctrinally maintains control of sufficient battlespace. If the Apache were not survivable, the Army's claim on an expansive battlespace—and a far-forward FSCL—would be less compelling.

The changing nature of conflict witnessed in Operation Anaconda resulted in some early tentative lessons, largely by nonmilitary observers, that would continue to be troublesome in Afghanistan—and eventually in Iraq—after the conclusion of decisive military operations. Stephen Biddle wrote about his concerns for the U.S. armed forces being able to learn the lessons implied by Afghanistan, lessons that, in particular, went against the Army's doctrinal grain. He believed that the analytical tools used by the U.S. military for force structure analyses "based largely on mounted or aerial warfare against exposed armored targets are dangerously misleading" because they "treat warfare mainly as a problem of interactions among armored vehicles and major weapon systems."[39] Biddle stressed that this analytical failure needed correction, because, in his view, "[w]arfare against dismounted, covered, concealed, and dispersed targets will . . . be the norm for American arms in the future. To assess military requirements using tools that cannot address such combat is to reach findings that are meaningless at best, and dangerous at worst."[40]

Anthony Cordesman wrote about the doctrinal implications that he believed Enduring Freedom highlighted:

---

[38] McElroy and Hollis (2002), p. 7.

[39] Biddle (2002), p. 51.

[40] Biddle (2002), p. 52.

Nothing that the U.S. and allied forces did in Operation Ana-conda or in independent search-and-destroy missions, however, has shown that the United States and its Western Allies have a solution to the problems of dispersed warfare against an enemy that is fluid and unwilling to fight. . . . Mid- and long-term success in building a stable nation in Afghanistan is as uncertain as it is in the Balkans and all of other countries where it has been attempted. In addition, the Taliban may rise up again in some form, or other warlords may offer sanctuary to terrorists.[41]

Four years after Cordesman offered this warning, coalition ground forces were continuing to conduct stability and support operations in Afghanistan, key al Qaeda leaders remained at large, and the central government had yet to establish its authority over outlying regions of Afghanistan. The Army also seems to understand the challenge:

Winning the combat was necessary but not sufficient to meet the nation's strategic goals. Transitioning Afghanistan to a stable and secure state that did not harbor terrorists required a long-term presence by an agile force capable of rapidly moving from stability operations to combat and back. While not required to participate substantively in the initial combat operations, the conventional Army served—and continues to serve on point as part of the coalition force—conducting sustained operations to secure the hard-won victory and achieve the nation's long-term goals.[42]

---

[41] Cordesman (2002), p. 27.

[42] Fontenot, Degen, and Tohn (2004), p. 25.

# CHAPTER SIX

# Iraq, 2003

## Background

On September 17, 2002, President Bush outlined a new *National Security Strategy* that would redefine how the United States viewed its military options. Until this point, the administration's strategy had been largely reactive and similar to that of the previous administration's, as it was laid out in the September 2001 *Quadrennial Defense Review Report*: "U.S. forces will remain capable of swiftly defeating attacks against U.S. allies and friends in overlapping timeframes."[1] President Bush's new policy envisioned a proactive approach to the threats facing the nation:

> The United States has long maintained the option of preemptive actions to counter a sufficient threat to our national security. The greater the threat, the greater is the risk of inaction—and the more compelling the case for taking anticipatory action to defend ourselves, even if uncertainty remains as to the time and place of the enemy's attack. To forestall or prevent such hostile acts by our adversaries, the United States will, if necessary, act preemptively.[2]

It soon became clear that Iraq would serve as the first application of this new national policy. On November 27, 2001, Secretary

---

[1]  U.S. Department of Defense (2001), p. 21.

[2]  The President of the United States, *The National Security Strategy of the United States of America*, The White House, 2002, p. 15.

of Defense Donald H. Rumsfeld called General Tommy Franks and told him, "[T]he President wants us to look at options for Iraq."[3] In the coming months, CENTCOM developed a four-phase plan for the invasion of Iraq and the toppling of Saddam Hussein's regime: Phase I—Preparation, Phase II—Shape the Battlespace, Phase III—Decisive Operations, and Phase IV—Post-Hostility Operations.[4] The following discussion focuses on Phase III.

The "D-Day" for the war against Iraq—termed Operation Iraqi Freedom (OIF)—began March 19, 2003, with the failed attempt to decapitate the Iraqi government by a strike on Dora Farm using Tomahawk land-attack cruise missiles and F-117s. CIA operatives believed Saddam and his two sons, Uday and Qusay, were at that location. U.S. special forces had also infiltrated Iraq and were particularly active in the Western area, where they worked to keep Scud missiles from firing and protecting the southern oil fields.[5]

"G-Day," the ground invasion across the Kuwaiti border into Iraq, began early in the morning of March 21 (D+2). "A-Day," the start of major air operations, began the evening of March 21. General Franks phased the initial ground and air operations as he did in an attempt to achieve operational surprise against the Iraqis. He believed that the enemy was anticipating an extended air campaign before a ground invasion, as had been the case in the first Gulf War. His concern was that the coalition air campaign would be the trigger for the Iraqis to begin sabotaging Rumilyah oil fields. By delaying A-Day, Franks planned to surprise the Iraqis and rapidly secure the oil fields with the 1st Marine Expeditionary Force. In General Franks's words,

> During months of planning, the length of air operations in preparation for ground attack had steadily decreased. Two months earlier, we had projected sixteen days and nights of air and SOF operations to "shape the battlespace" before the first Coalition armor crossed the berm. Now our Abrams tanks and Bradleys

---

[3]  Franks (2004), p. 315.

[4]  Franks (2004), p. 350.

[5]  Franks (2004), pp. 433–435.

would already be deep inside Iraq when Buzz Moseley's [CFACC] airmen delivered a possible knockout blow to the regime in Baghdad on the night of Friday, March 21.[6]

The decisive operations phase of the campaign progressed rapidly, and on April 9—twenty-one days after ground forces began combat operations—the Iraqi regime collapsed. On July 9, 2003, Secretary Rumsfeld and General Franks testified before the Senate Armed Services Committee. Secretary Rumsfeld believed that OIF had yielded several key lessons:

- The importance of *speed*, and the ability to get inside enemy's decision cycle and strike before he is able to mount a coherent defense;
- The importance of *jointness*, and the ability of U.S. forces to fight, not as individual de-conflicted services, but as a truly joint force—maximizing the power and lethality they bring to bear;
- The importance of *intelligence*—and the ability to act on intelligence rapidly, in minutes, instead of days and even hours;
- The importance of *precision*, and the ability to deliver devastating damage to enemy positions, while sparing civilian lives and the civilian infrastructure.[7]

Secretary Rumsfeld continued, perhaps pushing his department's transformation agenda and taking a poke at the "Powell doctrine" of overwhelming force:

Another lesson is that in the 21st century "overmatching power" is more important than "overwhelming force." In the past, under the doctrine of overwhelming force, force tended to be measured in terms of mass—the number of troops that were committed to a particular conflict. In the 21st century, mass may no longer be the best measure of power in a conflict. After all, when

---

6   Franks (2004), pp. 437–440, 489 (quote on pp. 439–440).

7   "Prepared Testimony by U.S. Secretary of Defense Donald H. Rumsfeld," before the Senate Armed Services Committee, July 9, 2003. Emphasis in the original.

Baghdad fell, there were just over 100,000 American forces on the ground. General Franks overwhelmed the enemy not with the typical three to one advantage in mass, but by overmatching the enemy with advanced capabilities, and using those capabilities in innovative and unexpected ways.[8]

General Franks expanded on Secretary Rumsfeld's points:

Decisive combat in Iraq saw a maturing of joint force operations in many ways. Some capabilities reached new performance levels. From a Joint Integration perspective, our experience in OPERA-TIONS Southern and Northern Watch, and Enduring Freedom helped to develop a joint culture in our headquarters and in our components. These operations helped to improve joint interoperability and improve our joint C4I [command, control, communications, computers, and intelligence] networks as joint force synergy was taken to new levels of sophistication. Our forces were able to achieve their operational objectives by integrating ground maneuver, special operations, precision lethal fires and non-lethal effects. We saw for the first time integration of forces rather than deconfliction of forces. This integration enabled conventional (air, ground, and sea) forces to leverage SOF capabilities to deal effectively with asymmetric threats and enable precision targeting simultaneously in the same battle space. Likewise, Special Operators were able to use conventional forces to enhance and enable special missions. Operational fires spearheaded our ground maneuver, as our forces sustained the momentum of the offense while defeating enemy formations in open, complex, and urban terrain.

We saw jointness, precision munitions, C2 [command and control], equipment readiness, state of training of the troops, and Coalition support as clear "winners" during OIF.[9]

---

[8]   "Prepared Testimony by U.S. Secretary of Defense Donald H. Rumsfeld" (2003).

[9]   "Statement of General Tommy R. Franks, Former Commander, US Central Command," before the Senate Armed Services Committee, July 9, 2003.

Clearly, the Iraqis were woefully outclassed by the enormous advantages in technical capabilities and force competence that the coalition employed. A key component of the technical overmatch was the coalition's impressive ability to "see" the battlefield—day and night, and all weather. General Franks's Joint Operations Center J-2 (intelligence staff) Fusion Cell combined the "all source intelligence" that flowed into it from an impressive array of reporting systems and sensors, which included Blue Force and Red Force Trackers; Force XXI Battle Command Brigade and Below (FBCB2); intelligence from satellites, JSTARS, UAVs, and reconnaissance aircraft (live video, digital photography, infrared detection, synthetic aperture radar, moving target indicator); and a modest CIA human intelligence network inside Iraq. Again, this intelligence capability gave the coalition an unprecedented strategic and operational view of the battlespace.[10] And it exploited this advantage to great effect with fires and maneuver.

The skill of the coalition made its technical edge all the more powerful against a largely incompetent Iraqi military, whose morale and readiness were very low before OIF. As Stephen Biddle explains in *Toppling Saddam: Iraq and American Military Transformation*:

> The Iraqis in 2003 were anything but highly proficient. Their poor training and leadership produced a combination of mistakes, ill-prepared fighting positions, poor marksmanship, and flawed dispositions that left them fatally exposed to Coalition technology at all ranges. This in turn enabled a relatively small coalition force to prevail in a short, relatively low-cost campaign.[11]

---

[10] Franks (2004), pp. 446–447. This is but a small sampling of the reporting systems and sensors employed in OIF. For an expanded discussion, see Fontenot, Degen, and Tohn (2004), pp. 58–66; U.S. Army 3rd Infantry Division, *Third Infantry Division (Mechanized) After Action Report: Operation Iraqi Freedom*, Fort Stewart, Ga., 2003, pp. 2–16, 63–82, 183–197; Air Combat Command, "Briefing: Airpower Lessons from Operation Iraqi Freedom, 25 Nov 03," Langley Air Force Base, 2003; and Mike Groen et al., *After Action Report, 1st Marine Division: Operation Iraqi Freedom*, Camp Pendleton, Calif.: Headquarters, 1st Marine Division, 2003, pp. 32–37.

[11] Biddle et al. (2004), p. 23.

Furthermore, the Iraqis' "inability to exploit complex terrain for cover and concealment left them exposed to Coalition standoff precision strike."[12] This was particularly true with respect to urban terrain:

> The Republican Guard and Iraqi Regular Army received no training whatsoever in urban warfare in the years leading up to the war. In fact, Guard and Army commanders found the entire concept of city fighting unthinkable. As one Iraqi colonel put it: "Why would anyone want to fight in a city?" His troops "couldn't defend themselves in cities."[13]

Nevertheless, the coalition suffered from inadequate intelligence in three major areas that affected decisive operations. First, it erroneously assumed that the Iraqis would employ chemical and possibly biological agents against its forces. This did not happen, but the precautions coalition forces took degraded operations. Second, the coalition was surprised by the appearance and ferocity of attacks by the paramilitary group Saddam Fedayeen on the battlefield. These light forces offered stiff resistance but were no match for coalition combat forces. They did, however, pose a significant threat to the coalition's extended ground lines of communication.[14] Finally, coalition forces expected a major battle for Baghdad. Fortunately, "pre-battle intelligence reports" had overestimated the resistance Iraqi conventional forces would mount in Baghdad.[15] Essentially, the leadership of the conventional Iraqi Army—as well as its surviving soldiers—had largely melted away as the coalition entered Baghdad. The 1st Marine Division's post-OIF

---

[12] Biddle et al. (2004), p. 29.

[13] Biddle et al. (2004), p. 28. Biddle notes that the Special Republican Guard was the only force that "was given any systematic training in conventional urban warfare, and even this was poor quality. The paramilitaries who shouldered much of the burden of city fighting in 2003 received no sustained conventional military training of any kind" (p. 28).

[14] Franks (2004), pp. 486–489. See also Michael R. Gordon and Bernard E. Trainor, *COBRA II: The Inside Story of the Invasion and Occupation of Iraq*, New York: Pantheon Books, 2006, pp. 498–499, 500–501, for a discussion of the Fedayeen and the United States' "failure to read the early signs of the insurgency and to adapt accordingly" (p. 501).

[15] Groen et al. (2003), p. 77.

after-action report succinctly summed up the continuing difficulties with taking the measure of an adversary: "As always, it had been easier to count enemy equipment than it was to judge the enemy's will."[16]

In the aftermath of the collapse of the Iraqi regime, the coalition began what it believed were Phase IV operations—the transition to post-conflict peace operations—on April 10.[17] On May 1, President Bush proclaimed from the deck of the USS *Abraham Lincoln*, "Major combat operations in Iraq have ended," while cautioning, "We have difficult work to do in Iraq."[18] Nevertheless, despite the rapidity of "decisive operations" in collapsing Saddam Hussein's regime, lessons about the relative roles of ground and air power in Iraqi Freedom have emerged in the public domain. These lessons are perhaps most apparent in the relationship between the U.S. Army V Corps (and its main effort, the 3rd Infantry Division) and the CFACC.

## A Joint Ground-Centric View

Coalition ground forces—the U.S. Army's 3rd Infantry Division and V Corps, the 1st Marine Expeditionary Force, and the British 1st Armoured Division—began crossing the Kuwait-Iraq border in the early morning hours of March 21, 2003, "G-Day." The mission statement issued by Lieutenant General David McKiernan, the combined force land component commander (CFLCC), in his March 19 execution order (CFLCC EXORD), was a masterpiece of brevity:

> Mission: CFLCC attacks to defeat Iraqi forces and control the zone of action, secure and exploit designated sites, and removes the current Iraqi regime. CFLCC conducts continuous stability operations to create conditions for transition to CJTF-Iraq.[19]

---

[16] Groen et al. (2003), pp. 77–78.

[17] Fontenot, Degen, and Tohn (2004), pp. 339.

[18] Bob Woodward, *Plan of Attack*, New York: Simon and Schuster, 2004, p. 412.

[19] Fontenot, Degen, and Tohn (2004), p. 95.

It was a "rolling start," beginning with the forces in theater, which would be reinforced during the campaign. This decision, which carried some risk, is discussed in the U.S. Army's history of OIF:

> Ground operations commenced while follow-on forces continued to flow into the theater. When 3rd ID's [Infantry Division's] main body crossed the berm on 21 March, it was the only Army division ready to fight out of the four that the original plan required. The remaining units were still moving into the theater, linking up with their equipment, or moving forward to attack positions. . . .
>
> With a clear understanding of the strategic situation and of the CFLCC's combat power, General Franks made the deliberate decision to start the ground fight before some of the designated forces were available and ready for combat. He balanced the strategic, operational, and tactical benefits of a rapid, early advance against the risk inherent in not having sufficient combat power to achieve the campaign's objective at the start of operations. The tensions within this balance affected the campaign's execution and are a defining characteristic of the entire operation.[20]

Aside from combat forces, the rolling start also affected the ability of CENTCOM to support and sustain operations:

> [T]he repercussions of starting the war with an immature logistics, long-distance communications, and transportation capabilities surfaced. As the soldiers and marines leapt forward, the logisticians, communicators, and transporters struggled to keep up. Meticulous planning for fuel, water, and ammunition paid off, yet at a cost. Delivery of just about every other commodity, to include repair parts, suffered as a consequence of inadequate means, limited ability to track supplies, and lack of an effective distribution system. These challenges became significant as the fight progressed toward Karbala and southern Baghdad.[21]

---

[20] Fontenot, Degen, and Tohn (2004), pp. 94.

[21] Fontenot, Degen, and Tohn (2004), p. 94–95.

From the Army perspective, coalition air power had made a crucial difference in the success of OIF, particularly in the availability of CAS and shaping fires. Lieutenant General William S. Wallace, V Corps Commander, recalled: "We've gotten more close air support and more availability of CAS and more access to CAS than I can ever remember. I go back to Vietnam, and we didn't have that kind of CAS in Vietnam." The Army history of OIF, *On Point*, reinforces General Wallace's accolades:

> CAS proved decisive in assuring tactical victory and, on more than one occasion, decisive in preventing tactical defeat. Perhaps just as important, CAS provided a strong boost to troops on the ground, who were profoundly grateful to the airmen who flew those missions. What had been a source of irritation has become a source of satisfaction and admiration.[22]

Air power, however, also made important contributions above the tactical level. General Franks, as already mentioned, believed that "operational fires spearheaded our ground maneuver."[23] The Army, in its history of OIF, acknowledged the contribution made by coalition air power:

> [I]t is difficult to overstate the importance of air operations in the context of OIF. By dominating the air over Iraq, coalition air forces shaped the fight to allow for rapid dominance on the ground. . . . integration of precision munitions with ground operations, supported by a largely space-based command and control network, enabled combat operations to occur in ways only imagined a decade ago.[24]

The air power employed against the Iraqi Army was formidable:

> Lethal combinations of A-10s, F-15s, F-16s, F/A-18s, B-1s, B-52s and a host of other aircraft were absolutely essential to the ground

---

[22] Fontenot, Degen, and Tohn (2004), p. 428.

[23] "Statement of General Tommy R. Franks" (2003), p. 5.

[24] Fontenot, Degen, and Tohn (2004), p. xxvi.

campaign's success. . . . Throughout the campaign, 79 percent of air operations (15,592 of 19,898 attacks) were CAS or kill box interdiction—direct targeting of Iraqi ground targets in support of coalition maneuver.[25]

The operational effect of these attacks was significant because they were "generally effective in hindering the bulk of the conventional forces from reaching cities, either by destroying them en route or by inducing the soldiers to abandon their equipment."[26] The only complaint Army commanders had was "the clearance of fires process was sometimes unwieldy."[27]

In General Wallace's mind, one particular occasion epitomized the powerful effects of joint ground-air operations. Toward the end of the drive to Baghdad, General Wallace executed several limited attacks whose objective was "to deceive enemy units into repositioning and to destroy enemy reconnaissance capabilities."[28] General Wallace later recalled:

> Now, the results of those five simultaneous actions, in my mind, caused the enemy to react. Late that afternoon, in beautiful sunlight, we started getting reports of the Republican Guard repositioning to what we believed to be their final defensive setup. My current thinking is that those actions caused the enemy commander to think that series of attacks was our main effort, that our main attack had started. . . . That was never our intention. But having done that, I believe our attacks caused him to react to our actions, fully knowing that if he did not react to them, given the limited successes that we had in those actions, then he would be out of position. So he started repositioning—vehicles, artillery, and tanks on [equipment transporters]—in broad daylight, under the eyes of the US Air Force.

---

[25] Fontenot, Degen, and Tohn (2004), pp. 249–250.

[26] Fontenot, Degen, and Tohn (2004), p. 250.

[27] Fontenot, Degen, and Tohn (2004), p. 250.

[28] Fontenot, Degen, and Tohn (2004), p. 259

I believe it was one of those classic cases of a maneuver action setting up operational fires which in turn set up for a successful decisive maneuver, which took place the following day and over the following 48 hours. Just 48 hours later, we owned Baghdad International Airport. . . . We had begun the encirclement of Baghdad. From my perch, my perspective, my retrospection, that was a tipping point in the campaign.[29]

This is different from what is frequently referred to as "the hammer and anvil" approach, in which air power serves as a "hammer," smashing enemy forces against the ground power "anvil."[30] Instead, it is more a case of ground power flushing the enemy, allowing air power to maul his forces, with ground power finishing the fight against the remnants and controlling the ground dimension in the aftermath of combat. This critical ground forces role was clearly demonstrated in OIF:

[G]round combat remains physically demanding. Ground operations remain central to toppling a regime by defeating its armed forces, seizing and holding territory, and controlling the population. While the campaign clearly took advantage of breathtaking technology, in the end, individual soldiers took the fight to the enemy in a personal, eyeball-to-eyeball manner. Humans, not high-tech sensors, remain indispensable, even in the 21st century.[31]

Nevertheless, the importance of "shaping" the battlefield with air power, enabled through high levels of operational situational awareness, was that it created a tactical condition whereby coalition ground forces never faced large conventional Iraqi formations "eyeball-to-eyeball." Enemy forces between Baghdad and Iraq's southern border could not maneuver in large formations without the possibility of being detected and accurately attacked, anytime, anywhere, day or night, *and*

---

[29] Fontenot, Degen, and Tohn (2004), p. 260.

[30] Pape (2004), p. 117.

[31] Fontenot, Degen, and Tohn (2004), p. xxvi.

*in any weather.*[32] There were no repetitions of the World War II Battle of the Bulge, when, in bad weather that grounded Allied air forces, the German Army achieved operational surprise when it attacked Allied forces with elements of 28 divisions out of the Ardennes.[33] Colonel William Grimsely, commander of the 1st Brigade, 3rd Infantry Division, acknowledged this new reality, recalling: "We never really found any cohesive unit of any brigade, of any Republican Guard Division."[34] Consequently, a relatively small coalition ground component could press on to Baghdad, facing mainly remnants of the less-than-competent Iraqi conventional forces and fanatical, but poorly equipped and trained, Saddam Fedayeen paramilitary forces, which were largely slaughtered when they made their suicidal attacks. In short, for coalition ground forces, OIF was a long series of tactical engagements that culminated in the strategic collapse of the Iraqi regime.

These tactical engagements, however, were often "meeting engagements" because technically enabled situational awareness did not always extend to the brigade level and below. Quite simply, as the Army's history of OIF notes, units could not "remotely identify and continuously track Iraqi units that chose to move by infiltration and to shield themselves where and when possible."[35] Although commanders had a sense of where they would encounter the enemy—either from intelligence or from their own assessment of possible enemy courses of action— "[m]ost tactical unit commanders claimed that they made every assault as a movement to contact."[36] Thus, situational awareness at the tactical level, as was the case in Operation Anaconda in Afghanistan, remained

---

[32] JDAM is revolutionary because it is an accurate, all-weather munition that has area effects, the parameters of which are relative to the target and the size bomb to which the JDAM kit is affixed.

[33] Forrest C. Pogue, *The Supreme Command: U.S. Army in World War II*, Washington, D.C.: U.S. Army Center of Military History, 1989, p. 360.

[34] Air Combat Command (2003), slide 19.

[35] Fontenot, Degen, and Tohn (2004), p. 422.

[36] Fontenot, Degen, and Tohn (2004), p. 423. This account concludes that "[t]he ability of Iraqis to hide, with some success, from the incredible array of technical intelligence available to the coalition may give pause to those advocating that US forces will be able to develop the situation out of contact and attack from standoff distances" (p. 422).

a particularly difficult problem. In short, "the experience of OIF seems a reminder that the enemy gets a vote" and that "[a]mbiguity is likely to remain a factor in combat operations indefinitely."[37] In OIF, heavy armor made up for tactical gaps in situational awareness.[38]

Perhaps OIF's most troublesome experience for proponents of a ground-centric approach to warfare was the performance of the AH-64 Apache helicopter units in executing deep attack operations. Army aviation doctrine stresses that it "operates in the ground regime" and that it is "a component of the combined arms team, not the air component of the US Army. . . . Aviation is composed of soldiers, not airmen."[39] Furthermore, members of the Army aviation community view their units as "maneuver forces engaged in shaping the battlespace and conducting decisive combat operations by employing direct fire and stand-off precision weapons in combined arms operations."[40]

Preeminent among Army aviation maneuver forces are the attack helicopter units flying the AH-64 Apache. They are a key component of the Army's vision of deep battle because "[t]he speed with which attack helicopters can mass combat power at chosen points in the battle area allows the force commander to influence the battle to a depth that

---

[37] Fontenot, Degen, and Tohn (2004), p. 424. See also David Talbot, "How Technology Failed in Iraq," *Technology Review*, November 2004. This article notes the difficulty of establishing adequate situational awareness below the division level:

> "What we uncovered in general in Iraq is, there appeared to be . . . a digital divide." . . . "At the division level or above, the view of the battle space was adequate to their needs. They were getting good feeds from the sensors." . . . But among front-line army commanders . . . as well as . . . in the U.S. Marines—"Everybody said the same thing. It was a universal comment: We had terrible situational awareness." The same verdict was delivered after the first Gulf War's ground battle, but experts had hoped the more robust technology used in the 2003 conflict would solve the problem.

[38] Biddle et al (2004), p. 9. Biddle describes the "Thunder Run" and the value of heavy armor:

> [W]hen 3ID's 2nd Brigade launched its "Thunder Run" into the city on April 5, it met a fusillade of Iraqi rocket propelled grenade (RPG) and small arms fire, at effectively point blank range, along its entire route. *Every single vehicle* in the brigade column was hit a least once by Iraqi RPGs and many took multiple hits. [Emphasis in the original.].

[39] U.S. Department of the Army, FM 1-100, *Army Aviation Operations*, 1997, p. 3.

[40] U.S. Department of the Army, FM 1-100 (1997), p. 3.

would otherwise be beyond his reach."[41] The doctrine for deep operations notes that

> Deep operations, or raids, are activities directed against enemy forces that are not currently engaged but that could influence division or corps close operations within the next 24 to 72 hours. . . . Deep attacks by corps ATKHBs [attack helicopter battalions] help the corps commander to shape the battlefield and set the terms for close operations.[42]

As V Corps moved north toward Karbala, General Wallace ordered the 11th Attack Helicopter Regiment (AHR) to execute deep strike operations against the Iraqi Medina Division. The mission's purpose was straight out of aviation doctrine:

> to shape the Corps' battlespace and thereby provide the 3rd ID freedom to maneuver in the Karbala area by destroying the artillery and armor forces of the 14th, 2nd, and 10th Brigades of the *Medina* Division.[43]

The 11th AHR employed elements of its organic 2-6th Cavalry Squadron and the 1-277th Attack Helicopter Battalion (AHB) (attached from the 1st Cavalry Division) in its deep operation the night of March 23.[44] From the beginning, the friction of war—problems with refueling, communications, and SEAD/CAS execution—plagued the operation. Nevertheless, 30 Apaches proceeded to their objectives. The 11th AHR ran into a hornet's nest of ground fire as it flew over

---

[41] U.S. Department of the Army, FM 1-112, *Attack Helicopter Operations*, 1997, p. 1-2.

[42] U.S. Department of the Army, FM 1-112 (1997), p. 1-6.

[43] Fontenot, Degen, and Tohn (2004), p. 180. Emphasis in the original.

[44] Fontenot, Degen, and Tohn (2004), p. 185. The 11th AHR had three squadron-sized units in OIF: the 2-6th and 6-6th Cavalry and the 1-277th AHB from the 1st Cavalry Division (attached). The 2-6th Cavalry and the 6-6th Cavalry each had 21 Apaches (the regiment had a total of 21 AH-64A Apaches and 21 AH-64D Longbow Apaches; the 1-277th AHB had 18 AH-64D Longbow Apaches).

built-up areas en route to its objectives.[45] The Iraqis, aware of American SEAD capabilities, "appear to have relied on ground observers who reported on cellular phones and low-power radios"[46] the approach of the Apaches. It was "a simple, yet sophisticated air defense 'system,'" largely reliant on optically directed small arms and machine-gun fire "that was virtually impossible to detect and suppress."[47] This system proved very effective against low-flying, relatively slow helicopters.

Neither of the regiment's battalions caused any appreciable damage to the Medina division before withdrawing in the face of withering ground fire. The regiment also suffered significant damage. All 30 Apaches were hit, with one battalion's helicopters, "[o]n average . . . sporting 15–20 bullet holes each." One Apache was lost in action and its crew captured.[48] On hearing of the travails of one of the 11th AHR's battalions, General Franks later recalled thinking at the time: "It's a blessing we didn't lose the whole battalion."[49]

V Corps conducted one more deep attack operation with attack helicopters on March 28. Two battalions of the 101st Aviation Brigade (101st Airborne Division) carried out the attack. The Apaches avoided built-up areas as they made their way toward their objectives—again the Medina Division—in the vicinity of Karbala. Additionally, SEAD and CAS were better coordinated.[50] Nevertheless, this second deep attack did not meet expectations. One battalion never found any targets. The second, in conjunction with Air Force and Navy fighters,

---

[45] See also Fontenot, Degen, and Tohn (2004), p. 186. The deep attack was executed by elements of the 6-6th Cavalry and the 1-277th AHB because there was sufficient fuel for only 31 of their Apache helicopters, and one of these crashed at the assembly area. Nevertheless, the "regiment leadership believed they had adequate resources" for the mission" (p. 185). See also *Battle Summary, OPERATION IRAQI FREEDOM, 6th Squadron, 6th U.S. Cavalry*, n.d., p. 5, which notes that "6-6 Cav had 5 mission capable aircraft that were not able to launch on the mission because they did not have fuel."

[46] Fontenot, Degen, and Tohn (2004), p. 191.

[47] Fontenot, Degen, and Tohn (2004), pp. 191.

[48] Fontenot, Degen, and Tohn (2004), p. 189.

[49] Franks (2004), p. 498.

[50] Fontenot, Degen, and Tohn (2004), pp. 192–195.

"destroyed six armored personnel carriers, four tanks, five trucks, and a fiber optic facility . . . [and] killed approximately 20 troops. . . not a high count by 'exercise standards.'"[51]

The 101st Aviation Brigade's Karbala mission was the last deep attack flown by attack helicopters during OIF. The focus shifted to a different set of missions. The post-Karbala experiences of the attack helicopters of the 101st Airborne Division, in particular, show the contributions—and potential—of Army attack helicopters in roles other than deep attack operations.

The 101st Airborne Division adapted to "enemy and environmental factors" and shifted its attack helicopter units to "daylight armed reconnaissance and security operations ISO [in support of] ground forces clearing urban areas and other tactical objectives."[52] The daylight armed reconnaissance missions—long-range attacks to protect the flank of V Corps[53]—were sophisticated joint operations that

> were often packaged with other air assets, such as USAF's E-8 Joint STARS radar, E-3 AWACS command and control aircraft, and F-16s with High speed Anti-Radiation Missiles, and Navy EA-6B electronic jamming aircraft. The Apaches would gather intelligence on how Iraqi forces were arrayed and scout for targets—but husband their own ordnance. If they came across hot targets, they'd call for strikes from Army artillery or from fixed-wing fighters overhead.[54]

Colonel Gregory P. Gass, commander of the 101st Aviation Brigade (Attack) during OIF later recalled why daylight operations became

---

[51] Fontenot, Degen, and Tohn (2004), p. 195.

[52] U.S. Army 101st Airborne Division (Air Assault), "Aviation Operations During Operations Iraqi Freedom," briefing, undated, slide 58.

[53] U.S. Army 101st Airborne Division (Air Assault) (undated), slide 58. Although the 101st Airborne Division conducted operations with attack helicopters after Karbala that "went deep," they were not the "deep attack" missions defined in Army aviation doctrine: "Deep attacks by corps ATKHBs [attack helicopter battalions] help the corps commander to shape the battlefield and set the terms for close operations" (U.S. Department of the Army, FM 1-112, 1997, p. 1-6).

[54] Richard J. Newman, "Ambush at Najaf," *Air Force Magazine*, October 2003, p. 63.

the norm after the Karbala deep attack, during which the brigade lost two helicopters to "mishaps, both at night with zero illumination."[55] Gass states: "Our accidents did convince us to re-evaluate some of our tactics, techniques and procedures—most notably conducting attacks in daylight rather than at night to minimize the dust's effects during takeoff and landing. Poor visibility remained an issue; dust storms lingered throughout the region."[56] Gass also writes that daylight operations were largely possible because of the absence of a sophisticated air defense threat during operations over enemy territory:

> Realizing the enemy's "iron sight" systems would be more effective during daylight, we drew on the Apache Target Acquisition and Designation System's ability to acquire and ID targets at much greater range in daylight, which provided increased standoff. Also, up to this point we had minimal radar activity from the enemy's integrated air defense systems.[57]

All these factors resulted in a pragmatic assessment by the 101st Airborne Division after the Karbala mission: "[E]nemy did not present a massed target array; consequently risks (especially night desert landings) of conducting deep attacks outweigh potential effects on target."[58]

The 101st's attack helicopters were also valuable in close combat attack missions, supporting ground operation in battles that "contributed to the liberation of Karbala, An Najaf, Al Hillah, Iskandiriyah, Al Mahmudiya, Qayyarah, Mosul."[59] As American

> troops punched through areas such as the Ramadi Gap, al Hillah, and Karbala, Apaches often hovered "over the shoulder" of ground units, guarding their flanks, protecting supply lines, and conducting standoff attacks of enemy troops up to five miles

---

[55] Gregory P. Gass, "The Road Ahead," *Rotor and Wing*, October 2003, p. 26.

[56] Gass (2003), p. 25.

[57] Gass (2003), p. 25.

[58] U.S. Army 101st Airborne Division (Air Assault) (undated), slide 58.

[59] U.S. Army 101st Airborne Division (Air Assault) (undated), slide 58.

ahead. At al Hillah, for instance, an Apache company from the 101st . . . was a key factor in the defeat of a Republican Guard battalion.[60]

Attack aviation also contributed by

filling the security vacuum created as the lead Army battalions briskly bypassed cities such as an Najaf and Karbala. When the 101st moved into some of those areas to begin peace enforcement operations, Apache helicopters turned out to be invaluable: Hovering over buildings gave them an ideal perch for intelligence gathering and taking direct action. They were far more effective than artillery when US ground forces needed offensive fire. When Iraqi irregulars belonging to the Fedayeen Saddam militia fired on a US brigade commander's convoy in Najaf, for instance, an Apache aircrew had the mobility—and the lethality—to track the attackers and destroy their vehicles. By the time US forces reached the Iraqi capital, Apache crews found themselves in an unprecedented role, essentially flying air combat patrols for troops engaged in urban combat.[61]

Apaches also supported air assault raids in the aftermath of major combat operations in Anbar province in the summer of 2003 (often with SOF forces and CAS) on terrorist sites and against high-value targets and provided a quick reaction force capability throughout the division's AO.[62]

---

[60] Newman (2003), p. 63. See also U.S. Army 101st Airborne Division (Air Assault) (undated), slide 58, which notes the damage inflicted by the 101st on the Iraqi army: 256 air defense artillery systems, 110 artillery systems, 287 maneuver systems, 47 radar systems, 11 surface-to-surface missile systems, 839 other pieces of equipment, and numerous enemy personnel.

[61] Newman (2003), p. 63. See also E. J. Sinclair, "Aviation in Operational Maneuver," briefing, U.S. Army Aviation Warfighting Center, undated, for a discussion of Army aviation in Afghanistan and Iraq.

[62] U.S. Army 101st Airborne Division (Air Assault) (undated), slides 39–52, 58. Some of the air assault raids covered long distances and were quite sizable. Operation McClellen, August 29–30, 2003, involved 96 aircraft from this division and the aerial movement of an infantry battalion task force over 430 kilometers (slide 50).

In Iraq, the Army—as it is in Kosovo and Afghanistan—remains engaged in stability and support operations; however, it is also contending with a difficult and deadly insurgency. In this environment, Army attack aviation continues to adapt and to provide critical support to ground forces as it did during OIF.

## A Joint Air-Centric View

Much of air power's contribution to ground operations during OIF has already been discussed. The Air Force understood the importance of its role in this regard. A briefing by the Air Force's Air Combat Command, "Airpower Lessons from Operation Iraqi Freedom," provides a succinct view of the impact of "air dominance" on the campaign:

- A new level of "freedom of action" could be exploited, our forces [were] free from air attack and able to strike at any point in the battlespace
- Ground forces able to operate immediately.[63]

Air power, however, had a much broader range of activity before and after OIF than shaping the battlespace for the ground campaign. Shaping for air dominance had occurred before the actual start of OIF. After November 2001, attacks on Iraqi ground-based air defenses intensified, and the United States and the United Kingdom "began an active campaign to suppress them in the summer of 2002 called 'Southern Focus.'"[64] Between June 2001 and March 19, 2003, coalition aircraft "flew 21,736 sorties, struck 349 Iraqi air defense targets, and fired 606 munitions" during Operation Southern Focus. This campaign centered on actively suppressing Iraqi air defenses in preparation for the impending war.[65] Thus,

---

[63] Air Combat Command (2003), slide 7.

[64] Anthony H. Cordesman, *The Iraq War: Strategy, Tactics, and Military Lessons*, Washington, D.C.: Center for Strategic and International Studies, 2003, p. 253.

[65] Cordesman (2003), p. 253.

[t]he coalition's ability to paralyze Iraq's air force and the systematic suppression of Iraqi air defenses allowed coalition air forces to
achieve nearly total air dominance shortly after the first air strikes
on March 19—a level of air superiority the United States and its
allies had never enjoyed in any previous major war.[66]

Although a significant portion of the air campaign focused on
Iraqi ground forces, the object of the campaign was to affect the Iraqi
regime as a system. This was not the "shock and awe" strategic attack
touted by proponents of a "notion of independent effects so powerful
they would put all other aspects of air warfare and joint operations
in the shade."[67] Instead, the coalition took advantage of advances in
command, control, communications, computers, intelligence, surveillance, and reconnaissance (C4ISR) and targeting technologies, and it
employed an effects-based approach to air operations to

> severely limit the number of targets it had to strike and then care-
> fully match weapon accuracy and reliability, and the size of the
> weapon to the right aim point necessary to destroy the function
> of a target without imposing unnecessary destruction or risk to
> the target and target area.[68]

---

[66] Cordesman (2003), pp. 253–254. See also Suzann Chapman, "The 'War' Before the
War," *Air Force Magazine*, February 2004.

[67] Rebecca Grant, "The Redefinition of Strategic Airpower," *Air Force Magazine*, Vol. 86,
No. 10, October 2003c. See also later in the article where Grant discusses the four roles of
strategic air power in OIF:

> In the 2003 Iraq war, strategic air power had four major roles. First, already achieved
> by March, was to guarantee access to the battlespace by neutralizing Iraq's integrated
> air defenses. Second, strategic attacks sought to "strategically dislocate" the regime and
> narrow command and control of Iraqi military forces to a trickle. Third, the air com-
> ponent moved to maintain air superiority and extend it by destroying SAM batteries in
> the north. The fourth role was to go after the three categories of time sensitive targets:
> leadership, terrorists, and weapons of mass destruction.

[68] Cordesman (2003), p. 29.

Consequently, the coalition sought "to paralyze and destroy a regime, not bomb a country."[69] In application, effects-based operations involved

> the selective use of precision air power to strike at targets to produce effects rather than simply maximize physical damage. Examples of such targeting include knocking out power communications, and fuel supplies to Iraqi military forces, rather than attacking major infrastructure facilities. Others include selectively bombing Iraqi regular army forces to paralyze or reduce their movement rather than destroy them by attrition, and using sensor platforms like the E-8C JSTARS to attack actual military units in movement, rather than blow bridges and attack lines of communication. Improved avionics and precision greatly reduced the need for multiple weapons to be used on a given target and for later restrikes. As one senior U.S. Air Force general put it, "Even in the Gulf War, the issue was always how many sorties it took to destroy a given target. In this war the issue is how many targets can be destroyed in a given sortie." Advances in precision also allowed the United States to reshape its targeting and choice of munitions to reduce civilian casualties and collateral damage. . . . Improvements in laser-guided systems and the use of GPS allowed the use of smaller bombs and often allowed 500-pound bombs to be used instead of 2,000-pound bombs.[70]

Some 1,800 coalition aircraft conducted approximately 20,000 strikes during OIF, with the vast majority (79 percent) focused on Iraqi ground forces.[71] The remaining sorties were directed

> against Iraqi government targets . . . Iraqi Air Force and Air Defense Command targets . . . [and] suspected sites, forces, and installations that might have weapons of mass destruction or surface-to-surface missiles.[72]

---

[69] Cordesman (2003), p. 29.

[70] Cordesman (2003), pp. 256–257.

[71] Cordesman (2003), p. 275.

[72] Cordesman (2003), p. 275.

Furthermore, the ability to rapidly retarget strike assets "enabled the United States to respond to active intelligence rather than bomb predetermined or fixed targets by the numbers."[73]

OIF was not, however, without friction. Battle damage assessment had significant shortcomings. Thus, the first-order "effects" of the effects-based campaign were not always determinable, much less the second- and third-order effects against enemy systems that underpin effects-based operations concepts. Air Combat Command later noted, "We perform force application better than we can assess its effects."[74] Additionally, "many of the strikes against Iraqi government targets did not do the damage originally estimated during the war, or they hit targets whose nature and value to the Iraqi war effort had not been accurately estimated, or they hit targets that had been largely evacuated." Strikes were also directed in other categories against "low-value or empty targets," and all the attacks against suspected weapons of mass destruction (WMD) targets were without basis, because the Iraqi regime had no WMD stockpiled capability at these sites or others as it appears to have turned out.[75] All that said, effects-based operations showed potential during OIF (and will be discussed later in this report) in that they demonstrated an effort to understand and attack the enemy as a system and to apply air power in a more efficient and intelligent way than had traditional target servicing. Nevertheless, effects-based operations in OIF remained more art than science.

In the area of deliberate planning, OIF, by its dynamic nature, presented several significant challenges. The ATO process did not always prove sufficiently flexible or keep pace with rapidly changing battlefield conditions. This was as much a result of the unanticipated speed of ground operations as it was the ATO process.[76] The 3rd Infan-

---

[73] Cordesman (2003), p. 282.

[74] Air Combat Command (2003), slide 10.

[75] Cordesman (2003), p. 275

[76] Cordesman (2003), p. 283. This opinion is not universally shared. See Air Combat Command (2003), slide 13, which notes that "ATO Cycle and CAOC Operations tremendously responsive."

try Division's after-action report, reflecting on the pace of operations caused by its 19-day, 600-kilometer advance, is instructive:

> Rapid decisive operations executed by the division resulted in changes in how we planned, coordinated, and executed fires. The normal AI [air interdiction] planning process based on 24, 48, 72, 96–hour target refinement, nomination, and submission proved not conducive based on movements of the DTAC [division tactical command post] and division main command post (DMAIN). . . . One of the biggest hurdles the division faced was the ability to conduct target refinement during a rapid advance.[77]

Nevertheless, whatever its shortcomings, the coalition air effort in OIF was critical because it set the conditions for successful major combat operations. The combination of air dominance, vastly improved C4ISR, precision, and all-weather, day-or-night capabilities gave coalition air power an unprecedented capability to seek out and strike the enemy under virtually any conditions. Thus, the coalition was able "to locate and target Iraq forces under weather conditions the Iraqis felt protected them from the air."[78]

The Air Combat Command briefing "Airpower Lessons from Operation Iraqi Freedom" contains several quotes from Iraqi officers that illustrate the impact of coalition air power on their forces. Captain Khalidi, of the Iraqi Republican Guard, recalled the impact of all-weather bombing:

> It was night and in the middle of a severe sandstorm. The troops and vehicles were hidden under trees. The soldiers thought they were safe, but two enormous bombs and a load of cluster munitions found their targets. Some soldiers left their positions and ran away. When the big bombs hit their targets, the vehicles just melted away.[79]

---

[77] U.S. Army 3rd Infantry Division (2003), p. 32.

[78] U.S. Army 3rd Infantry Division (2003), p. 304.

[79] Air Combat Command (2003), slide 17.

We were surprised when they [U.S. pilots] discovered this place. . . . [T]his affected the morale of the soldiers, because they were hiding and thought nobody could find them. . . . In the end, when [U.S. troops] entered Baghdad, everything was messed up . . . there were no orders . . . commanders . . . we didn't know what to do.[80]

Colonel Ghassan, a member of the Iraqi General Staff, spoke of the effect coalition air power had on the overall ability of the Iraqi Army to respond to coalition ground force maneuver:

Defeat was in large part due to our inability to move troops and equipment because of devastating US air power . . . our divisions were essentially destroyed by air strikes when they were still about 30 miles from their destinations. Before elements of the 3rd Infantry Division were in a position to launch their main assault, the [Iraqi] Medina Division had disintegrated.[81]

After its mauling by coalition air dominance, the Iraqi army largely ceased being an operational threat to the coalition.[82]

---

[80] Air Combat Command (2003), slide 16.

[81] Air Combat Command (2003), slide 18.

[82] For a report on the level of the air effort in OIF, see T. Michael Moseley, "Operation Iraqi Freedom—By the Numbers," Central Air Forces, 2003. See also Kevin M. Woods, Michael R. Pease, Mark E. Stout, Williamson Murray, and James G. Lacey, *Iraqi Perspectives Project: A View of Operation Iraqi Freedom from Saddam's Senior Leadership*, Suffolk, Va.: U.S. Joint Forces Command, Joint Center for Operational Analysis, 2006, p. 128, which notes:

> Precision air attacks in the first days of the war may have failed to decapitate the regime, but they had a devastating effect on the Iraqi armed forces—even when they missed. The Commander of the Al-Nida Republican Guards Division, whose division dissolved from the psychological impact of the air attacks, commented to an interviewer after the war:

> The early air attacks hit only empty headquarters and barracks buildings. It did affect our communications switches which were still based in those buildings. We primarily used schools and hidden command centers in orchards for our headquarters—which were not hit. But the accuracy and lethality of those attacks left an indelible impression on those Iraqi soldiers who either observed them directly or saw the damage afterwards.

## Areas of Ground-Air Tension

The "jointness" of the OIF campaign was also better than in previous campaigns. Unlike the 1991 Gulf War, which was largely an air campaign followed by a ground campaign, OIF witnessed unprecedented levels of—in the new term of art—"joint interdependence." CENT-COM had taken significant steps since Afghanistan to improve joint relationships. General Franks's CFACC for OIF, Lieutenant General T. Michael Moseley, was in the same position during Operation Anaconda. He was determined not to repeat the ground-air coordination problems that had plagued Anaconda and placed

> a two-star general [Major General Daniel Leaf] inside the ground component commander's Kuwait headquarters during the 2003 war against Iraq, to serve as his personal representative in coordinating air-ground operations.

This enabled General Moseley to "offer air and space expertise from the very beginning, from the genesis of the motion, whether it's ever executed or not."[83] Furthermore, "[b]andwidth and information connectivity resulted in a high degree of interoperability" between the components, and there was "seamless integration of service component efforts in the CAOC," resulting in "unprecedented cooperation among components."[84]

Thus, in OIF,

> land power reinforced air power and vice versa. Iraqi land forces were forced to expose themselves by the speed of land operations and then were hit hard from the air, which in turn sharply reduced the Iraqi threat to U.S. and British land forces. Jointness took on a new practical meaning.[85]

---

[83] Grossman (2004b).

[84] Air Combat Command (2003), slide 14.

[85] Cordesman (2003), p. 216.

Nevertheless, despite the significant improvements in ground-air effectiveness, some lingering issues remained. These included, as already mentioned, the responsiveness of air support to Army forces. Nevertheless, it appears from the evidence available that the single greatest issue between the Army and the Air Force during OIF was the old one of battlespace management. Ironically, this issue also surfaced between the various echelons of the ground component—that is, the 3rd Infantry Division, V Corps, and the CFLCC.

One of the unintended consequences of vastly improved battlespace awareness at all echelons of command is the temptation of higher echelons to meddle in the business of lower echelons, which often do not have the C4ISR systems to "see" what the higher echelons can see or the systems to attack the targets that are seen. In OIF, this was a continuing point of frustration for the 3rd Infantry Division, as pointed out in its OIF after-action report:

> The division was consistently challenged by CFLCC/CFACC and corps attempting to engage targets with CAS and air interdiction (AI) inside 3ID (M) AO. Instead of passing intelligence information down to the division and allowing 3ID (M) elements to engage targets, higher headquarters insisted upon engaging the targets themselves. On several occasions no known coordination was attempted.

> One more topic worthy of discussion is the argument of engaging targets based on who has "eyes on." On many occasions, either with Hunter, Predator, or SOF, corps had more SA [situational awareness] on the target than the brigade who owned the battlespace. Corps used this information as an argument that they should control the aircraft. The problem lies in the fact that corps may have more SA on the target; however, they do not have more SA on friendly forces in the area. Corps needs to either push the ISR asset down to the division or they need to coordinate with division for operations in our AO.[86]

---

[86] U.S. Army 3rd Infantry Division (2003), pp. 140–141.

Additionally, tension existed between the 3rd Infantry Division and V Corps over so-called corps CAS. This involved creating "an imaginary line approximately 30 km in front of the forward line of own troops (FLOT) that was established to delineate between divisional CAS responsibility and corps use of fixed wing aviation to engage targets." The effect of this innovation was that V Corps "continually engaged targets short of the FSCL in 3ID (M)'s zone without requesting kill boxes be opened," and deconfliction of divisional and corps CAS was often not conducted.[87] These battlespace control issues identified by the 3rd Infantry Division are ones that need to be sorted out in Army and joint ground-centric doctrine.

The other issue—ground-air battlespace management—is more problematic because it involves resolving different notions of how to execute operations. Again, the Army deep attack concepts and the placement of the FSCL are at the heart of the matter.

During OIF, the CFLCC was responsible for placing the FSCL. In the V Corps AO, the CFLCC deferred to the corps for its placement. V Corps routinely requested an FSCL at 100 or more kilometers past the forward edge of the battle area (FEBA).[88] Figure 6.1 depicts the doctrinal manner in which the Army divides its AO into close, deep, and rear areas and the area in which the FSCL is placed.

---

[87] U.S. Army 3rd Infantry Division (2003), p. 106. This report was also explicit in its views about corps CAS: "3ID (M) believes that the CFACC is better prepared to engage targets to effectively shape the battlefield versus V Corps' use of corps CAS" (p. 108). For the corps commander's views about corps CAS, see William S. Wallace, "Joint Fires in OIF: What Worked for the Vth (US) Corps," briefing, U.S. Army Combined Arms Center, 2003. General Wallace was focused, per Army doctrine, on shaping the V Corps AO. In his view (slide 6), "Corps Shaping sorties beyond the Division Forward Boundary were 270% more effective (targets destroyed/sortie) than Killbox interdiction in V Corps AO" (slide 8). Wallace also noted that corps CAS was more timely in support of the V Corps: "Targets outside ARTY range were destroyed in MINUTES not hours or days by alternate (air) means." Emphasis in the original.

[88] U.S. Army 3rd Infantry Division (2003), p. 102. See also Michael B. McGee, Jr., *Air-Ground Operations During Operation Iraqi Freedom: Successes, Failures, and Lessons of Air Force and Army Integration*, thesis, Air War College, 2005, p. 17. McGee notes that the FSCL was usually 30 nautical miles beyond the forward line of troops (approximately 55 kilometers).

**Figure 6.1**
**Army Close, Deep, and Rear Areas and FSCL Placement**

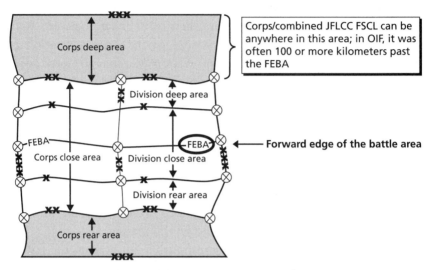

RAND *MG405-6.1*

**NOTES:** U.S. Department of the Army, FM 3-0 (2001), p. 4-26. Although acknowledging "the increasing nonlinear nature of operations," the Army recognizes that "there may be situations where commanders describe decisive, shaping, and sustaining operations in spatial terms" (p. 4-25), as shown here. In practice, this spatial description is the norm for major combat operations, providing boundaries and control measures within an AO. Army doctrine for deep, close, and rear areas is as follows (pp. 4-25 to 4-27):

> **Close Areas.** When designated, **the close area is where forces are in immediate contact with the enemy and the fighting between the committed forces and readily available tactical reserves of both combatants is occurring, or where commanders envision close combat taking place. Typically, the close area assigned to a maneuver force extends from its subordinates' rear boundaries to its own forward boundary.** Commanders plan to conduct decisive operations through maneuver and fires in the close area and position most of the maneuver force within it. . . . The activities of forces directly supporting fighting elements also occur in the close area. Examples of these activities are field artillery fires and combat health support. Within the close area, depending on echelon, one unit may conduct the decisive operation while others conduct shaping operations. Commanders of forces engaged in the close area may designate subordinate deep, close, and rear areas. . . .

**Figure 6.1—Continued**

**Deep Areas.** When designated, **the deep area is an area forward of the close area that commanders use to shape enemy forces before they are encountered or engaged in the close area. Typically, the deep area extends from the forward boundary of subordinate units to the forward boundary of the controlling echelon.** Thus, the deep area relates to the close area not only in terms of geography but also in terms of purpose and time. The extent of the deep area depends on the force's area of influence—how far out it can acquire information and strike targets. Commanders may place forces in the deep area to conduct shaping operations. Some of these operations may involve close combat. However, most maneuver forces stay in the close area. . . .

**Rear Areas. When designated, the rear area for any command extends from its rear boundary forward to the rear boundary of the next lower level of command. This area is provided primarily for the performance of support functions and is where the majority of the echelon's sustaining operations occur.** Operations in rear areas assure freedom of action and continuity of operations, sustainment, and C2. Their focus on providing CS and CSS leaves units in the rear area vulnerable to attack. Commanders may designate combat forces to protect forces and facilities in the rear area. In some cases, commanders may designate a noncontiguous rear area due to geography or other circumstances. In this case, the rear area force protection challenge increases due to physical separation of forces in the rear area from combat units that would otherwise occupy a contiguous close area. [Emphasis in the original.]

See also p. 4-20. FM 3-0 also discusses noncontiguous AOs: "Commanders typically subdivide some or all of their AO by assigning AOs to subordinated units. Subordinate unit AOs may be contiguous or noncontiguous. . . . When AOs are contiguous, a boundary separates them. When AOs are noncontiguous, they do not share a boundary; the concept of operations links the elements of the force. The higher headquarters is responsible for the area between noncontiguous AOs." Thus, large surface AOs with boundaries and fire support coordinating measures will exist on nonlinear battlefields as well as in the largely linear case depicted here.

This placement of the FSCL enabled V Corps to employ its organic systems—Apache helicopters and ATACMS—out to the limits of their range.[89] It also allowed V Corps to control air power employed within its AO short of the FSCL as it conducted corps shaping operations because of the coordination requirements imposed by the FSCL.[90] As a consequence, "joint targeting operations in the V Corps area of responsibility were extremely restrictive" for other than V Corps systems.[91] Indeed, the 11th AHR operation on the night of March 23 essentially shut down fixed-wing aircraft operations:

> The helicopter attack also had a limiting effect on other air power operations. Sorties by fixed-wing aircraft were reduced to make way for the Apache action, and the fire support coordination line in the sector was moved dozens of miles farther out in front of coalition forces.
>
> The decision to move the FSCL "cost us, basically, a full night of fixed-target strikes inside the FSCL," said [Lieutenant General Daniel P.] Leaf. "We—the entire coalition team—had not hit our stride in achieving the command and control required to operate in volume effectively inside the fire support coordination line."[92]

---

[89] U.S. Army 3rd Infantry Division (2003), p. 106.

[90] Wallace (2003), slide 8. General Wallace implies the importance of corps control of assets: in the several of the points noted on this briefing slide: "Executed per Vth Corps direction," "Targets matched with best available aircraft/bomb combination from CAS flow to kill," "More efficient Shaping," "Ability to execute in Open or *Closed* Killboxes." Emphasis in the original. See also McGee (2005), p. 66. McGee, who served in the ASOC with the V Corps during OIF, writes: "ASOC-controlled Corps shaping was [the] most efficient and effective destruction of enemy targets by airpower short of the FSCL." He also notes:

> Only one $C^2$ agency should control assets short of the FSCL; the ASOC. No other $C^2$ organization knows the real-time artillery deconfliction, current friendly conventional ground, SOF, and rotary wing operations. Due to the "fog and friction" and the speed of maneuver warfare, a CFACC organization (the ASOC) co-located with the owning ground commander must be the single $C^2$ of aircraft employing fires in the ground commander's AO. Different $C^2$ agencies cannot control air assets within the same airspace.

[91] U.S. Army 3rd Infantry Division (2003), p. 108.

[92] Rebecca Grant, "Saddam's Elite in the Meat Grinder," *Air Force Magazine*, September 2003b, p. 43. The article continues, noting: "It became clear that fixed-wing attack aircraft—USAF bombers and Air Force, Navy, Marine Corps, and allied fighters—were the

The Air Combat Command OIF briefing highlighted in rather neutral language this issue of fire control measures: "Doctrinal limitations of fire control procedures sub-optimizes [sic] the attainment of joint force objectives."[93] The 3rd Infantry Division report was much more direct, forcefully recommending to

> [p]lace the FSCL close enough to the FEBA so that organic indirect fires would be able to range most targets short of the FSCL. Targets beyond the FSCL could be engaged by the CFACC (AI) or by corps/division deep attack assets. The coordination for corps or division deep attacks would have to be coordinated regardless of the FSCL placement, so this is not an additional requirement. Placing the FSCL closer to V Corps maneuver allows the CFACC to adequately resource, conduct ISR, attack, and provide feedback. . . . The argument seems to be that CFACC would not adequately address V Corps targeting requirements; 3ID (M) violently disagrees. CFACC is a component, manned and equipped to effectively manage this battlespace forward of the FSCL; V Corps is not and has demonstrated their inability to manage said battlespace. 3ID (M) believes CFACC is better prepared to engage targets to effectively shape the battlefield.[94]

One sentence in the 3rd Infantry Division report, however, perhaps best sums up the solution to ground-air tensions in the post-OIF era: "The U.S. Army must redefine the battlespace based on our ability to influence it."[95]

---

weapon of choice for destroying the Republican Guard. Leaf noted, too, that 'FSCL placement became somewhat less of an issue,' because the air-ground team got better at coordinating actions within the various kill boxes." General Leaf was director of the air component coordination element with the CFLCC.

[93] Air Combat Command (2003), slide 27.

[94] U.S. Army 3rd Infantry Division (2003), p. 108.

[95] U.S. Army 3rd Infantry Division (2003), p. 108.

# CHAPTER SEVEN

# What Has Been Learned and What Has Not?

This review of post–Cold War operations shows that the United States has a unique military capability that has grown ever more impressive since the 1991 Gulf War. In the realm of large-scale theater warfare, today's U.S. armed forces are clearly without peer. Furthermore, the services have made significant accommodations to joint operations. Nevertheless, in the area of ground and air operations, important war-fighting lessons either have not been learned, have been ignored, or have been interpreted within service perspectives.

This study assessed several post–Cold War operations to test the hypothesis that a shift has occurred in the relative roles of ground power and air power in warfighting. Table 7.1 shows the results of this assessment and notes two trends. First, across the five cases examined here, air power showed growing levels of effectiveness and robustness and played commensurately growing roles. Second, the cases illustrate a gradual acceptance by Army officers of this reality.[1] Nevertheless, as will be discussed later in this chapter, despite the apparent acceptance of the increased warfighting effectiveness of air power by Army officers, Army doctrine is not being revised to accommodate this new reality.

---

[1] The cases examined in this study represent all the "warfighting" cases since the end of the Cold War. Consequently, one significant qualification pertains to all of the cases: In its post–Cold War conflicts, the United States and it coalition partners have never faced a first-rate (and some would say second-rate) opponent.

**Table 7.1**
**Case Assessment Results**

| Case | Ground Centric | Air Centric | Integrated | End State |
|------|----------------|-------------|------------|-----------|
| Iraq, 1991 | Ground campaign decisive after air softened Iraqi forces. | Air power set the conditions for overwhelming success—all but won the war. | Air campaign significantly weakened an incompetent opponent who was defeated by ground power. | Containment and sanctions for 10+ years; OIF |
| Bosnia | Croat-Muslim ground offensive principally responsible for Serb concessions. | Decisive and precise air power forced Serb concessions. | Combination of ground threat and air attack and low stakes for Serbs resulted in concessions; rapidity yields false expectations about Serb will to resist. | MOOTW |
| Kosovo | Threat of a ground invasion caused Milosevic to yield; center of gravity Serb Forces in Kosovo; a minor view held that KLA influenced decision. | Air power forced Milosevic to yield after stepping up modest initial campaign; center of gravity "downtown"—what Milosevic valued; attacking forces in Kosovo a waste of bombs. | Air attack against infrastructure targets changed the political dynamic. This use of air power, coupled with diplomatic isolation (Russians) and NATO unity, caused Milosevic to yield. Ground threat a future consideration and may have influenced to a lesser degree. | MOOTW |

Table 7.1—Continued

| Case | Ground Centric | Air Centric | Integrated | End State |
|---|---|---|---|---|
| Afghanistan | Anti-Taliban Afghan ground forces, enabled by air power, overcame Taliban and al Qaeda. CAS not responsive during Operation Anaconda, when U.S. ground forces necessary to root out remnants. | Air power decisive in giving Anti-Taliban Afghans the edge. Also key in Operation Anaconda in protecting U.S. ground forces. | Air power decisive in giving Afghans the edge, but U.S. ground forces needed to do the searches and rooting out that surrogate Afghan forces did not want to do. Air power critical in Operation Anaconda. | MOOTW |
| Iraq, 2003 | "Shock and awe" did not obviate the need for ground combat; "boots on the ground" were needed to destroy Saddam's regime and occupy Iraq. Nevertheless, air power was a key enabler in achieving these objectives. | Air power set the conditions for rapid success on the ground, despite being in a supporting role. However, control of the FSCL by ground commanders limited air power's contribution in the "deep battle" (as defined by the Army and Marine Corps). | Air power precluded effective positioning and employment of Iraqi ground forces even in bad weather or darkness, often shattering units before they could close with coalition ground forces. This not only reduced the costs, risks, and duration of the coalition campaign to remove Saddam's regime but largely left coalition ground units to mop up the remnants of shattered enemy formations in close battle where friction persisted unabated. | MOOTW |

This shift in the relative roles of ground and air power was most apparent in OIF, from whose assessment several conclusions emerge:

- The operational level of warfighting against large conventional enemy forces was dominated by flexible, all-weather, precision strike air power, enabled by ISR.
- The tactical level of war and the exploitation of the operational effects of air power were the primary domains of ground power, and despite significant increases in ISR-enabled situational awareness at the strategic and operational levels, uncertainty at the tactical and close combat levels of war continues.
- Successful major combat operations did not necessarily result in either the desired strategic political end state or conflict resolution. A protracted postwar U.S. presence in military support to stability, security, transition, and reconstruction (SSTR) operations is the norm.
- The Army and the Air Force experience the greatest interservice tension over the relative roles of ground power and air power in warfighting. This tension is largely the result of deep, culturally rooted differences in warfighting perspectives. Joint doctrine, however, mainly defers to the surface components' views in how it designates and defines AOs, and these views are supportive of the Army's about deep operations. Generally, AOs are expansive to promote an aggressive surface scheme of maneuver and to enable the maximum use of the organic capabilities of the surface components. The Army's doctrine tends to retain control over a large AO so that a corps can control and shape the operational environment for its fight and employ its organic assets (ATACMS and attack helicopters) to the limits of their capability as part of its shaping efforts. Not surprisingly, Army operational commanders want to control the resources used in their AOs. Such control is accomplished by establishing fire support coordinating measures—for example, the fire support coordination line (FSCL) within the corps or combined/joint force land component commander's AOs, which are permissive for Army systems but restrictive for the systems of other components.

- In reality, despite improved joint "interdependence," U.S. military operations remain an amalgamation of component operations, designed for optimal employment of their organic capabilities.

If these conclusions are correct, then the question that logically follows is: How are they influencing joint, Army, and Air Force concepts and doctrine? The record of joint, Army, and Air Force "learning" in this area is mixed, essentially for three reasons:

- Joint doctrine defers to surface components in the establishment of AOs.
- The Army's retention of control of large AOs in support of its preferred warfighting role—offensive operations at the operational level—constrains the potential effectiveness of joint fires across the theater of operations.
- The Air Force's continued push of its decades-long quest for equality (some would say preeminence) creates tension between it and the other services, most notably with the Army.

## The Inadequacies of Joint Doctrine

In the aftermath of OIF, changes are being made to joint doctrine, including the September 2006 publication of a new JP 3-0, *Joint Operations*, which consolidates JP 3-07, *Joint Doctrine for Military Operations Other than War*, and JP 3-0, *Doctrine for Joint Operations*.[2] This new publication has a much more sophisticated and expansive discussion of the range of military operations than did the 2001 version:

> The United States employs its military capabilities at home and abroad in support of its national security goals in a variety of operations that vary in size, purpose, and combat intensity. The use of joint capabilities in **military engagement, security cooperation, and deterrence** activities helps shape the operational environment and keeps the day-to-day tensions between nations or

---

[2]  U.S. Joint Chiefs of Staff, JP 3-0 (2006), p. iii.

groups below the threshold of armed conflict while maintaining US global influence. A **crisis response or limited contingency operation** can be a single small-scale, limited-duration operation or a significant part of a major operation of extended duration involving combat. The associated general strategic and operational objectives are to **protect** US interests and **prevent** surprise attack or further conflict. When required to achieve national strategic objectives or protect national interests,the US national leadership may decide to conduct a **major operation or campaign** involving large-scale combat, placing the United States in a wartime state. In such cases, the general goal is to **prevail** against the enemy as quickly as possible, conclude hostilities, and establish conditions favorable to the host nation (HN) and the United States and its multinational partners.[3]

The new JP 3-0 emphasizes that "JFCs integrate and synchronize the actions of military forces and capabilities to achieve strategic and operational objectives through joint campaigns and operations."[4] JP 3-0 also stresses that "functional and Service components of the joint force **conduct supported, subordinate, and supporting operations, not independent campaigns.**"[5] Nevertheless, the new JP 3-0, as did its predecessor, still defers to the surface components in the establishment of surface AOs for major operations and campaigns:

> JFCs establish land and maritime AOs to decentralize execution of land and maritime component operations, allow rapid maneuver, and provide the ability to fight at extended ranges. The size, shape, and positioning of land or maritime AOs will be based on the JFC's CONOPS and the land or maritime commanders' requirements to accomplish their missions and protect their forces.[6]

---

3   U.S. Joint Chiefs of Staff, JP 3-0 (2006), p. xi. Emphasis in the original.

4   U.S. Joint Chiefs of Staff, JP 3-0 (2006), p. II-4.

5   U.S. Joint Chiefs of Staff, JP 3-0 (2006), p. II-12. Emphasis in the original.

6   U.S. Joint Chiefs of Staff, JP 3-0 (2006), p. V-21.

Thus, the JP 3-0 definition of *area of operations* is critical in determining the intercomponent relationships in a joint operation:

> **Area of Operations.** JFCs may define AOs for land and maritime forces. AOs typically do not encompass the entire operational area of the JFC, but should be large enough for component commanders to accomplish their missions and protect their forces. Component commanders with AOs typically designate subordinate AOs within which their subordinate forces operate. These commanders employ the full range of joint and Service control measures and graphics as coordinated with other component commanders and their representatives to delineate responsibilities, deconflict operations, and achieve unity of effort.[7]

Also important is how this central joint doctrinal publication sets the terms of the supported-supporting relationship within surface AOs:

> **Within these AOs, land and maritime commanders are designated the supported commander for the integration and synchronization of maneuver, fires, and interdiction.** Accordingly, land and maritime commanders designate the target priority, effects, and timing of interdiction operations within their AOs. Further, in coordination with the land or maritime commander, a component commander designated as the supported commander for theater/JOA–wide interdiction has the latitude to plan and execute JFC prioritized missions within a land or maritime AO. If theater/JOA–wide interdiction operations would have adverse effects within a land or maritime AO, then the commander conducting those operations must either readjust the plan, resolve the issue with the appropriate component commander, or consult with the JFC for resolution.[8]

Further elaboration makes clear that within a ground AO, the supported commander makes the rules:

---

[7]  U.S. Joint Chiefs of Staff, JP 3-0 (2006), p. V-21. Emphasis in the original.

[8]  U.S. Joint Chiefs of Staff, JP 3-0 (2006), p. V-21. Emphasis in the original.

The land or maritime commander should clearly articulate the vision of maneuver operations to other commanders that may employ interdiction forces within the land or maritime AO. The land or maritime commander's intent and CONOPS should clearly state how interdiction will enable or enhance land or maritime force maneuver in the AO and what is to be accomplished with interdiction (as well as those actions to be avoided, such as the destruction of key transportation nodes or the use of certain munitions in a specific area). Once this is understood, other interdiction-capable commanders normally can plan and execute their operations with only that coordination required with the land or maritime commander. However, the land or maritime commander should provide other interdiction-capable commanders as much latitude as possible in the planning and execution of interdiction operations within the AO.[9]

As demonstrated in both Gulf wars, JFCs generally defer to the ground commander's desire to have an expansive AO to execute a service doctrine, as delineated in JP 3-31, *Command and Control for Joint Land Operations*: "JFCs should allow Service tactical and operational assets and groupings to function generally as they were designed. The intent is to meet the needs of the JFC while maintaining the tactical and operational integrity of the Service organizations."[10]

The operational doctrines for the Army and the Marine Corps both include similar discussions of the parameters of an AO. The relevant Army doctrine appears in FM 3-0, *Operations*:

An AO is an operational area defined by the JFC for land and naval forces. AOs do not typically encompass the entire operational area of the JFC but should be large enough for component commanders to accomplish their missions and protect their forces. AOs should also allow component commanders to employ their organic, assigned, and supporting systems to the limits of

---

[9]    U.S. Joint Chiefs of Staff, JP 3-0 (2006), p. V-21.

[10]    U.S. Joint Chiefs of Staff, JP 3-31 (2004), p. III-2.

their capabilities. Within their AOs, land and naval commanders synchronize operations and are supported commanders.[11]

The Marine Corps doctrine for an AO emerges in Marine Corps Doctrinal Publication (MCDP) 1-0, *Marine Corps Operations*:

> An AO is an operational area defined by the joint force commander for land and naval forces. AOs do not typically encompass the entire operational area of the joint force commander, but should be large enough for the Marine Corps component commander and his subordinate units to accomplish their missions and protect their forces. The AO is the tangible area of battlespace and is the only area of battlespace that a commander is directly responsible for. AOs should also be large enough to allow commanders to employ their organic, assigned, and supporting systems to the limits of their capabilities. The commander must be able to command and control all the forces within his AO. He must be able to see the entire AO—this includes coverage of the AO with the full range of collection assets available to the Marine Corps component command and MAGTF [Marine air-ground task force], to include reconnaissance, electronic warfare aircraft, unmanned aerial vehicles, remote sensors, and radars. He must be able to control the events and coordinate his subordinates' actions. Finally, the commander must be able to strike and maneuver throughout the AO.[12]

---

[11] U.S. Department of the Army, FM 3-0 (2001), p. 4-19.

[12] U.S. Department of the Navy, MCDP 1-0, *Marine Corps Operations*, Headquarters, United States Marine Corps, 2001, pp. 4-5, 4-6. See also p. 6-3 for a discussion of what constitutes a "battlespace." Battlespace is the environment, factors, and conditions that must be understood to successfully apply combat power, protect the force, and accomplish the mission. This includes the air and sea, space, and enemy and friendly forces, infrastructure, weather, and terrain within the assigned AO and the commander's area of interest. Battlespace is conceptual—a higher commander does not assign it. Commanders determine their own battlespace based on their mission, the enemy, and their concept of operations and force protection. They use their experience and understanding of the situation and mission to visualize and adapt their battlespace as the situation or mission changes. The battlespace is not fixed in size or position. It varies over time and depends on the environment, the commander's mission, and friendly and enemy actions. Battlespace normally comprises an AO, area of influence, and area of interest.

As well, both the Army and the Marine Corps have doctrine for deep operations. But their capabilities for these operations are markedly different.

MCDP 1-0, *Marine Corps Operations*, contains the following guidance on deep operations:

> Deep operations shape the battlespace to influence future operations. They seek to create windows of opportunity for decisive action, restrict the enemy's freedom of action, and disrupt the cohesion and tempo of his operations. Deep operations help the commander seize the initiative and set the conditions for close operations. Because of its operational reach, *deep operations are normally conducted by the ACE* [aviation combat element], although the GCE [ground combat element] and CSSE [combat service support element] may play significant roles. MAGTF intelligence assets, e.g., force reconnaissance and signals intelligence and ACE and GCE surveillance and reconnaissance assets (UAVs and ground surveillance radars) contribute to the conduct of deep operations.[13]

The Marine Corps relies heavily on its ACE, particularly its fixed-wing fighter aircraft, to execute deep operations. Furthermore, a MAGTF component commander in a joint operation can generally count on maintaining control of its ACE, since JP 0-2, *Unified Action Armed Forces (UNAAF)*, specifies the following:

> **The MAGTF commander will retain OPCON** [operational control] **of organic air assets.** The primary mission of the MAGTF aviation combat element is the support of the MAGTF ground combat element. During joint operations, the MAGTF air assets normally will be in support of the MAGTF mission. The MAGTF will make sorties available to the JFC, for tasking through the joint force air component commander (JFACC), for air defense, long-range interdiction, and long-range reconnaissance. Sorties in excess of MAGTF direct support requirements will be provided to the JFC for tasking through the JFACC for

---

[13] U.S. Department of the Navy, MCDP 1-0, (2001), p. 6-21. Emphasis added.

the support of other components of the joint force or the joint force as a whole.[14]

The authority of the Marine Corps component commander to retain control of organic aviation resources is further defined in JP 3-30, *Command and Control for Joint Air Operations*:

> **Only the JFC has the authority to reassign, redirect, or real-locate component's air capabilities/forces. . . . Component air capabilities/forces are those air capabilities/forces organic to a component that are used by the component to accomplish its assigned mission.** These organic assets should appear on the air tasking order (ATO) to enable coordination and minimize the risk of fratricide. The inclusion of component air assets on the ATO does not imply any command or tasking authority over them, nor does it restrict component commander flexibility to respond to battlespace dynamics.[15]

Thus, the Marine Corps component commander retains a robust fixed-wing aviation capability to conduct deep operations within his AO.[16] The aircraft available to him are roughly equivalent to U.S. Air Force fixed-wing fighter aircraft in their flexibility, speed, relative immunity to surface fires and their ability to conduct deep operations. Nevertheless, Marine aviation is focused on the Marine fight and, unlike the Air Force, normally does not allocate any resources to the strategic level of warfighting. The Army's organic systems, as will be discussed shortly, are not nearly as capable of conducting deep operations.

---

[14] U.S. Joint Chiefs of Staff, JP 0-2, *Unified Action Armed Forces (UNAAF)*, 2001, p. V-4. Emphasis in the original.

[15] U.S. Joint Chiefs of Staff, JP 3-30, *Command and Control for Joint Air Operations*, 2003, p. viii. Emphasis in the original.

[16] See U.S. Joint Chiefs of Staff, JP 3-0 (2006), p. iii, which states that JP 3-0 "Replaces the term 'battlespace' with the term 'operational environment.'"

## The Relationship of Service Cultures to Joint Culture

Stephen K. Scroggs, in his book *Army Relations with Congress: Thick Armor, Dull Sword, Slow Horse* uses a definition of culture from Edgar H. Schein's *Organizational Culture and Leadership* to explain Army culture as a way to understand its dealings with Congress. Schein defines culture as a

> pattern of shared basic assumptions that the group learned as it solved its problems of external adaptation and internal integration, that has worked well enough to be considered valid and, therefore, to be taught to new members as the correct way to perceive, think, and feel in relation to those problems.[17]

Scroggs goes on to note that culture results in "patterns of shared basic assumptions that color the way an organization views and approaches a problem."[18] Although Scroggs was writing about the Army, Schein's definition is useful in understanding the cultures of all the services.

Service culture is manifested in service doctrine.[19] In the U.S. military, doctrine is a culturally shaped paradigm, similar to the paradigms employed by scientific communities, described by Thomas Kuhn in his classic study, *The Structure of Scientific Revolutions*. Kuhn described scientific paradigms in two ways. First, in a sociological sense, paradigms defined "the entire constellation of beliefs, values, techniques, and so on shared by the members of a given community."[20] Second, the paradigm provided "exemplary past achievements" that give "the concrete puzzle solutions which, employed as models or examples, can replace explicit rules as a basis for the solution of the remaining puz-

---

[17] Edgar H. Schein, *Organizational Culture and Leadership*, 2nd ed., San Francisco: Jossey-Bass, 1992, p. 12, quoted in Stephen K. Scroggs, *Army Relations with Congress: Thick Armor, Dull Sword, Slow Horse*, Westport, Conn.: Praeger, 2000, p. xii.

[18] Schein (1992), p. 12, quoted in Scroggs (2000), p. xii.

[19] This section on doctrine as paradigm comes from Johnson (1997), pp. vi–viii.

[20] Thomas S. Kuhn, *The Structure of Scientific Revolutions*, 2nd ed., Chicago: University of Chicago Press, 1962, p. 175.

zles of normal science."[21] Kuhn also described how paradigms change. Essentially, paradigms shift when they fail to provide solutions to the problems against which they are applied. These conditions of failure, or anomalies, can result in two responses. First, the community can "devise numerous articulations and *ad hoc* modifications of [its] theory in order to eliminate any apparent conflict."[22] The institutional Army's response to the failure of the 11th AHR's attack in OIF is an example in this regard. Thus, the anomaly remains such and is not the basis for a fundamental rethinking of the validity of the paradigm—in this case, examining the underlying premises of corps operations and deep attack and the Air Force's insistence on the independent control of air power. Second, if the discontinuities are clearly not solvable with the existing paradigm—a situation Kuhn refers to as a crisis—a new paradigm will emerge. It is yet to be seen if the difficulties the Army is experiencing in dealing with the post-OIF insurgency in Iraq may cause a rethinking of its belief that an undifferentiated Army can be full-spectrum capable. If such a fundamental recasting of doctrine does occur, Kuhn would assert that a paradigmatic revolution has taken place.[23]

Thus, doctrine is important in understanding the culture of the services.

While the services are not unsophisticated, monolithic entities marching blindly to the beat of a rigid set of rules, their "institutional essence" is defined by their doctrine.[24] In short, doctrine is the frame of reference, derived from its culture, that fundamentally defines the activities of each of the Armed Forces by

---

[21] Kuhn (1962), p. 175.

[22] Kuhn (1962), p. 78.

[23] Kuhn (1962), pp. 66–91.

[24] Morton H. Halperin, *Bureaucratic Politics and Foreign Policy*, Washington, D.C.: Brookings Institution, 1974. I rely on Halperin's definition of "organizational essence" when I refer to "institutional essence." Halperin notes that: "Organizations have considerable freedom in defining their missions and the capabilities they need to pursue these missions. The organization's essence is the view held by the dominant group in the organization of what the missions and capabilities should be. Related to this are convictions about what kinds of people with what expertise, experience, and knowledge should be members of the organization" (p. 28).

- Prescribing the shared worldview and values as well as the "proper" methods, tools, techniques, and approaches to problem solving within and among the services.
- Providing a way in which the services view themselves
- Governing how the services deal with each other and with other governmental and nongovernmental agencies.
- Prescribing the questions and the answers that are considered acceptable within the institution or school of thought covered by the paradigm.[25]

Kuhn's logic resonates in service doctrines, but it is less compelling in the definition of joint doctrine contained in JP 1, *Joint Warfare of the US Armed Forces*:

> Joint doctrine enables the Armed Forces of the United States to conduct the most effective joint activities and unified action. Joint doctrine is based on extant capabilities and incorporates time-tested principles for successful military action as well as contemporary lessons that together guide aggressive exploitation of US advantages against adversary vulnerabilities.[26]

This capstone joint publication goes on to note what this study has pointed out is one of the principal weaknesses of U.S. joint doctrine—that it relies on *promoting a common perspective* from which to plan, train, and conduct military operations in combat and non-combat situations"[27] rather than demanding one and thus continues to defer to the services. Consequently, at this juncture in the evolution

---

[25] Johnson (1997), pp. vii–viii,

[26] U.S. Joint Chiefs of Staff, JP 1, *Joint Warfare of the Armed Forces of the United States*, 2000, p. I-8.

[27] U.S. Joint Chiefs of Staff, JP 1 (2000), p. I-8. Emphasis added. Contrast this with the less deferential language in the 1991 version of JP 1, *Joint Warfare of the US Armed Forces*, which stated, "Because we operate and fight jointly, we must all learn and practice joint doctrine, tactics, techniques, and procedures; feed back to the doctrine process the lessons learned in training and exercises, and operations; and ensure Service doctrine and procedures are consistent. This is critical for our present and future effectiveness. *Joint doctrine offers a common perspective from which to plan and operate, and fundamentally shapes the way we think about and train for war*" (p. 6). Emphasis in the original.

of the U.S. armed forces, service cultures and doctrinal paradigms still largely trump joint culture and doctrine.

## The Army Future Force as a Reflection of Army Culture

The Army is learning and has made adaptations in the aftermath of OEF and OIF to cope with the realities it is facing in today's operational environment. Army Chief of Staff General Peter Schoomaker has embarked the Army on a major restructuring effort; it is in the process of "modularizing" from a division- to a brigade-based force. The plan is to create brigade combat teams and to have more of them in the Active Component Army than the 33 currently in the 10 divisions before the implementation of modularity.[28] Thus, the Army would have "a larger pool of units to fulfill strategic commitments."[29] Adding National Guard brigades to the mix will further help increase the time between deployments for Army units. Furthermore, the Army is shedding some of its Cold War structure, which includes "decreasing the number of field artillery, air defense, engineer, armor and ordnance battalions while increasing military police, transportation, petroleum and water distribution, civil affairs, psychological operations and biological detection units," which will give the Army more capability to support ongoing operations.[30] Finally, the Army recently published a new field manual that provides guidance on combating insurgencies, informed by ongoing operations.[31] Thus, the Army is taking significant steps to adapt to the operational environment within which it finds itself. The Army is also, in many ways, adapting its warfighting-

---

[28] Gary Sheftlick, "Army to Reset into Modular Brigade-Centric Force," Army News Service, February 24, 2004.

[29] U.S. Department of the Army, "Army Campaign Plan Briefing," undated.

[30] Anne Plummer, "Army Chief Tells President Restructuring Force Could Cost $20 Billion," *Inside the Army*, February 9, 2004, p. 2.

[31] See U.S. Department of the Army and Marine Corps Combat Development Command, U.S. Department of the Navy, FM 3-24/MCWP 3-33.5, *Counterinsurgency*, 2006.

focused culture to enable better performance in the missions the nation is demanding of it.

Longer-term Army transformation efforts—plans for the Future Force—are, however, largely focused on warfighting. Once again, the fundamental assumption is that Army forces optimized for warfighting can handle other operations as lesser-included cases.[32]

The centerpiece of Army transformation is the FCS-equipped unit of action (UA), a self-contained combined arms maneuver "brigade." The Army has high expectations for the UA: "The FCS equipped UA represents a capability critical to the Future Force and the accomplishment of the goals of the Joint Vision, Army Vision, and the applicable policy documents. . . . [I]t is the Future Force's capability to conduct decisive operations that is the most relevant to the Joint Force." The Army expects the UA to be both strategically deployable—"it has the responsiveness and deployability to achieve the 96-hour deployment goal"—and operationally and tactically responsive—"it is designed with the durability, endurance, and stamina to fight battles and engage-

---

[32] See Andrew F. Krepinevich, *Transforming the Legions: The Army and the Future of Warfare*, Washington, D.C.: Center for Strategic and Budgetary Assessments, 2004, pp. i–ii. Krepinevich argues that the future missions the Army will have to accomplish for the nation require

> a balanced force among four Army types: *The Territorial Army*: This Army, concerned primarily with homeland defense, characterized the US Army during the early part of the nation's history. *The Constabulary Army*: This Army, concerned primarily with stability operations, has seen it role wax and wane throughout the nation's history. The Constabulary Army experienced dramatic decline following the Vietnam War, but the demand for its services increased following the Cold War's end, and has jumped dramatically following the US-led invasions of Afghanistan and Iraq. *The Expeditionary Army*: This is the Army that dominated during the world wars, when the United States projected the bulk of its ground combat power from the continental United States. Its role declined during the Cold War but has increased again with the shift in focus away from Europe and toward the "Arc of Instability" that stretches from the Middle East across South and Central Asia, through Southeast Asia up into Northeast Asia. *The Frontier Army*: This forward-deployed Army dominated the Cold War era, but has declined with the withdrawal of substantial US forces from overseas following the Soviet Union's collapse. While today's Army is primarily a legacy of the Frontier Army that manned the western alliance's perimeter during the Cold War, there is clearly a need for an increase in Territorial, Constabulary and Expeditionary Army forces, with a corresponding decline in the Frontier Army. . . . However, the Service has focused the bulk of its [transformation] efforts on enhancing the Expeditionary Army, while underemphasizing the Constabulary Army, and perhaps the Territorial Army as well."

ments for the duration of a campaign, focused on decisive points and centers of gravity."[33]

The critical enablers for the UA concept are the Future Combat Systems, a new "system of systems":

> FCS are comprised of a family of advanced, networked air and ground-based maneuver, maneuver support, and sustainment systems that will include manned and unmanned platforms. FCS are networked via a C4ISR architecture including networked communications, network operations, sensors, Battle Command system, training, and both manned and unmanned Reconnaissance and Surveillance (R&S) capabilities that will enable levels of SA [situational awareness] and synchronized operations heretofore unachievable. FCS will operate as a Family of Systems (FOS) that will network existing systems, systems already under development, and new systems to be developed to meet the needs of the UA. The Battle Command Network will enable improved Intelligence, Surveillance, and Reconnaissance (ISR), enhanced analytical tools, Joint exchange of blue and red force tracking down to the tactical level, battle command, real time sensor-shooter linkages, and increased synergy between echelons and within small units. It will also enable the UA to connect to UE [unit of employment—echelon(s) above the UA] and Joint, Interagency, and Multinational (JIM) capabilities, making these capabilities available to the small units of the UA as well as with adjacent, non-contiguous units.[34]

The level of situational awareness imparted by the FCS will enable the UA to fight wars in radically different ways than today's forces:

---

[33] U.S. Army Training and Doctrine Command, *Change 3 to TRADOC Pamphlet 525-3-90 O & O: The United States Army Future Force Operational and Organizational Plan, Maneuver Unit of Action*, draft, Fort Knox, Ky.: Unit of Action Maneuver Battle Lab, 2004, pp. 4–5. Army Chief of Staff General Shinseki first established the 96-hour deployment goal for a brigade combat team in 1999. See also Vick et al. (2002) for an assessment of the difficulty the Stryker Brigade Combat Teams will have in meeting General Shinseki's deployment goals (96 hours to employ a brigade anywhere in the world after wheels up), which could also inform a discussion of FCS-based UA deployability.

[34] U.S. Army Training and Doctrine Command (2004), p. 4.

[The UA] employs its revolutionary Battle Command Network architecture to expand or contract its span of control and integrate UE or JTF supporting capabilities to accomplish missions. The hallmark of UA operations will be the significant abilities to develop situations out of contact, engage the enemy in unexpected ways, maneuver to positions of advantage with speed and agility, engage enemy forces beyond the range of their weapons, destroy enemy forces with enhanced fires, and assault at times and places of our choosing.[35]

The UA also adheres to the Army culture of optimizing for warfighting and assuming that other operations are lesser-included cases: "Although optimized for offensive operations, the FCS-equipped UA will be capable of executing stability and support operations."[36] This future-focused statement maintains continuity with the Army's cultural predilections, most recently reaffirmed in the 2001 version of FM 3-0, *Operations*: "The Army's warfighting focus produces a full spectrum force that meets the needs of joint force commanders. . . . In peace, Army forces train for war."[37]

Fundamentally different in the Army's goals for the future force is its quest for rapid strategic deployability and a robust intratheater mobility capability. Consequently, the UA concept stresses that

FCS equipped UA must be transportable by inter/intra-theater land, sea vessel and airlift anywhere in the world; more deployable with reduced deployment tonnage; and transportable by C-130 profile aircraft with full fighting loads (including a full load of ammunition), 3/4 tank of fuel, and crew with personal equipment. When available, comparable advanced vertical lift or theater support vehicle will be employed to move the UA. Rationale for this capability is to introduce the UA at multiple points of entry that are unpredictable to overcome enemy access denial, to

---

[35] U.S. Army Training and Doctrine Command (2004), pp. 4–5.

[36] U.S. Department of the Army, *2005 Army Modernization Plan*, Office of the Deputy Chief of Staff, G-8, 2005, p. 32.

[37] U.S. Department of the Army, FM 3-0 (2001), pp. 1–3.

be able to leverage austere points of entry to increase force flow, to increase transport options available to the combatant commander using C-130/C-17 aircraft and fast sealift, to conduct operational maneuver to positions of advantage during a campaign, and to pursue future vertical lift concepts that are follow-on to C-130.[38]

All this said, however, the central reason to require FCS transportability by "C-130 profile aircraft" is to enable the UA "to conduct operational maneuver to positions of advantage during a campaign, and to pursue future vertical lift concepts that are follow-on to C-130."[39] Incorporating required capabilities into the FCS, however, has resulted in a weight increase that makes its transportability by a C-130 problematic. Consequently, the Army is attempting to create a requirement for new platforms to execute its concepts of vertical maneuver with FCS-equipped forces.[40] The recently released TRADOC Pamphlet 525-3-0, "The Army in Joint Operations: The Army's Future Force Capstone Concept, 2015–2024, Version 2.0," specifically states a need for such a capability: "Vertical maneuver of *mounted* forces, employing SSTOL [supershort takeoff and landing] or HVTOL [heavy lift vertical takeoff and landing] aircraft, puts large areas at risk for the adversary and will often lead to rapid tactical decision, shortening durations of battle, and contributing to the more rapid disintegration of the enemy force."[41]

---

[38] U.S. Army Training and Doctrine Command (2004), p. 185.

[39] U.S. Army Training and Doctrine Command (2004). For a discussion of Army concepts for the Future Force, and possible alternatives, see Peter A. Wilson, John Gordon IV, and David E. Johnson, "An Alternative Future Force: Building a Better Army," *Parameters*, Vol. 33, No. 4, Winter 2003–2004.

[40] See Army Science Board, *Challenges and Opportunities for Increments II and III Future Combat Systems (FCS)*, Summer 2003, pp. 4, 37, 43. This briefing makes the case for a Joint Transport Rotorcraft (JTR) by noting that it would enable "Forced entry," "Over the shore logistics," and "Eases weight constraint [on the FCS]" (p. 37). The briefing further makes the case for a JTR by citing the limitations of the C-130 ("Must use APODs"; "Cannot unload ships" [p. 43]) and implies that the FCS will weigh more than originally postulated because of "Current vehicle weight projections and historical weight growth" (p. 4).

[41] U.S. Army Training and Doctrine Command, TRADOC Pamphlet 525-3-0, *The Army in Joint Operations: The Army's Future Force Capstone Concept, 2015–2024, Version 2.0*, Fort

This air transportability requirement persists despite continuing lessons about the vulnerability of low-flying, slow aircraft in distributed, noncontiguous operational environments and the reality that the Army is not developing organic systems to provide ISR and strike to forces executing vertical maneuver over long distances.[42] The other services, absent an organic Army capability, would have to provide the crucial enabling capabilities to support the Army's emerging concepts for operational maneuver.

The strategic deployability and air transportability imperatives, which limit the weight of any potential FCS and thus, probably, its potential capability, were also key factors in selecting the Stryker vehicle in the aftermath of the experience of Task Force Hawk during Operation Allied Force in Kosovo. Aside from limiting the weight of combat systems, the Army is streamlining its organizations to meet the rapid deployment timelines.[43] Again, the Army seems to be assuming that its future relevance is contingent on getting to the fight rapidly, because, if it can, its fundamental cultural belief can be realized: "Land operations determine the outcome of major theater wars. . . . Army forces are the decisive forces for sustained land combat, war termination, and postwar stability."[44]

In light of the enormous—and steadily growing—U.S. increases in sensors to locate targets and precision strike air power systems to attack them with relative impunity, the Army vision for the future is out of synchronization with what appears to be "the new operational reality." This reality, at least for the foreseeable future, is one that makes

---

Monroe, Va., 2005, p. 23. Emphasis in the original. See also Robert Scales, "The Shape of Brigades to Come," *Armed Forces Journal*, October 2005, p. 32. Scales argues that "the challenge of future warfare on land cannot be met without building modular, FCS-equipped aero-mechanized brigades that will form the aerial blitzkrieg force of the future."

[42] See Jon Grossman, David Rubenson, William Sollfrey, and Brett Steele, *Vertical Envelopment and the Future Transport Rotorcraft: Operational Considerations for the Objective Force*, Santa Monica, Calif.: RAND Corporation, MR-1713-A, 2003, for an assessment of "the technical risk, cost and survivability" of HVTOL aircraft (p. xii).

[43] John Gordon IV and Jerry Sollinger, "The Army's Dilemma," *Parameters*, Summer 2004, p. 33.

[44] U.S. Department of the Army, FM 3-0 (2001), pp. 1-10, 1-11.

it increasingly likely that air power will be the instrument "that risk averse senior civilian and military decisionmakers will reach for first." And making an "air-first" response to any crisis does have compelling logic:

> Why risk deploying ground forces quickly into a dangerous situation when a period of precision attack possibly could achieve the desired results? Even if precision attack does not by itself accomplish the desired military or political goals, at least the decisionmakers will have the satisfaction of knowing that when ground forces do have to be committed, the enemy already will have been mauled by precision strike operations.[45]

One final point needs to be made about the Army's plans for the near and long term. Because of enduring Army deep operations concepts, these plans inherently guarantee interservice tension with the Air Force over the control of the operational environment. These concepts are questionable in light of post–Cold War operational experiences.

### The Problems with Army Concepts for Deep Operations

Army doctrine for operations in deep areas, contained in FM 3-0, *Operations*, is similar to that of the Marine Corps:

> **Deep Areas.** When designated, the *deep area* is an area forward of the close area that commanders use to shape enemy forces before they are encountered or engaged in the close area. Typically, the deep area extends from the forward boundary of subordinate units to the forward boundary of the controlling echelon. Thus, the deep area relates to the close area not only in terms of geography but also in terms of purpose and time. The extent of the deep area depends on the force's area of influence—how far out it can acquire information and strike targets. Commanders may place forces in the deep area to conduct shaping

---

[45] Gordon and Sollinger (2004), p. 38.

operations. Some of these operations may involve close combat. However, most maneuver forces stay in the close area.[46]

The depth to which an Army corps can acquire information is becoming almost limitless. The depth to which it can strike targets, however, is physically limited by its organic resources and logically by the increased effectiveness of fixed-wing air power.

The Army has two principal organic systems that it can use to attack targets within its AO beyond the approximately 40-kilometer range of organic cannon and MLRS indirect fire systems—ATACMS and attack helicopters. All versions of ATACMS have a range in excess of 100 miles. Nevertheless, the ATACMS has one weakness that limits its effectiveness in deep area operations when compared with air power: It cannot be retargeted in flight. Thus, the sensor-to-shooter-to-impact time is critical for using ATACMS targets with mobility. This, and the high cost and relatively small payload of the missile, largely limits the ATACMS to high-payoff stationary targets.[47]

The AH-64 Apache attack helicopter is the other organic resource an Army division or corps commander has at his disposal to conduct deep area operations. Ironically, the attack helicopter was developed by the Army in the aftermath of the Korean War because Army officers doubted the Air Force's commitment to providing the aerial fires they needed on the battlefield.[48] Army concerns about the adequacy of CAS during Operation Anaconda are the latest example of soldiers not being convinced that the Air Force, focused on other missions, will be there when they need it. Nevertheless, post–Cold War operational

---

[46] U.S. Department of the Army, FM 3-0 (2001), p. 4-26. Emphasis in the original.

[47] See also U.S. Department of the Army, "Army RDT&E Budget Item Justification (R-2 Exhibit): 0604768A, Brilliant Anti-Armor Submunition (BAT)," February 2003, pp. 623–624. The Army was pursuing a more capable warhead for the ATACMS—the Brilliant Anti-Armor Submunition or BAT. The ATACMS Block II missile would carry 13 BAT or BAT P31 submunitions (a more capable BAT munition with millimeter wave and imaging infrared sensors). This document reported that "[t]he ATACMS BLK II and BAT P31 programs have been terminated after FY03 in order to fund Transformation and other higher priority Army programs" (p. 624).

[48] Frederic A. Bergerson, *The Army Gets an Air Force: Tactics of Insurgent Bureaucratic Politics*, Baltimore, Md.: Johns Hopkins University Press, 1980, p. 52.

experience shows that three issues call into question the ability of the AH-64 Apache to adequately support Army operations, particularly deep area operations: available platforms, speed, and survivability.

The number of attack helicopters available to a corps commander to shape his AO is small. As already noted, during OIF, V Corps had its 21 AH-64As and 21 AH-64Ds in the two organic attack squadrons in its 11th AHR, as well as the 18 AH-64Ds of the 1st Cavalry Division's 1-277th AHB (attached to the 11th AHR for OIF). On the eve of OIF, V Corps and its subordinate units had a total of 151 AH-64A/Ds in theater (18 in the 3rd Infantry Division, 72 in the 101st Airborne Division, and 61 in the 11th AHR).[49] Normally, however, the divisional attack helicopter units are not available to the corps commander because they are supporting division-level operations.[50] In contrast to the two deep attack missions flown by the 11th AHR and the 101st Airborne Division—whose combined sorties totaled fewer than 80 on the two missions—the 735 fighters and 51 bombers in the coalition air forces flew 20,733 sorties between March 19 and April 18, 2003, and struck more than 15,592 killbox interdiction/CAS desired mean points of impact.[51] All the sorties allocated by the CJFACC during OIF supported the JFC's plan, and more than half were allocated against targets to "[s]upport CFLCC to achieve defeat or compel capitulation" of Iraqi ground forces and to support security and stabilization operations.[52]

In addition to the small number of attack helicopters available to the corps commander, the operational characteristics of attack helicopters are also a constraint on shaping a large AO. The Apache is a relatively slow aircraft in the environment within which it typically operates during deep attack operations: low level, night flights, and often over unfamiliar terrain. In these circumstances, the Apache cannot fly

---

[49] Fontenot, Degen, and Tohn (2004), p. 80.

[50] U.S. Department of the Army, Field Manual, 3-04.111, *Aviation Brigades*, 2003, Chapter 1. See also "Army Accelerates Aviation Transformation," September 7, 2001. This article details Army plans to reduce corps-level attack helicopter battalions from 24 Apaches to 21, and heavy division attack helicopter battalions from 24 Apaches to 18.

[51] Moseley (2003), pp. 2, 5–8.

[52] Moseley (2003), pp. 4–5.

at its 150+ knot maximum speed. Indeed, during the 101st Aviation Brigade's deep operation in OIF, it took one battalion 40 minutes to fly the 100 kilometers from its forward arming and refueling point to its objective.[53] Furthermore, the Apache is subject to environmental conditions that limit its employability. During several crucial days during OIF, sandstorms grounded the Army's helicopter fleet. Fixed-wing aircraft, however, continued to operate.

> Although hampered by severe sandstorms, coalition [fixed-wing] aircraft continued to attack air defense, command and control, and intelligence facilities in the Baghdad area. Coalition aircraft continued to achieve high sortie rates despite the weather. The focus of strike missions began to shift to the Republican Guard divisions in the vicinity of Baghdad. Control of the air allowed the employment of slow-moving intelligence-gathering aircraft such as the E-8C Joint Surveillance Target Attack Radar System (JSTARS) and the RC-135 Rivet Joint, which gathers signals intelligence and UAVs. In the days just prior to the sandstorms, the air component flew an average of 800 strike sorties daily. The majority of the effort was against discrete targets designed to achieve specific effects against the regime, to interdict enemy movement, or in close support of ground forces. Even during the sandstorms, surveillance aircraft continued to provide data that enabled the coalition to target Iraqi units over an area of several hundred square miles during weather the Iraqis thought would shield them from air attack. On 28 March, the weather cleared, allowing coalition forces to increase the number of strikes on Baghdad and Republican Guard units. Coalition air forces operated against strategic, operational, and tactical targets, demonstrating both the efficacy and flexibility of air power.[54]

---

[53] Fontenot, Degen, and Tohn (2004), p. 194. During OIF (and OEF), Army attack helicopter units operated from secure locations. During the deep attack operations of the 11th AHR and the 101st Aviation Brigade, elements of these units displaced forward to a tactical assembly area or forward arming and refueling points, respectively, to reduce their flight time to their objectives.

[54] Fontenot, Degen, and Tohn (2004), pp. 141–142. See also U.S. Army 3rd Infantry Division (2003), p. 30. The all-weather precision capability of the JDAM was an important capability during the sandstorms.

Thus, the ability of fixed-wing aircraft to cover an extended operational environment and to operate with precision under adverse operational conditions is much superior to rotary-wing aircraft, including attack helicopters. During OEF and OIF, fixed-wing aircraft routinely operated throughout the operational environment, making them readily available to ground units in the form of CAS or to the CFACC or JFC for interdiction[55]. The performance challenges endemic to rotary-wing aircraft, however, pale in comparison to the principal issue constraining the capability of the AH-64 Apache to reliably conduct deep operations: the helicopter's vulnerability in the post–Cold War operational environment.

The record of the AH-64 Apache in conducting operations against dispersed and adaptive enemies has spawned a debate about its survivability against low-altitude air defense systems, ranging from small arms to man-portable air defense systems. One side argues that the helicopter is inherently vulnerable on the contemporary battlefield, as shown in Operations Allied Force, Enduring Freedom, and Iraqi Freedom. The other side argues that improvements in tactics will enable the AH-64 to continue conducting effective deep area operations.

General Merrill McPeak, former Air Force Chief of Staff, is representative of the "Apache is too vulnerable camp." He believes that

> the AH-64 and other attack helicopters should have their operations restricted to short-range missions directly in combat support of land forces. . . . [He] argues that nothing can give attack helicopters the stealth and speed necessary to survive, and that aircraft like the A-10 and fighters using standoff precision weapons are far more effective in the mission.[56]

---

[55] During OIF (and OEF), the fixed-wing aircraft available to the JFC were cycled through the AO in such a manner that they were generally very responsive to ground commanders for CAS and supportive of the interdiction requirements of the JFC and the CFLCC. See U.S. Army 3rd Infantry Division (2003), p. 30. During OIF, the 3rd Infantry Division was particularly impressed with "CAS stacks" and "push CAS," techniques that ensured "effective fires within 5–10 minutes."

[56] Cordesman (2003), p. 323.

Thus, in General McPeak's view, attack helicopters "should stay close to the front lines or work in tandem with Air Force strike jets" because, when "[y]ou start operating helicopters over hostile territory, I think you've got very serious problems."[57]

Senior Army commanders in OIF were also concerned about the risks involved in employing helicopters in the environment in which they were operating. After the deep attack by the 101st Airborne Division, General Wallace later recalled that "we did no more deep operations with the Apaches. . . . I gave my Corps AH-64s to 3rd Infantry Division for close support. . . . I sent the 101st up there [to the west] to do armed reconnaissance."[58] Major General Buford C. Blount, commanding the 3rd Infantry Division, also chose not to use his divisional attack helicopters in deep operations given the experience of the 11th AHR:

> I ordered attack helicopters to stay west of the Euphrates after [the] abortive attack by [the] 11th Aviation Regiment. The area west of the river was too heavily built-up and there was too much potential ground fire. We did not need to take the added risk of operating attack helicopters in this environment.[59]

Nevertheless, Army officials, most notably Army Vice Chief of Staff General Richard Cody, are not willing to concede the vulnerability of the Apache. They have argued that the 11th AHR's problems in Iraq were an anomaly that can be corrected through better tactics. Thus, "The mission was proper, but it was poorly executed."[60] General Cody, himself an attack helicopter pilot, remained supportive of Army doctrine and attack helicopters: "I disagree with people saying the attack helicopter's role has been diminished by that mission. I think we

---

[57] "Proponents Defend Army Helicopters," *Columbia (Mo.) Daily Tribune*, August 1, 2004.

[58] RAND interview with Lt. Gen. (U.S. Army) William S. Wallace, Arlington, Va., October 6, 2003.

[59] RAND interview with Maj. Gen. (U.S. Army) Buford C. Blount, Arlington, Va., November 18, 2003.

[60] "Proponents Defend Army Helicopters" (2004).

gave the attack helicopters a mission that wasn't quite suited for them at the time."[61]

Army aviation is adapting to the conditions encountered in Iraq (and Afghanistan). Training at the Army Aviation Center is incorporating combat lessons:

> There is no doubt that the wars fought yesterday are much different from those we will fight tomorrow, and current combat actions in Operation Iraqi Freedom and Operation Enduring Freedom prove that. Both OIF and OEF have provided the Aviation Center with valuable lessons learned—lessons that have prompted modifications to the way we train our aviators in order to be more lethal and survivable on the battlefield.

> Maneuvering flight and diving fire are two primary examples of the way aviation flight training is being modified. . . . Today, Fort Rucker's flight students receive training on how to conduct maneuvering flight to take full advantage of their aircraft's flight capabilities. The result is increased survivability for our pilots and their aircraft.

> For years, diving fire from attack helicopters seemed to be a lost art. During the Cold War, gunnery tactics called for our helicopters to engage the enemy from static hovering positions. While this technique was certainly appropriate for yesterday's fight, it is not so for today's or tomorrow's. Recent experience from OIF and OEF has shown that on today's battlefield, hovering fire positions can place our attack aircraft in dangerous circumstances.

> Diving fire fits the AH-64 Apache's capabilities far better. By training to attack targets from altitude in a fast, steep dive, not only is accuracy improved, but so too is survivability. And, when put together with newly taught maneuvers such as the "pitch back attack," a technique used to quickly reengage targets via a tight

---

[61] "Proponents Defend Army Helicopters" (2004).

turn back to the target area, our aviators can deliver far more lethal blows to the enemy.[62]

The Army aviation community is also transforming in response to recommendations from an aviation task force, chartered by the Army Chief of Staff, to transform Army aviation for its roles in future wars and in stability operations, including the recapitalization of the aviation fleet and expanding the roles of UAVs. To resource an aviation transformation strategy focused on "fixing Army aviation while supporting combat operations," the Army in 2004 terminated the Comanche helicopter program.[63] Furthermore, "The Army's aviation fleet is undergoing a total overhaul, and the main priority is increasing survivability."[64] Nevertheless, the *2004 Army Transformation Roadmap* shows that the Army still believes that deep attack is a central mission for Army attack aviation in the future:

> The aviation brigade will be fully capable of planning, preparing for, executing and assessing mobile strike operations and deep attacks using attack helicopters. It will retain a fully capable fire support element that possesses suppression of enemy air defense, maintains the intelligence links to track targets, and includes the Army aviation battle command element to coordinate airspace control measures as necessary—all linked to the appropriate joint systems.[65]

---

[62] Frederick Rice, "Army Aviation—Preparing For the Future," Fort Rucker, Ala., undated.

[63] U.S. Army Training and Doctrine Command, "TRADOC Futures Center Feedback on RAND Study: 'Learning Large Lessons: The Evolving Roles of Ground Power and Air Power in the Post–Cold War Era'—Part III, Army Aviation Transformation: Army Attack Aviation for a Campaign Quality Army with Joint and Expeditionary Capabilities," PowerPoint briefing, Fort Monroe, Va., August 31, 2005. This briefing also notes that, as of August 2005, the U.S. Army had "lost 80 aircraft (with 23 more undergoing assessment) in hostile and non-hostile incidents since 1 October 2001, including 12 that were lost by hostile fire." See also U.S. Department of the Army, *2005 Army Modernization Plan*, 2005, p. 30.

[64] U.S. Department of the Army, *2004 Army Transformation Roadmap*, 2004, p. 3-10.

[65] U.S. Department of the Army, *2004 Army Transformation Roadmap*, 2004, p. 3-8. See also U.S. Department of the Army, Field Manual (Interim) 3-04.101, *UEx Aviation Brigade Organization, Training, and Operations*, 2005, which notes: "Mobile strike operations are

This is not to argue that attack helicopters have no role to play in modern combat. During OIF, as already discussed, the Apache proved itself a useful member of the Army combined arms team in many roles aside from deep operations. Furthermore, ongoing stability operations in Iraq show the value and viability of an air platform directly responsive to the ground commander in many mission areas, including reconnaissance, close combat attack, and convoy escort.[66] But the fundamental reality is that these aircraft must operate in a flight regime in which they can be engaged by large numbers of visually and infrared-guided systems that cannot, under most circumstances, be suppressed reliably.

Nevertheless, the debate about the utility and survivability of the attack helicopter in deep attack or mobile strike operations is an important one because its resolution is key to determining the dimensions of the AO allocated to ground or air power by the combatant commander. Absent the Apache's ability to function as the key component of Army deep operations, the argument to place the FSCL much closer to the FEBA is logical and similar to the recommendation in the 3rd Infantry Division's OIF after-action report: that the FSCL be routinely placed at the outer limit of divisional indirect fire systems (cannon and MLRS).[67] These organic ground indirect fire systems are particularly responsive in close combat and counterfire (fires against enemy artillery and mortars) missions. Again, the problem the 3rd Infantry Division faced with a deep FSCL (100 kilometers or more beyond the FEBA) was that it had no systems that could cover the gap between the range of its M109A6 Paladin howitzers and M270 MLRSs and the FSCL. To the division, as noted in its after-action review, "The question quickly became: 'How do we target enemy forces located beyond

---

extended combat operations that capitalize on the ability of attack aviation to maneuver to the full depth of the UEx AO, deliver massed fire, and employ precision munitions in support. The UEx executes mobile strikes outside of the BCT areas against targets that are capable of maneuvering to avoid precision strikes."

[66] TRADOC, "TRADOC Futures Center Feedback on RAND Study, Part III," pp. 2, 19.

[67] U.S. Army 3rd Infantry Division (2003), p. 106.

the range of our organic artillery but short of the FSCL?' The answer was equally apparent: 'Air-delivered fires.'[68] The CFLCC FSCL, however, made the use of air-delivered fires short of the FSCL less effective than desired.

Interestingly, Marine Corps forces did not experience the same integration problems that the Army and the Air Force did, for two reasons. One was procedural, the other cultural. From the procedural perspective, the 1st Marine Expeditionary Force employed a battlefield coordination line (BCL), which the 3rd Infantry Division's OIF after-action report recommended the Army adopt, which was defined as:

> A supplementary fire support coordination measure, established based on METT-T [mission, enemy, terrain and weather, troops and support available—time available] which facilitates the expeditious attack of surface targets of opportunity between the measure (the BCL) and the fire support coordination line (FSCL). When established, the primary purpose is to allow MAGTF aviation to attack surface targets without approval of a ground combat element commander in whose area the targets may be located. To facilitate air delivered fires and deconflict air and surface fires, an airspace coordination area (ACA) will always overlie the area between the BCL and the FSCL. Additionally, ground commanders may strike any targets beyond the BCL and short of the FSCL with artillery and/or rockets without coordination as long as those fires do not violate the established BCL ACA. This includes targets in an adjacent (OPCON) ground commander's zone which fall within the BCL-FSCL area.[69]

---

[68] U.S. Army 3rd Infantry Division (2003) p. 106.

[69] U.S. Army 3rd Infantry Division (2003), p. 108. See Rebecca Grant, "Marine Air in the Mainstream," *Air Force Magazine*, June 2004, for a discussion of the relationship between the CFACC and Army and Marine Corps forces during OIF. Opinion within the Marine Corps about the efficacy of the BCL is not unanimous. See *Richard K. Hilberer, John C. Barry,* and *Dawn N. Ellis,* "Go Ugly, Early," *Marine Corps Gazette*, May 2005, p. 30. This article poses the question: "For simplicity's sake, should the MEF simply drop the BCL concept and have the DASC control everything up to the fire support coordination line like the air support operations center (ASOC) does in support of the Army?"

Consequently, during OIF, the "Marines defined a battlefield coordination line much closer to friendly forces [than the FSCL] and opened all kill boxes beyond this line, an approach that promoted a much more efficient use of air power."[70]

The ease with which 1st Marine Expeditionary Force employed the BCL in OIF, however, indicates more than procedural flexibility in Marine Corps operations. It also reflects a cultural dimension mentioned earlier, which helps to explain why the Marine Corps can incorporate fixed-wing aircraft—both its own and those of the Navy and the Air Force—into its operations more readily than the Army can.

From the earliest days of American military aviation, the Marine Corps and the Navy resisted efforts led by Army Air Service air power advocates, most notably Brigadier General Billy Mitchell, to create an air arm separate from their services. The comments of one Marine officer perhaps best captured the views of Marine pilots during this formative period: "Marine aviation is not being developed as a separate branch of the Service that considers itself too good to do anything else. Unlike the army air service, we do not aspire to be separate from the line or to be considered as anything but regular marines."[71]

This is not to say that Marine aviators then, or now, viewed close support of ground forces as their only mission. Indeed, in 1940, the Marine Corps specified that

> the use of attack aviation to supplement the firepower of ground arms is generally discouraged, as it may result in the neglect of more distant and perhaps more vital objectives. As a ground rule, attack aviation should be used in lieu of artillery only when the time limit precludes the assembly of sufficient artillery units to

---

[70] Bruce R. Pirnie, Alan Vick, Adam Grissom, Karl P. Mueller, and David T. Orletsky, *Beyond Close Air Support: Forging a New Air-Ground Partnership*, Santa Monica, Calif.: RAND Corporation, MG-301-AF, 2005, p. 68.

[71] Lt. Col. Edward C. Johnson, *Marine Corps Aviation: The Early Years, 1912–1940*, Headquarters, U.S. Marine Corps, 1977, p. 35, in Williamson Murray and Allan R. Millett, eds., *Military Innovation in the Interwar Period*, Cambridge, UK: Cambridge University Press, 1996), p. 176.

provide the necessary preparation, and when such absence of artillery may involve failure of the campaign as a whole.[72]

Today, Marine Corps doctrine specifies a wide range of missions for its aviation component:

> Marine aviation provides the MAGTF with the operational flexibility it needs to accomplish its mission across the range of military operations. It extends the operational reach of the MAGTF and enables it to accomplish operational objectives designed to achieve strategic goals. . . . Since most ground- and ship-based fires have a limited range and ground-based mobility systems are limited by speed, range, and the terrain, the MAGTF's ACE allows the MAGTF commander to conduct the deep fight. . . .
>
> The ACE's role is to project combat power, conduct air operations, and contribute to battlespace dominance in support of the MAGTF's mission, and it organizes, trains, and equips for that role. . . .
>
> The MAGTF's single-battle concept exploits the combined-arms nature of MAGTF operations. It allows the MAGTF commander to fight a single battle with an integrated, task-organized force of ground, aviation, and logistic forces. Based on this concept, operations performed by Marine aviation are rarely undertaken in isolation since its greatest value is in its integrated contribution to the MAGTF's overall mission. It is designed to function most effectively as an integral part of the MAGTF and cannot be separated without a significant loss of capability. Marine aviation provides enhanced mobility and close fires for units in contact and augments ground and naval indirect fires. Marine aviation also gives a Marine expeditionary force (MEF), which would otherwise be a light infantry force, the operational reach of a corps-level force.
>
> Marine aviation performs a variety of roles and tasks in support of national objectives. Marine aviation provides the MAGTF with

---

[72] Johnson, *Marine Corps Aviation*, p. 79, in Murray and Millett (1996), pp. 177–178.

six specific functions: antiair warfare (AAW), offensive air support (OAS), assault support, air reconnaissance, electronic warfare (EW), and control of aircraft and missiles.[73]

Additionally, the MAGTF contains organizations to provide air direction, air control, and airspace management.[74]

This close integration of aviation by the Marine Corps since the 1920s, and the belief by Marine aviators that they are Marines who happen to fly, results in a service culture that routinely relies on integrating air power routinely into its operations. Again, this goes beyond CAS. The MAGTF commander, who does not have Apache helicopters or ATACMS[75] at his disposal, must rely on air power, which he "owns," as his principal instrument in his deep fight.[76]

The Marine culture is based on trust, unity of command, and a common mission:

> Inside the Corps the belief is that collective trust in the Officer Corps is deliberately generated and is based on shared culture because Marine officers attend a common bonding experience at both Officer's Candidate School (for all but Academy grads)

---

[73] U.S. Department of the Navy, MCWP 3-2, *Aviation Operations*, U.S. Marine Corps, 2000, pp. 1-1, 1-2.

[74] U.S. Department of the Navy, MCWP 3-2 (2000), pp. 4-7, 4-8.

[75] See James A. Pace, "Myths, Misperceptions, and Reality of the Ground Fires Triad," *Marine Corps Gazette*, June 2005. The Marine Corps is in the process of acquiring deep fire rocket capabilities by fielding two high-mobility artillery rocket systems (HIMARS, the truck-mounted version of MLRS, capable of firing ATACMS). As a consequence, the "MAGTF and division commanders will have the organic ground fire support capability to fight the deep fight, conduct long-range counterfire, and weight the main effort that is currently limited to air and the number and range of current cannon artillery systems" (p. 16). Thus, rather than having to rely on existing Army MLRS/ATACMS resources within a theater, the Marine Corps is adding two battalions at the expense of existing structure and capabilities.

[76] See U.S. Department of the Navy, *Aviation Training and Readiness (T&R) Manual, AH-1, Marine Corps Order 3500.48*, U.S. Marine Corps, May 13, 2003, p. 3. The Marine Corps, like the Army, employs attack helicopters. The Marine Corps organizes its attack helicopters in light attack squadrons. The Mission Essential Task List for these units does not include the deep attack mission contained in Army doctrine for attack helicopter operations.

and the six month long Basic Course. This common schooling in Marine warfighting philosophy instills a common approach to warfighting that does not place primacy in a particular dimension, but rather, emphasizes the synergy of combined arms and the Marine Air Ground Team. . . . The Marines believe in balancing both air and ground maneuver synergistically and think in terms of combined arms, not air or ground dominance. Their doctrine reinforces this, and their force structure demands it because they lack the ground combat power of traditional conventional armies.[77]

The common culture and trust among Marine officers are also reflected in the unified approach to warfighting in Marine organizations:

The two most important and distinguishing characteristics of the MAGTF are (1) the fact that all Marines are Marines first and pilots, infantry officers, or FACs [forward air controllers], second—thus every Marine pilot and naval flight officer knows firsthand the challenges facing the GCE [ground combat element] Marine, and (2) there is no question in the Marine Corps who is the supported unit. Although the ACE [air combat element] can be employed as a maneuver element, it primarily supports the GCE.[78]

This perspective is clearly evident in a statement in the chapter on planning for OIF in the *After Action Report, 1st Marine Division*: "As part of the vision, the Division planned to be the most 'air-centric division in history', crushing the Iraqi indirect fire capability with air power, preserving artillery ammunition for fights it could not win by air alone."[79] This "air-centricity," however, is different from the "air-centric" perspective of air power advocates discussed throughout this study. From the Marine perspective, air power—and all other forms of combat power—are harnessed to the central aim of supporting the mission

---

[77] F. G. Hoffman, letter to Cynthia Cook, RAND, March 30, 2005.

[78] Staff of the Marine Corps Center for Lessons Learned, "Operation Iraqi Freedom Lessons Learned," *Marine Corps Gazette*, May 2005, p. 79.

[79] Groen et al. (2003), p. 4.

of the MAGTF in its AO. As with the Army corps commander in his AO, the MAGTF commander is king. The basic difference is that the MAGTF commander owns his own fixed-wing air power and is only reliant on the other services for reinforcing capabilities. Again, the Marines are more adept at integrating fixed-wing air power from the Air Force because they are accustomed to directing their own aircraft.

This situation holds some irony. In the abstract, the MAGTF would appear to be a model of how to integrate ground power and air power across the theater in a joint campaign. In practice, however, the MAGTF operates as independently as the Army in its own AO, controlling—and largely withholding—its organic air assets from the larger theater campaign.

Thus, the adoption of a BCL as an Army fire support coordinating measure, although it would facilitate the attack of targets within a division's AO, would still not address the larger issue of the AO retained by a corps commander to employ organic corps systems (ATACMS and attack helicopters). And Army commanders are not inclined to contract their AOs for what are largely issues of trust between the Army and the Air Force.

Army officers prefer to rely on organic systems—or CAS that they control—for deep operations because they do not believe that the Air Force will provide the resources necessary to shape the battlefield adequately. Past experiences have created a cultural perception that conditions Army officers to believe that the Air Force will not always be there when it is needed, and therefore the Army must have organic capabilities to conduct deep battle. Leaving aside for a moment the propensity of air officers in past conflicts to focus on the independent "air campaign," before the advent of JDAM this supposition was correct in weather that grounded fixed-wing aircraft or conditions that obscured the target area. Experiences in OEF and OIF, however, would argue that air power, enabled by sensors ranging from satellites to soldiers, can be relied upon to be available all-weather, day or night.

For its part, Air Force culture similarly inhibits close integration with the Army. While senior Air Force officers today are committed to supporting land operations and have proven willing to allocate very large portions of the overall air effort to this task, they still do not trust the Army on its own to employ airpower properly. And they are extremely reluctant to cede operational control of their instrument to nonairmen.[80]

Given the post–Cold War evidence of the increasing capability of air power—and the Marine example in OIF of the effective integration of ground and air power—the Army has a compelling need to reassess its corps deep battle doctrine and fire support coordinating measures. Again, this was clearly articulated in the 3rd Infantry Division's OIF report: "The U.S. Army must redefine the battlespace based on our ability to influence it."[81]

This lesson about the Army's organic limitations to conduct deep operations is not, however, being reflected in plans for the Future Force. The Army of the future will still have two principal means to directly affect conditions in its AO: ATACMS and attack helicopters. As already noted, the Army's position is that attack helicopter operations are still viable, even though the Army will have to rely on the AH-64 Apache Longbow attack helicopter for the foreseeable future following the cancellation of the RAH-66 Comanche helicopter. In the category of indirect fire systems, however, the Army is still intent on increasing its capability:

> To shape the battlespace and conduct decisive operations, the Army is also moving toward common munitions and a suite of long-range precision-strike weapons. The corps commander will have a true organic deep-strike capability with rockets and mis-

---

[80] The continued reluctance of the Air Force to integrate closely with the Army is apparent in the latest version of U.S. Department of the Air Force, AFDD (Air Force Doctrine Document) 2-1.3, *Counterland Operations*, 2006, p. 5, which notes:

> The purpose of interdiction is to attack the enemy's ability to fight by targeting tactical and operational forces and infrastructure with either lethal or non-lethal means. . . . The Air Force defines AI as air operations conducted to divert, disrupt, delay, or destroy the enemy's military potential before it can be brought to bear effectively against friendly forces, or to otherwise achieve JFC objectives. AI is conducted at such distance from friendly forces that detailed integration of each air mission with the fire and movement of friendly forces is not required. [Emphasis in the orginal.]

[81] Groen et al. (2003). Such an assessment of corps deep operations and Army AOs would also have to consider the probability that ATACMS should be controlled by the CFACC as a component of strategic attack or interdiction or SEAD to support these uses of air power.

siles that have longer ranges, more lethality, and increased precision than those currently fielded.[82]

The Army will surely press for a larger AO so that it can employ its desired long-range precision strike capabilities to their limits. The UA concept states as much and provides the criteria for the size of, and a commander's authority within, an AO:

> AOs should be large enough for component commanders to employ their organic, assigned, and supporting systems to the limit of their capabilities. For Army forces, it's a geographical area, including the airspace above, usually defined by lateral, forward, and rear boundaries assigned to a commander, by a higher commander, in which he has responsibility and the authority to conduct military operations.[83]

Indeed, the UA concept acknowledges the requirement for a larger Army component AO: "The AO of the UA will often be significantly larger than that of a brigade today."[84] One could logically expect the same to be true for Army echelons above the UA. And within its AO, per joint doctrine, the Army component would remain the supported force.

The Army's plans for its Future Force guarantee future tension between the Army and the Air Force similar to that experienced during both Gulf wars. This is unfortunate in a period when ground forces are

---

[82] U.S. Department of the Army, *United States Army Transformation Roadmap, 2003*, p. A-4.

[83] U.S. Army Training and Doctrine Command (2004), pp. 4–8.

[84] U.S. Army Training and Doctrine Command (2004). The UA concept notes the UA has an Area of Influence (AI) (defined as "a geographical area wherein a commander . . . is directly capable of influencing operations by maneuver or fire support systems normally under his command or control") with a 75-kilometer radius. Furthermore, one could also expect the smaller, more capable forces the Army envisions in the Future Force being more widely distributed within their AOs, which could further increase the need to rely on air power as a means to attack the enemy beyond the range of ground systems. See also Rocky G. Samek, "ATACMS: Fires for the Objective Force," *Field Artillery*, May–June 2003, p. 22. This article notes, "The UA most likely will have an AO radius in excess of 75 kilometers with its UE's AO likely to be up to 250 kilometers."

becoming increasingly dependent on air power for information and fire support. The Army's plans for the future also place it in the potentially untenable bureaucratic position of maintaining "as a result of tradition and inclination" its "focus on the high end of the spectrum of conflict—precisely the point of the spectrum where the still-increasing [air power] capabilities of the Air Force and Navy provide the greatest appeal to risk-averse decisionmakers." This argument is based both on prudent risk aversion and the greater capabilities of air power to perform effectively at the operational and strategic levels.[85]

### The Enduring Nature of Army Culture and Self-Perception

The Army's culture and self-perception, as reflected in its plans for the future, indicate that post–Cold War lessons either are not being absorbed or are being viewed from a ground-centric perspective. John Gordon and Jerry Sollinger, writing in *Parameters*, succinctly summed up the essence of Army culture:

> The Army has long seen itself as the "supported service," the one with the primary responsibility to win the nation's wars. Indeed, the Army's vision statement describes "fighting and winning our nation's wars" as its "nonnegotiable contract" with the American people. It does not qualify the vision by indicating that it wins the wars in conjunction with the other services. . . .
>
> This view has important implications. Chief among them is that the Army, a believer in joint operations, perceives the role of the other services as being, fundamentally, to support the Army. The Air Force and Navy get the Army to the theater and provide it such important combat support as naval gunfire, interdiction, and close air support. The Marines are regarded as the "junior partner" in land operations. To be sure, the sister services fulfill other roles: clearing the air of enemy aircraft and the seas of enemy vessels. But in the Army view, these are subsidiary roles and ultimately intended to facilitate the Army's mission of win-

---

[85] Gordon and Sollinger (2004), p. 41.

ning the land battle. The Army closes with and destroys enemy forces, with the other services in support.[86]

In the post–Cold War era, when events have called the singular decisiveness of ground power into question, the Army has responded by either pointing to ground power surrogates in wars (such as in Bosnia and Kosovo) or attributing to itself a much greater degree of operational decisiveness than the evidence would support (in both Gulf wars and Afghanistan). OIF, however, is the most instructive. In this war, operational decisions by Army commanders about how to control their AO, principally by extending the depth of the FSCL to facilitate the use of organic V Corps resources, constrained the ability of air power to contribute to the overall JFC's effort. Furthermore, the employment of V Corps attack aviation assets in deep area operations, which necessitated this extended AO (and which was in full consonance with Army doctrine), had virtually no positive influence on the strategic and operational outcome of the war.

### What Is the Future of Ground Power?

Important positive ground power lessons from the post–Cold War era, particularly from OIF, illuminate the possible future of ground warfare. It is clear that the Army remains a vital component of the overall joint effort in successfully concluding decisive operations. But its role, at least in these conflicts, was different from what it has been in the past. Although the Army will still have to close with and destroy the enemy, the enemy will likely be engaged in smaller units than in the past. At this moment in the history of warfare, the United States has a C4ISR and strike advantage, made possible by air dominance, that makes it extraordinarily difficult for substantial mounted ground formations to hide or move without being engaged by air power or, for that matter, Army indirect fire systems that can range them. Therefore, those attempting to frame the present with past metaphors (e.g.,

---

[86] Gordon and Sollinger (2004), pp. 34–35.

"hammer and anvil"[87]) are missing the key dimensions of what appears to be an emerging new operational reality.

Major General Bob Scales takes on the question of what has changed in his book *Yellow Smoke: The Future of Land Warfare for America's Military*. One of his recommendations is to "[a]dopt an operational maneuver doctrine based on fire power doctrine and area control" because "[o]n a vastly more expanded and lethal battlefield, where maneuver supports fire, a force will succeed only if freed from the traditional constrictions of linear maneuver and direct control."[88] Scales then goes on to challenge one of the tenets of U.S. Army doctrine— that of ground forces closing with and destroying the enemy, fundamental to Army doctrine since at least 1923, stating:

> The task of destroying the enemy now belongs to firepower, not maneuver, systems. Close-combat forces today perform the paralyzing function formerly reserved for firepower systems. Instead of closing with and destroying the enemy with fire and maneuver, close-combat soldiers will exploit superior maneuverability to first find and then fix the enemy long enough for precision to do the killing.[89]

*Yellow Smoke* was published before OIF, and Scales draws on the Afghanistan experience to "demonstrate the power inherent in the reversal of the roles between firepower and maneuver and serve as a model for how this function will be performed in the future."[90] In Scales's view, "Small discrete maneuver elements [will] cautiously move in to just outside the lethal range of the enemy's weapons and begin the deadly and methodical process of directing precision fires."[91] This is what happened with special operating forces that supported

---

[87] Pape (2004), pp. 116–130.

[88] Robert H. Scales, Jr., *Yellow Smoke: The Future of Land Warfare for America's Military*, Lanham, Md.: Rowman and Littlefield, 2003, p. 156.

[89] Scales (2003), p. 157.

[90] Scales (2003), p. 157.

[91] Scales (2003), p. 157.

the Northern Alliance by directing air strikes against Taliban forces. In OIF, however, ground maneuver continually advanced, exploiting the effects of fires. Relatively small, but lethal and competent, Army ground forces advanced rapidly and inexorably toward Baghdad. In the process, they directly or indirectly caused Iraqi formations to reposition to meet their advance. This repositioning exposed the Iraqis to devastating aerial attack, and they were rendered ineffective as large units. Consequently, coalition air power shattered conventional Iraqi ground force units; ground forces dealt with the remnants. The ground action that followed the coalition air attacks on Iraqi formations, for those needing a traditional doctrinal anchor, most resembles *exploitation*, defined in JP 1-02, *Department of Defense Dictionary of Military and Associated Terms*, as: "Taking full advantage of success in military operations, following up initial gains, and making permanent the temporary effects already achieved."[92]

This assessment of post–Cold War lessons shows that since the 1991 Gulf War, ground maneuver forces have performed three unique roles that should be incorporated into Army plans for its Future Force. First, the presence of a ground component in OEF and OIF forced the adversary to react to its presence. In OEF, this was largely accomplished at the operational level through surrogate Afghan forces, enabled by air power. In OIF, coalition ground forces, through their maneuver, induced movement in Iraqi forces, which in turn exposed them to devastating air attack.

Second, ground forces in OEF and OIF have, as always, taken on the tough, dirty business of going after pockets of tenacious resistance in the aftermath of major combat operations and have contended with insurgencies in the wake of both wars. General Robert Foglesong,

---

[92] U.S. Joint Chiefs of Staff, JP 1-02, *Department of Defense Dictionary of Military and Associated Terms*, 2001, p. 152. Coalition ground forces also faced the paramilitary Saddam Fedayeen. These forces, poorly trained and armed, relative to coalition forces, were generally slaughtered when they were engaged. Ironically, the need to have an enemy react to one's forces to make him susceptible to discovery and strike may require a rethinking of traditional notions of operations security. In the future, friendly force movements may have to be unmasked so the opponent can see and move to respond to them.

commander of U.S. Air Forces in Europe, seems to understand this grim reality:

> I was reminded of [that fact] again in Afghanistan. Jack [Army Gen. John M. Keane] and I kind of laughed about this—not in a humorous way—but [USAF] took great credit . . . in the air campaign that went on in Afghanistan, [but] guess who had to go into those caves and pull those people out? Well, it wasn't [USAF]. We may have been on the ground down there with them to assist them to a degree, but it was that inspirational and intimidating Army.[93]

Third, ground forces have remained in the countries where rapid victories have turned into enduring stability and support missions: keeping the peace in Bosnia and Kosovo and trying to bring peace to Afghanistan and Iraq. Again, General Foglesong's comments are instructive:

> I'm always reminded of when I was doing some interesting work in the negotiation business in Kosovo—what a great air war that was for us; . . . it was a great chance for us to beat our chest and proudly proclaim what air power can do—[but] three days later I happened to go to Pristina and guess who was standing on the street corners up there? I'll tell you who it wasn't. It wasn't the United States Air Force. It was the United States Army and the Marine Corps.[94]

There are also cautionary lessons from OIF that should resonate deeply within the Army: Despite the remarkable capacity of U.S. ISR systems to find large units, smaller formations often went undetected until they were in direct fire range of Army ground combat units. To play off the title of Admiral Bill Owens's book *Lifting the Fog of War*, although there is a higher probability of finding and striking large mounted units, a thick bank of ground fog at the tactical

---

[93] "Springboard for Airpower," *Air Force Magazine*, Vol. 87, No. 3, March 2004.

[94] "Springboard for Airpower" (2004).

level still remains. Again, as already noted, the Army's own history of OIF, *On Point*, recognized this, noting, "Most tactical unit commanders claimed that they made every assault as a movement to contact."[95] Consequently, in OIF, genuine situational awareness in the rush to Baghdad was most often achieved by 3rd Infantry Division soldiers only when they made unexpected contact with small groups of Iraqi soldiers and Saddam Fedayeen. The U.S. advantage was that its soldiers were protected by the armor of their Abrams tanks and Bradley fighting vehicles. The 3rd Infantry Division after-action report is clear in this regard:

> This war was won in large measure because the enemy could not achieve effects against our armored fighting vehicles. While many contributing factors, such as air interdiction (AI), close air support (CAS), Army aviation, and artillery helped shape the division battlespace, ultimately any war demands closure with an enemy force within the minimum safe distance of supporting CAS and artillery. U.S. armored combat systems enabled the division to close with and destroy heavily armored and fanatically determined enemy forces with impunity, often within urban terrain. Further, the bold use of armor and mechanized forces striking the heart of the regime's defenses enabled the division to maintain the initiative and capitalize on its rapid success in route [*sic*] to Baghdad. During MOUT, no other ground combat system currently in our arsenal could have delivered similar mission success without accepting enormous casualties.[96]

In retrospect, it appears that the Army is selectively applying lessons learned in post–Cold War operations to its vision of its Future Force. In near-term operations, it is adapting to the operational environment, but the lessons from ongoing operations across the globe are being incorporated as "TTPs" (tactics, techniques, and procedures)

---

[95] Fontenot, Degen, and Tohn (2004), p. 423.

[96] U.S. Army 3rd Infantry Division (2003), p. 22. On the value of heavy armored vehicles in OIF, see also John Gordon IV and Bruce R. Pirnie, "Everybody Wanted Tanks: Heavy Forces in Operation Iraqi Freedom," *Joint Force Quarterly*, No. 39, October 2005, pp. 84–90.

rather than making their way into Army doctrine. The Army is taking on the tough, long-term missions of controlling terrain and populations. These are missions that only ground forces can accomplish. They also appear to be enduring missions that will require long-term institutional solutions across the doctrine, organization, training, materiel, leadership, personnel, facilities (DOTMLPF) categories that inform how the Army conceptualizes and manages change.

This is not to say that the Army should abandon its warfighting focus. Instead, it is to argue that a narrow view of the range of military operations that turns warfighting, particularly at the operational level, into the institution's defining raison d'être, with all else being lesser-included cases, limits the effectiveness of the Army and shortchanges the nation. The nation expects and deserves to have an Army that is the world's best warfighting force and SSTRO force, and equally prepared across the DOTMLPF for the entire range of military operations. Here again, Gordon and Sollinger are instructive:

> It is essential to remember that the US Army, the premier land force of the world's sole superpower, must maintain primarily a warfighting focus in its culture, organization, training, and modernization plans. That is unassailable as the Army's central focus. The issue for the Army is one of balance. Given the changing realities in how the United States will conduct future joint operations, plus the fact that mid- to low-intensity missions will clearly dominate in the coming decade or more (and the Army is the optimal force for such missions), the Army has to reexamine how it will balance its traditional focus on high-end combat operations with the need to perform the other missions that will predominate in the coming years.[97]

The Army has to be prepared for any eventuality that threatens the interests of the nation—now, ten years from now, and forever—across the range of military operations. Nevertheless, the Army has to accept as an institution that the nation will look to it after major combat operations are over to provide a secure environment in which

---

[97] Gordon and Sollinger (2004), p. 44.

new institutions of governance can be established. This issue is central to the ultimate goal of reaching a satisfactory strategic political end state. And it is an issue a warfighting-focused Army has yet to fully embrace. A report prepared by the U.S. Army War College Strategic Studies Institute on the eve of OIF eloquently stated the consequences of getting the post-conflict operation wrong:

> In recent decades, U.S. civilian and military leadership have shied away from nation-building. However, the current war against terrorism has highlighted the danger posed by failed and struggling states. If this nation and its coalition partners decide to undertake the mission to remove Saddam Hussein, they will also have to be prepared to dedicate considerable time, manpower, and money to the effort to reconstruct Iraq after the fighting is over. Otherwise, the success of military operations will be ephemeral, and the problems they were designed to eliminate could return or be replaced by new and more virulent difficulties.[98]

The paper also emphasized that "[t]he U.S. Army has been organized and trained primarily to fight and win the nation's major wars. Nonetheless, the Service must prepare for victory in peace as well."[99]

All this balancing and refocusing, however, will be extraordinarily difficult for the Army, because "[i]t requires nothing less than a cultural change, and these are neither lightly undertaken nor easily accomplished, particularly in conservative military organizations. Furthermore, it will require the Army to revisit important aspects of the transformation that it has been pursuing for the past four years."[100]

---

[98] Conrad C. Crane and W. Andrew Terrill, *Reconstructing Iraq: Insights, Challenges, and Missions for Military Forces in a Post-Conflict Scenario*, Carlisle, Pa.: Strategic Studies Institute, U.S. Army War College, 2003, p. iv.

[99] Crane and Terrill (2003), p. vi.

[100] Gordon and Sollinger (2004), p. 44.

## The Future Air Force as an Evolving Idea

Unlike the Army, whose learning has been largely framed by its constancy in adhering to its traditional central doctrinal tenet that wars are won by ground forces closing with and defeating the enemy, the Air Force has shown a greater capacity for adaptation throughout its history. In many ways, it was a service focused on proving an idea: that independent air power can be a decisive, war-winning instrument in and of itself. In the post–Cold War period, the Air Force has employed warfighting strategies whose broad conceptual approaches were quite diverse in the pursuit of this idea. In the 1991 Gulf War, the air campaign was initiated at the start of Desert Storm, and it combined counterair, SEAD, strategic attack, and interdiction. During the ground war, these components of the air campaign continued, but the Air Force also provided CAS to ground forces. In Operation Allied Force, Air Force officers believed that the appropriate use of air power was to employ it against strategic targets in Belgrade, rather than against Serb forces in Kosovo. In Afghanistan, air power showed its greatest utility in attacking Taliban and al Qaeda forces in the field, tipping the battlefield balance against these forces and in favor of the Northern Alliance and other Afghan forces. Finally, in OIF, the Air Force selectively attacked strategic targets but made its most significant contribution during major combat operations by shattering Iraqi forces in the field. During war the basic idea of the decisiveness of air power evolved to meet operational realities.

Lessons from recent operations have also made their way into Air Force doctrine. In the area of "strategic attack," there is a fundamental difference between the 1992, 1997, and 2003 versions of the Air Force's principal doctrine manual. The 1992 manual noted that "[t]he objective of strategic attack is to destroy or neutralize an enemy's war-sustaining capabilities or will to fight."[101] The 1997 doctrine was more expansive and included categories of fielded forces as potential centers of gravity worthy of strategic attack:

---

[101] U.S. Department of the Air Force, AFM 1-1 (1992), p. 6.

> Strategic attack is defined as those operations intended to directly achieve strategic effects by striking at the enemy's COGs [centers of gravity]. These operations are designed to achieve their objectives without first having to necessarily engage the adversary's fielded military forces in extended operations at the operational and tactical levels of war. . . . Strategic attack objectives often include producing effects to demoralize the enemy's leadership, military forces, and population, thus affecting an adversary's capability to continue the conflict. . . . Strategic attack may also be conducted against fielded forces. For example, strategic attack may be conducted against identified COGs such as major reserves or politically significant military formations, space launch and support elements, or forces used for strategic nuclear attack. Strategic attacks can be conducted independently by air and space forces.[102]

Finally, in the 2003 version of Air Force Basic Doctrine, strategic attack had evolved to effects-based operations against an enemy system writ large and explicitly recognized its contribution to the ground scheme of maneuver:

> Strategic attack is defined as offensive action conducted by command authorities aimed at generating effects that most directly achieve our national security objectives by affecting the adversary's leadership, conflict-sustaining resources, and strategy. Strategic attack is a concept, not just a function. As a concept, strategic attack builds on the idea that it is possible to directly affect an adversary's sources of strength and will to fight without first having to engage and defeat their military forces. Strategic attack may also be used to prevent the enemy from attacking our vulnerable points, essentially denying them their war aims. Adding in the concept of effects-based operations takes it further.
>
> Military forces are highly interconnected entities. Through strategic attack, military commanders can directly affect adversary leadership perceptions (either by isolation, deception, or exploi-

---

[102] U.S. Department of the Air Force, AFDD 1 (1997), p. 51.

tation) and cut off their fielded forces from their leadership and societies, as well as directly attack the adversary's capacity to sustain military forces in the field. While strategic attack may not totally eliminate the need to directly engage the adversary's fielded military forces, it can shape those engagements so they will be fought at the time and place of our choosing under conditions more likely to lead to decisive outcomes with the least risk for friendly forces.[103]

Thus, strategic attack evolved in just over a decade from a function focused on affecting the adversary's will and capacity to sustain warfare—largely ignoring military forces in the field—to an approach that recognized adversaries as complex systems, whose military forces were also centers of gravity.

Air Force counterland doctrine has also adapted, with the 2003 version of Air Force Basic Doctrine incorporating the OEF experience. Although still acknowledging the objectives of counterland as "operations to dominate the surface environment and prevent the opponent from doing the same," and noting that air power could conduct counterland operations without friendly surface forces, the manual went on to note that they could also be conducted "with only small numbers of surface forces providing target cueing," capturing the SOF support to Afghan forces experience from OEF.[104] The manual, however, went further. Instead of focusing on "halting" an adversary in a reactive response to aggression, the new manual adopts a more proactive posture: "This independent or direct attack of adversary surface operations by air and space forces is the key to success when seizing the initiative during the early phases of a conflict."[105] Furthermore, some within the Air Force argue that because "[t]he Air Force has developed the capability to directly engage and render ineffective an adversary's land forces," counterland doctrine should be expanded. They advocate

---

[103] U.S. Department of the Air Force, AFDD 1 (2003), pp. 40–41.

[104] U.S. Department of the Air Force, AFDD 1 (2003), pp. 43–44.

[105] U.S. Department of the Air Force, AFDD 1 (2003), p. 44.

adding "direct attack" (formerly "battlefield air operations") to the existing counterland interdiction and CAS mission categories.[106]

Implicit in the arguments for direct attack as a mission category is the requirement for the air component commander to control these operations. The air component commander would also be given the resources to plan direct attack and could be the supported commander.[107] In advocating direct attack, Major General David A. Deptula and his coauthors addressed these points in a Winter 2003 *Air and Space Power Journal* article:

> The current intelligence and C2 architectures and processes necessary to plan and execute DA missions are principally provided by and located within the land-component headquarters. How, then, does the CFACC develop the capability to engage the adversary's fielded forces without ready access to the current intelligence and C2 architectures and processes—particularly when there is no CFLCC? Another important challenge is to define the doctrinal tenets for employing land-maneuver forces in a supporting role to air forces. The first step in solving these challenges is the formal codification of DA [direct attack].
>
> Intelligence can best be provided by the appropriate land-warfare experts to assist in the planning and execution of DA missions. This expertise is not normally resident in the CFACC staff or in the combined air operation center (CAOC) and should be provided by land component forces—whether or not land forces are deployed or the JFC has designated a CFLCC. Even when land forces are present, it is still critical to the efficient planning and execution of DA for this expertise to work formally for the

---

[106]David A. Deptula, Gary L. Crowder, and George L. Stamper, Jr., "Direct Attack: Enhancing Counterland Doctrine and Joint Air-Ground Operations," *Air and Space Power Journal*, Winter 2003, p. 12. See also David A. Deptula and Sigfred J. Dahl, "Transforming Joint Air-Ground Operations for 21st Century Battlespace," *Field Artillery*, July–August 2003, pp. 21–25, and Phil M. Haun, "Vortices: Direct Attack—A Counterland Mission," *Air and Space Power Journal*, Summer 2003, pp. 9–16.

[107]Deptula, Crowder, and Stamper (2003), pp. 9–12.

CFACC, rather than as part of the CFLCC's battlefield coordination detachment.[108]

Although only implied in the article, direct attack could place the air component commander in charge of all attack operations other than those within the range of ground force organic systems. The use of long-range ground systems, e.g., ATACMS and attack helicopters, would presumably have to be coordinated with the new owner of the AO—the air component commander. Therefore, concepts such as direct attack are guaranteed to raise concerns among the ground components. They would likely be perceived as a power grab by air power advocates who, having clearly gained equality with the surface components, now want preeminence. This preeminence will affect both war-fighting concepts and, perhaps even more importantly, influence service bureaucratic imperatives and budgets. From a warfighting perspective, the new arrangements delineated in the direct attack article are probably unnecessary if the issues of AO designation, fire support coordinating measures, and support of the JFC are adequately addressed.

Another emerging change in Air Force (and joint) doctrine is the notion of "effects-based" operations, in which operational functions are "tied to specific effects":

> Effects are outcomes, events, or consequences resulting from specific actions; effects should contribute directly to desired military and political outcomes. This requires commanders and planners to explicitly and comprehensively link, to the greatest extent possible, each tactical action to strategic and operational objectives. This linkage is at the heart of effects-based operations (EBO), which are those actions taken against enemy systems designed to achieve specific effects that contribute directly to objectives. Commanders and planners must have a clear understanding of national security and campaign objectives and those actions nec-

---

[108] Deptula, Crowder, and Stamper (2003), p. 11. Emphasis in the original.

essary to create effects that cumulatively result in the desired end state.[109]

As discussed earlier, however, effects-based operations are still partly, if not largely, an art more than a science, given the difficulty that per-

---

[109]U.S. Department of the Air Force, AFDD 1 (2003), p. 38. See also U.S. Joint Forces Command, *Pamphlet 7: Operational Implications of Effects-Based Operations (EBO)*, Suffolk, Va.: Joint Warfighting Center, 2004, p. 2. This document provides the JFCOM "working definition of EBO":

> Operations that are planned, executed, assessed, and adapted based on a holistic understanding of the **operational environment** in order to influence or change **system** behavior or capabilities using the **integrated application** of selected **instruments of power** to achieve **directed policy aims**. [Emphasis in the original.]

See also U.S. Joint Forces Command, *Joint Forces Command Glossary,* undated. The glossary provides the following definitions for the various effects-based operations and their components:

> **Effects Based Operations (EBO)**—A process for obtaining a desired strategic outcome or "effect" on the enemy, through the synergistic, multiplicative, and cumulative application of the full range of military and nonmilitary capabilities at the tactical, operational, and strategic levels.
>
> **Effects Based Planning (EBP)**—An operational planning process to conduct EBO within RDO. EBP is results-based vice attrition-based. EBP closely mirrors the current joint planning process, yet focuses upon the linkage of actions to effects to objectives. EBP changes the way we view the enemy, ourselves, and what is included and emphasized in the planning process. EBP uses a flexibly-structured battle rhythm that leverages a collaborative knowledge environment and capitalizes on the use of fewer formal joint boards. It employs virtual, near-simultaneous planning at all echelons of command.
>
> **Effects Based Strategy**—The coherent application of national and alliance elements of power through effects-based processes to accomplish strategic objectives.
>
> **Effects Based Targeting**—The focus of the targeting process is to produce COAs [courses of action] that will change the enemy's behaviors and compel him to comply with our will. The behavioral changes we attempt to create are the result of effects that flow from the employment of our lethal and nonlethal capabilities. Thus, effects-based targeting is distinguished by the ability to generate the type and extent of effects necessary to create outcomes that facilitate the realization of the commander's objectives.
>
> **Effects Based Warfare**—The application of armed conflict to achieve desired strategic outcomes through the effects of military force.

See also U.S. Joint Forces Command, *Commander's Handbook for an Effects-Based Approach to Joint Operations*, Suffolk, Va.: Joint Warfighting Center, 2006. This document is a "predoctrinal follow-on" to the U.S. Joint Forces Command's Pamphlet 7, which is "**intended to provide sufficient detail to help joint force commanders (JFCs) and their staffs understand and apply an effects-based approach to joint operations**" (p. I-1). Emphasis in the original.

sists in obtaining reliable pre-strike intelligence and post-strike battle damage assessment. Absent exquisite intelligence (and a C4ISR-strike capability that can adapt in near real time to measurable changes in the adversary's system), it will be difficult to determine with any certainty the first-order, much less the second- or third-order, effects whose achievement will be necessary to have the desired overall effects on an enemy's system. This is particularly true if the objective of a given effects-based operation is to achieve psychological or cognitive effects, which are inherently much more difficult to plan and assess than a campaign whose objective is the physical destruction of the components of an enemy system, with the reasonable expectation that such destruction will also have some levels of effect on enemy will and morale. Nevertheless, effects-based operations, focused on the potential of producing multiplicative, cascading effects that will collapse enemy systems, is more strategically appealing than an air campaign focused only on destroying enemy targets in a war of attrition.[110] The caution for effects-based operations advocates is to be cognizant of the constraints on the realization of the concept and to promise only what they can deliver.[111]

Intellectually, effects-based operations are similar to World War II strategic bombing theory: It is largely assumption driven, and its decisiveness is highly context dependent. In World War II, the resilience of the German industrial web frustrated the expectations put forth in AWPD-1. Effects-based operations are analogous in many ways to this earlier air power strategic concept, whose intellectual underpinnings relied on achieving a singularly decisive, war-winning strategic effect through aggregated tactical means (bombing). This is not to say that

---

[110] See also Paul K. Davis, *Effects Based Operations: A Grand Challenge for the Analytical Community*, Santa Monica, Calif.: RAND Corporation, MR-1477-USJFCOM/AF, 2001, for a discussion of the analytical challenges posed by effects-based operations.

[111] One should not, however, lose sight of the fact that in some operational circumstances attrition might be the desired effect or the best approach to achieving a desired indirect effect. Attacks on enemy fielded forces can have the direct effect, through attrition, of diminishing their combat effectiveness by destroying equipment and killing or wounding personnel. These attrition attacks can also have the indirect effect of demoralizing enemy forces, affecting their will, and perhaps triggering large-scale desertions or surrenders.

in World War II air power did not play a vitally important role. It did. What it did not do, however, was live up to the prewar exhortations of its most strident advocates to win wars independently. Nevertheless, the prevailing cultural view within the Air Force, a culture discussed below, is that "technology will catch up with doctrine" and the idea of air power will be realized. One can assume that the current prevailing belief in effects-based operations will be no exception.[112]

## Air Force Culture and Interservice Cooperation

Air Force culture is one that, in the words of Carl Builder,

> could be said to worship at the altar of technology. The airplane was the instrument that gave birth to independent air forces. The airplane has, from its inception, been an expression of the miracles of technology. . . . If flight is a gift of technology, and if the expansion of technology poses the only limits on the freedoms of that gift, then it is to be expected that the fountain of technology will be worshiped by fliers and the Air Force. If the Air Force is to have a future of expanding horizons, it will come only from understanding, nurturing, and applying technology. There is a circle of faith here: If the Air Force fosters technology, then that inexhaustible fountain of technology will ensure an open-ended future for flight (in airplanes or spacecraft) that, in turn, will ensure the future of the Air Force.[113]

However, another dimension to Air Force culture persists despite the advances in its capabilities and its obvious value in operations since the end of the Cold War: a tendency to continue to assert its independence and equal status with land and naval power.

> Early air power advocates argued that air power could be decisive and could achieve strategic effects. While this view of air power was not proved during their lifetimes, the more recent history of air and space power application, especially since the 1991 Persian

---

[112] Earl H. Tilford, "Review of *Fast Tanks and Heavy Bombers: Innovation in the U.S. Army, 1917–1945*," *Naval War College Review*, Winter 2000.

[113] Builder (1989), p. 19.

Gulf War, has proven that air and space power can be a dominant and frequently the decisive element of combat in modern warfare. *Air and space power is a maneuver element in its own right, coequal with land and maritime power*; as such, it is no longer merely a supporting force to surface combat. As a maneuver element, it can be supported by surface forces in attaining its assigned objectives. Air and space power has changed the way wars are fought and the manner in which the United States pursues peacetime efforts to protect the nation's vital interests.[114]

The highlighted section in this passage from the 2003 version of Air Force Basic Doctrine is remarkably similar to the statement in the 1943 FM 100-2, *Command and Employment of Air Power*, written when the Air Force was still part of the Army: "LAND POWER AND AIR POWER ARE CO-EQUAL AND INTERDEPENDENT FORCES; NEITHER IS AN AUXILIARY OF THE OTHER."[115] Clearly, there is broad recognition of the critical contribution of air and space power to warfighting throughout DoD. But Air Force culture requires formal acceptance of its equality with the other services, lest that equality be jeopardized by relegating it to the role of a supporting force. Furthermore, the section in *Air Force Basic Doctrine* that states that air power can be a maneuver element and "supported by surface forces in attaining its assigned objectives" is, at best, confusing and, at worst, has the potential to heighten interservice tension.

Air Force doctrine writers appear to be attempting to force a round Air Force idea into a square surface component doctrine hole, perhaps in the hopes of being designated the premier and "supported" service. The latest version of the Air Force Doctrine Manual 2-1.2, *Strategic Attack*, also appears to be reverting to the "air power as the decisive war-winning instrument" argument of the past. The manual argues that

Operation DESERT STORM proved the efficacy of strategic attack and Operations DELIBERATE FORCE, OAF, OEF, and

---

[114] U.S. Department of the Air Force, AFDD 1 (2003), p. 16. Emphasis added.

[115] U.S. War Department, FM 100-2 (1943), p. 1. Capitalization in the original.

OIF further refined it. In these operations, air and space assets conducting strategic attack proved able to deny enemy access to critical resources, defeat enemy strategies, and decisively influence enemy decisions to end hostilities on terms favorable to US interests. *Today's Air Force possesses an independent war-winning potential distinct from and complementary to its ability to decisively shape surface warfare.*[116]

Again, all of this strains the language of warfighting and impedes efforts to attain a joint solution to achieving national strategic objectives. Quite simply, although air power has clearly demonstrated its ability to make a significant contribution to major combat operations, it has not shown that it can independently obtain a strategic political end state. If it could, U.S. forces would not be in Kosovo, Afghanistan, and Iraq today.

## The Future of American Warfighting

At the risk of being overly simplistic, the debate between the Army and the Air Force over the relative roles of ground and air power is one that has, with varying degrees of stridency, been ongoing since 1918. Furthermore, the institutional perspectives and cultures of the two services fundamentally affect how they view their operational experiences and learn lessons. The Army uses lessons and adapts technologies to buttress its warfighting doctrine, which it believes is fundamentally sound and inherently guarantees its place as the supported force. The Air Force evolves its doctrine, rooted in the idea of the decisiveness of air power and a desire to be the preeminent warfighting supported service, to accommodate the empirically proven promise of ever-improving air power and related technologies. Given the divergence between these culturally based perspectives, one should expect tension between the two services until these issues are addressed and resolved.

---

[116] U.S. Department of the Air Force, AFDD 2-1.2, *Strategic Attack*, 2003, p. 1. Emphasis (italics) added.

Nevertheless, the dominance of air power at the operational and strategic levels of warfighting can no longer be ignored. In the aftermath of Operation Desert Storm, Thomas Keaney and Eliot Cohen raised the question of whether the "remarkable outcome" of the war "presages a new relationship between air forces and ground forces."[117] They also noted that the issue would "no doubt, be debated for years to come."[118] More than a decade later, after the example of the efficacy of air power against the same enemy, the conclusion by these authors "that some threshold in the relationship between air and ground forces was first crossed in Desert Storm" seems unassailable.[119] Keaney and Cohen's caution about the lessons from Desert Storm—"We may require a sterner test against a more capable adversary"[120]—is an important one. It is clear that the United States must prepare for sterner tests than it has faced since the end of the Cold War. This challenge is recognized in the *National Security Strategy*, which states the imperative to transform U.S defense capabilities "to assure our allies and friends; dissuade future military competition; deter threats against U.S. interests, allies, and friends; and decisively defeat any adversary if deterrence fails."[121]

It is also clear that U.S. military transformation plans and programs to meet the challenges of the future must reflect the reality that U.S. air forces have repeatedly demonstrated the ability to dominate regional adversaries at the operational and strategic levels of warfighting and the fact that Army deep attack systems—in the current inventory or planned for the future—are not adequate to the task of shaping large ground AOs called for in Army doctrine. Consequently, the task of shaping the theater—strategically and operationally—should be an air component function, and joint and service doctrines and programs should change accordingly. Nevertheless, a critical transformation challenge confronting the United States is to ensure that air

---

[117] Keaney and Cohen (1993), p. 246.

[118] Keaney and Cohen (1993), p. 246.

[119] Keaney and Cohen (1993), p. 247.

[120] Keaney and Cohen (1993), p. 246.

[121] The President of the United States of America (2002), p. 29.

power can operate effectively against future, first-class opponents, who will undoubtedly pose significantly more formidable challenges to its employment than has been the case in the post–Cold War conflicts discussed in this study.

Specifically, joint doctrine for determining AOs and implementing fire support coordinating measures, particularly the FSCL, should be modified to exploit the capability of air power to attack military forces, other than those in contact with ground forces, more effectively than organic ground power means. This, in essence, is how the Marine Corps employs its organic fixed-wing aircraft. This will be particularly difficult for the Army, given its operational warfighting focus. Although it is apparent that the Army is cognizant of the increasing effectiveness of air power, as witnessed in its own internal assessments of OIF, to accept this reality will raise important questions about Army doctrine, organizations, and equipment. Specifically, it would require the Army to reassess the viability of the Apache helicopter and ATACMS as Army deep battle assets. This assessment would be particularly difficult, given the Army's investment in these systems, from both a cultural and fiscal perspective.[122] The most difficult component of such an evaluation, however, would be the possibility that the Army would have to consider ceding control of the cornerstone of its operational doctrine—corps control of deep operations—to the Air Force as the agent of the JFC.

Thus, in the future, the principal roles of the Army (and Marine Corps) in joint theater warfighting would be to employ its overwhelming tactical dominance to

- force enemy reaction at the operational and strategic levels by forcing concentration and/or movement, thus making him vulnerable to air attack

---

[122]Attack helicopters are at the core of the institutional essence of the Army's aviation branch, and deep attack is an important mission to this community. ATACMS, though not as central as cannon artillery to the self-image of the Army's field artillery branch, are the principal means through which that branch contributes to the deep battle central to Army operational doctrine. One could expect these Army constituencies to resist any efforts to radically change the missions or control of either of these systems.

- close with and finish enemy tactical remnants, exploit success, and seize and hold ground
- deal with the post-conflict security environment until the desired strategic political end state is reached.

Air power roles should be to

- shape the theater at the operational and strategic levels
- provide close air support (CAS), intelligence, surveillance, and reconnaissance (ISR), and lift to support ground combat operations
- provide CAS, ISR, and lift for ground-force operations to secure and stabilize the theater.

Again, accepting and implementing these doctrinal changes will be particularly difficult for the Army, given its focus on operational-level warfighting.

Ironically, General McPeak, on the eve of his retirement as Air Force Chief of Staff, proposed a radical restructuring of service roles and missions that attempted to end service redundancies and capitalize on the most effective service contributions to the joint fight. His views from a decade ago still resonate today, given the insights from the cases assessed in this study:

> In my view, modern land warfare can be seen as containing four "battles"—the rear battle, which includes all the base and supporting elements; the close battle, in which the main opposing ground forces engage one another; the deep battle, which includes hostile territory well beyond the line of contact; and the high battle, the arena of air and space combat. . . . The rear and close battles should be the responsibility of a ground forces commander, an Army or a Marine Corps officer. His forces should be capable of relatively autonomous operations—they should be capable of engaging the enemy in the friendly rear and immediately in front of them, without a lot of outside help. True, the ground commander has a deep and abiding interest in what goes on overhead in the high battle or over the horizon in the deep battle and he

may even have some capability to get into these fights. But, his forces are not the most effective for the high or deep battle. Air assets provide the best, most often the only capability to operate in these parts of the battlefield. . . . [T]his approach to dividing battle space provides a logical starting point for identifying unnecessary overlap and duplication. If you accept the scheme I just laid out, it follows that the commander with responsibility for the close battle does not require systems or capabilities that reach across the boundaries into the deep and high battles. If there are such systems in the field or on the drawing board, they might be good candidates for retirement or transfer to another service. Alternatively, the commander with responsibility for the deep battle does not need forces that are configured for direct support of close combat operations. If there are any, they too could be transferred out.[123]

General McPeak's comments highlight the central issue, which is much broader than a discussion of how best to employ ground or air power within the Army component commander's AO. The real question that needs to be addressed is: How best are all the means within the joint force used to satisfy the operational and strategic intent of the JFC? Despite all the self-congratulatory talk of "interdependence" and "seamless joint operations" emerging from OIF, the reality remains that within their AOs, component commanders called the shots, perhaps at the cost of overall joint effectiveness. Furthermore, the two components of the CFLCC—V Corps and 1st Marine Expeditionary Force—each pursued a different service doctrine, particularly regarding the employment of air power. In OIF and past operations, this has resulted in the suboptimal use of air power at the operational level, which left Air Force officers justifiably frustrated. They believe that making air power the supporting component to the ground force is an anachronistic idea, akin to "flying artillery," and an unnecessary constraint on their instrument.

---

[123]"The Military Must Be Different," *Aviation Week & Space Technology*, Vol. 141, No. 13, September 26, 1994.

The Air Force, for its part, should continue training, organizing, and equipping forces for the flexible application of air power at the strategic and operational levels—while also providing responsive close air support—to support the JFC's campaign and, specifically, his scheme of maneuver. Furthermore, the targeting process should be closely integrated with the JFC's scheme of maneuver and intent. In short, air power, while conducting strategic attack in support of the theater campaign, must also be prepared to operate interdependently with ground forces at the operational and tactical levels. Therefore, the selection of strategic targets and the design of kill boxes for interdiction must have the purpose of achieving the effects required to support the JFC's campaign design. Although this study has held up the Marine Corps as an example of how the integration of Air Force air power was accomplished more effectively than with Army units, the OIF experience also shows that more needs to be done between these two services as well, given the comments by the Commanding General, 1st Marine Division:

> Target tracking and assessment was extremely difficult during OIF. There was no reliable and responsive process or means to determine whether Air Interdiction (AI) targets on the PTL [priority target list] were serviced and successfully attacked during and after ATO execution. The impact was that targeting personnel/LNOs [liaison officers] could not consistently and reliably provide the necessary feedback to MSC [major subordinate command] commanders that their AI target nominations were being serviced or not. Further, there was no consistent or reliable method for the MSCs and Force Fires to track their target nominations on the DS ATO. Ostensibly due to system constraints, TBMCS [theater battle management core system] would not accept the MEF Target Reference Number from the PTL. Hence when the ATO was published there was no easy way to associate the target reference number (TRN) with the assigned aircraft mission number on the ATO. The customer would have to cull through the ATO searching for other data elements like BE [basic encyclopedia] number, location or target description

that matched the TRN. Often the ATO did not consistently list the BE numbers, locations and/or target descriptions. . . .

During OIF the 72-hour deliberate targeting process did not keep pace with the dynamics of the battlefield. The key reason was due to the fact that the planning to execution cycle was too long and the process did not react quickly enough to changes in the scheme of maneuver. As a result the AI shaping effort often did not focus on the enemy forces I MEF would actually fight in 48 hours.[124]

The ongoing interservice rivalries discussed in this study have deep cultural and institutional origins. At the heart of the issue is the persistent reality that the services do not feel confident that they can rely absolutely on each other when the chips are down. Thus, they maintain redundant capabilities and develop service warfighting concepts that are largely self-reliant. This lack of trust is most evident between the Army and the Air Force. The Army does not trust the Air Force to be there when it is needed, and the Air Force does not trust the Army to employ air power properly if it is in control of the resource.

The fact that these rivalries and "service ways of doing things" have persisted in the two decades since the passage of the Goldwater-Nichols Department of Defense Reorganization Act of 1986 shows how deeply embedded these views are. Indeed, some literature supports the premise that interservice rivalry actually promotes innovation.[125] Nevertheless, it would seem self-evident that service doctrines should be subordinated to the central idea that *the JFC is the supported commander* and that the components exist to support his warfight and efforts to achieve national objectives.

---

[124]Commanding General, 1st Marine Division, "Operation Iraqi Freedom (OIF): Lessons Learned," MEF-FRAGO 279-03, May 29, 2003, quoted in Cordesman (2003), pp. 282–283.

[125]An alternative perspective, with which I largely disagree, views interservice rivalry as a positive force. See Rosen (1993), which argues: "The defense establishment should not turn a blind eye to the warp in which creative competition among the services can encourage the development of new capabilities in even a period of fiscal constraint."

Clearly, the issues identified in this study demand joint solutions. Fortunately, processes are in place within DoD to implement the necessary reforms. The Joint Staff and the Joint Forces Command have the authorities to promulgate joint doctrine and to experiment with new operational concepts, and they should exercise them more rigorously.[126] Regarding enhanced cooperation and integration between the Army and the Air Force specifically, a historical example worthy of emulation is the period between 1973 and 1990. During those years, the Army and the Air Force peacetime partnership, although perhaps unusual in the context of their overall historical relationship, was as strong as it has ever been as the two services worked together to defend NATO. Nevertheless, any meaningful change to service warfighting doctrines and organizations will likely meet with service resistance. Recall that the last significant attempt at sweeping joint reform—Goldwater-Nichols—was bitterly resisted by the services as an infringement of their prerogatives at the time of its enactment.[127]

Thus far, emerging joint concepts have largely been a consensus view about how service capabilities are going to be incorporated, not about what capabilities are needed in joint warfighting and which service should provide them. The comments of Admiral E. P.

---

[126]See U.S. Code, Title 10, Subtitle A, Part I, Chapter 5, Section 153. This section of Title 10 describes the functions of the Chairman of the Joint Chiefs of Staff. They include: "Advising the Secretary on the extent to which the program recommendations and budget proposals of the military departments and other components of the Department of Defense for a fiscal year conform with the priorities established in strategic plans and with the priorities established for the requirements of the unified and specified combatant commands" and "Developing doctrine for the joint employment of the armed forces." See also U.S. Joint Forces Command (undated), which states: "The 2001/2002 Unified Command Plan gave USJFCOM a 'laser focus' to become the incubator for new transformational concepts to build the military of the 21st century. As a result of the 2002 Unified Command Plan, the USJFCOM missions are: Joint Force Provider; Joint Force Integrator; Joint Force Trainer; [and] Joint Concept Development and Experimentation."

[127]For discussions of service resistance to the Goldwater-Nichols Act, see James R. Locher, *Victory on the Potomac: The Goldwater-Nichols Act Unifies the Pentagon*, College Station, Tex.: Texas A&M University Press, 2002, and Gordon Nathaniel Lederman, *Reorganizing the Joint Chiefs of Staff: The Goldwater-Nichols Act of 1986*, Westport, Conn.: Greenwood Press, 1999.

Giambastiani, Commander of Joint Forces Command, are instructive in this regard:

> We visited all the combatant commanders and service chiefs—and their staffs—to help us focus on producing a list of challenges affecting future Joint operations that Joint Forces Command could work on. We took their insights, perspectives and recommendations as a mandate to produce the joint operational concepts and capabilities that would enable coherently joint, effects-based operations. These inputs led to the development of the common joint context we have embedded into service wargames.
>
> The joint context allows services to examine for themselves how well their future capabilities can operate in a Joint environment. They can then begin to acquire service capabilities that are "Born Joint." This process is a fundamental shift in the force development paradigm.[128]

Consequently, absent significant reform, the joint system will continue to produce concepts that are largely an amalgamation of service doctrines and capabilities—and which are often based on service preferences—rather than demanding that the services develop capabilities specifically designed to support joint doctrine. Therefore, the final warfighting recommendation of this study is that joint doctrine—and the processes by which it is derived and promulgated—be overhauled. As its stands now, joint doctrine frequently reflects a consensus view of what the services will tolerate, rather than a truly integrated joint perspective. Service doctrines and capabilities—whether redundant or conflicting—are often accommodated. A signal example of this reality is the FSCL, as employed by the Army in both Gulf wars, which is permissive to ground component commanders (and established by the land component commander) but restrictive to the employment of air power. The FSCL, however, is merely symptomatic of the Army's desire to control a large AO—and all the resources of the other services

---

[128]E. P. Giambastiani, "Remarks for AFCEA West 'Born Joint?' Conference," transcript, February 4, 2004.

entering that AO—to execute its operational doctrine. This limits the employment and effectiveness of fixed-wing air power—which is more effective than organic Army systems for deep operations—in operations short of the FSCL, but forward of the range of divisional indirect fire systems.

An essential first step in reforming joint doctrine is to eliminate the principle that joint doctrine must defer to that of the services. At present, guidance to joint commanders is that "JFCs should allow Service tactical and operational assets and groupings to function generally as they were designed."[129] Rather, the guidance should stipulate that the services organize and equip themselves in ways that provide the JFC capabilities and organizations that best realize the theaterwide campaign plan by providing integrated fire and maneuver. A lesser but still critical step would be to withhold to the JFC the authority to establish all fire support coordinating measures that could affect the theater campaign plan. These measures would begin the process of building a new American warfighting construct that is truly joint and not a collection of service perspectives.

## Reforms Beyond Warfighting

Another related issue looms large in American security affairs. What has emerged in the American way of war is an unmatched capacity to conduct operations and win battles. This capacity is reflected in the 2004 *National Military Strategy*, which "directs a force sized to defend the homeland, deter forward in and from four regions, and conduct two, overlapping 'swift defeat' campaigns. Even when committed to a limited number of lesser contingencies, the force must be able to 'win decisively' in one of the two campaigns."[130] Winning decisively in a military campaign is a warfighting, operational capability. Unfortunately, it is not a recipe for strategic victory, as evidenced by the fact that U.S. forces, as already noted, remain in Kosovo, Afghanistan, and

---

[129] U.S. Joint Chiefs of Staff, JP 3-31 (2004), p. III-2.

[130] U.S. Joint Chiefs of Staff, *National Military Strategy of the United States*, 2004, p. 21.

Iraq with no end in sight. In the words of Antulio Echevarria, "the new American way of war . . . appears geared to fight wars as if they were battles and, thus, confuses the winning of campaigns or small-scale actions with the winning of war."[131] Echevarria recommends that U.S. political and military leaders "habituate themselves to thinking more thoroughly about how to turn combat successes into favorable strategic outcomes."[132]

Thus, the irony of this study's assessment of the relative relationship of American air and ground power is tied to this reality: In a world in which the United States is the sole remaining superpower, its operational prowess and immense technological advantages do not necessarily guarantee an end state that is favorable to U.S. strategic interests. As events in Kosovo, Afghanistan, and Iraq have shown, substantial and often specialized investments, particularly in ground forces, are required to turn warfighting successes into the desired strategic political end states and the realization of national policy objectives. Furthermore, absent a coherent and comprehensive national strategy that transcends military operations, military means are not sufficient to achieve national political objectives.

Improving service capabilities to translate successful warfighting operations into the achievement of national goals will be at least as difficult as addressing competing service warfighting perspectives. There does, however, appear to be an emerging sense within DoD that, in the future, the United States will require capabilities beyond those optimized for warfighting.

In November 2005, DoD promulgated a directive (3000.05) that raised stability operations to a level equivalent with warfighting, stating "DoD policy" as follows:

> Stability operations are a core U.S. military mission that the Department of Defense shall be prepared to conduct and support. They shall be given priority comparable to combat operations and be explicitly addressed and integrated across all DoD activities

---

[131] Echevarria (2004), p. vi.

[132] Echevarria (2004), p. vii.

including doctrine, organizations, training, education, exercises, materiel, leadership, personnel, facilities, and planning.[133]

Prior to the release of DoD Directive 3000.05, an article in the *Wall Street Journal* speculated about its origins, asserting that it "highlights the extent to which the [U.S.] military, built to fight high-tech conventional wars against other armies, is still struggling more than three years after the Sept. 11 attacks to refashion itself for the far different demands of the war in Iraq and the broader war on terror."[134]

Furthermore, the article went on to report that the draft directive "reflects a broader push by senior Pentagon officials to divert spending and manpower away from weapons systems and units built to fight state-on-state wars in favor of units better suited to guerrilla warfare, counterterrorism and what the military calls 'pre- and post-conflict stability operations.'" The article also notes that the Army would be the service most affected by the implementation of the directive.[135] Given the Army's cultural and institutional predilection for warfighting, the changes implied in the directive could be quite wrenching.

The last time an administration attempted to get the Army to shift its focus to counterinsurgency warfare was during the Kennedy administration. General George H. Decker, Army Chief of Staff at the time, "shrugged off preparation for counter-guerrilla warfare as something it [the Army] can take in stride," telling the President that "any good soldier can handle guerillas."[136] Decker also noted in an *Army* article that his service was, and always had been, prepared for "unconventional operations," and that

> Army doctrine today establishes proficiency in unconventional warfare as a normal requirement for its versatile, modern ground

---

[133]U.S. Department of Defense, Directive 3000.05, *Military Support for Stability, Security, Transition, and Reconstruction (SSTR) Operations*, November 28, 2005, p. 2.

[134]Greg Jaffe and David S. Cloud, "Pentagon's New War Planning to Stress Postconflict Stability," *Wall Street Journal*, October 25, 2004.

[135]Jaffe and Cloud (2004).

[136]Lloyd Norman and John B. Spore, "Big Push in Guerrilla Warfare," *Army*, March 1962, pp. 32–33.

forces. We believe that a thorough grounding in the basic skills of soldiering provides the foundation upon which to build this proficiency.[137]

In the aftermath of the Vietnam War, the Army returned to its doctrinal heritage of preparing for the worst case and assuming that a force thus prepared could handle any lesser contingencies. The first post-Vietnam version of FM 100-5, *Operations*, reflected this conventional, warfighting perspective, emphasizing that

> Battle in Central Europe against forces of the Warsaw Pact is the most demanding mission the US Army could be assigned. Because the US Army is structured primarily for that contingency and has large forces deployed in that area, this manual is designed mainly to deal with the realities of such operations. The principles set forth in this manual, however, apply also to military operations anywhere in the world.[138]

Clearly, the remarks of General William E. DuPuy, commander of U.S. Army TRADOC and the driving force behind the new FM 100-5, reflected a consensus of the Army's senior leadership at the time: "The Vietnam war—combat with light and elusive forces—was over. . . . The defense of central Europe against large, modern, Soviet armored forces once again became the Army's main, almost exclusive mission."[139]

In the nearly three decades since the end of the Vietnam War, the Army has become the world's preeminent conventional ground force. Nevertheless, its doctrine, training, organizational, materiel, and leader development efforts have remained focused almost exclusively on warfighting combat operations, based on the enduring belief that its prin-

---

[137] "Guerrilla Warfare—As the High Command Sees It," *Army*, March 1962, p. 42.

[138] U.S. Department of the Army, FM 100-5 (1976), p. 1-2.

[139] William E. DePuy, "FM 100-5 Revisited," *Army*, November 1980, p. 12. See also Donald B. Vought, "Preparing for the Wrong War?" *Military Review*, Vol. 57, May 1977, p. 32. Vought quotes Lieutenant General Donn Starry, then commander of V Corps German and eventually a U.S. Army TRADOC commander, as saying: "After getting out of Vietnam, the Army looked around and realized it should not try to fight that kind of war again."

cipal responsibility is to fight and win America's wars and that other operations can be dealt with by an Army prepared for warfighting. This results in a cultural belief that effective combat units can adapt to any challenge across the range of military operations. General Henry H. Shelton, former Chairman of the Joint Chiefs of Staff, echoes a common viewpoint: "[P]rofessional soldiers, trained for combat operations, clearly provide the best type of manpower for peace operations."[140] The newest version of the Army's core doctrinal manual, FM 3-0, *Operations*, also emphasizes the centrality the warfighting ethos: "Battle-focused training on combat tasks prepares soldiers, units, and leaders to deploy, fight, and win."[141] Furthermore, current Army doctrine is explicit in its warfighting focus, even for peace operations:

> Training and preparation for peace operations should not detract from a unit's primary mission of training soldiers to fight and win in combat. *The first and foremost requirement for success in peace operations is the successful application of warfighting skills.*[142]

This study does not argue that warfighting skills are not important. Instead, it posits that they are not enough and that other skills and capabilities are necessary for the Army to be effective across the range of military operations. A comment by Lieutenant Colonel Jeffrey Ingram, of Task Force 2-70 Armor in Iraq, summed up the difficulty of the post-major combat environment quite eloquently: "Peace enforcement is wearing everybody out. . . . This is much harder [than combat]."[143]

The Army will be the service expected to provide many of the new capabilities for military operations across the range of military operations. As noted earlier, the Army, to its credit, is energetically adapting to the situations in which it now finds itself. It is creating

---

[140] Henry H. Shelton, "Peace Operations: The Forces Required," *National Security Studies Quarterly*, Summer 2000.

[141] U.S. Department of the Army, FM 3-0 (2001), p. 1-17.

[142] U.S. Army, FM 100-23 (1994), p. C-1. Emphasis in the original.

[143] Fontenot, Degen, and Tohn (2004), p. 427.

more combat brigades and more specialized units, e.g., civil affairs and military police. Furthermore, tactics, techniques, and procedures are being developed and implemented to respond to the tactical lessons the Army in the field is learning.[144] Nevertheless, a review of the Army's concepts for the future reveals a remarkable consistency in the belief that well-trained combat forces are capable of performing any task. This is a tenet that has its origins in the earliest experiences of the U.S. Army. Historian Robert M. Utley's description of the response of Army leaders to the Indian Wars of the nineteenth century is one that is strikingly similar to the war in Vietnam and the situation the Army finds itself in today:

> In part the generals were motivated by a desire to place the Army on a more enduring basis than afforded by Indian warfare. But in part, too, they were genuinely concerned about national defense. . . . the army they fashioned was designed for the next conventional war rather than the present unconventional war.[145]

The parallels among the frontier Regular Army of the Indian Wars, the U.S. Army in Vietnam, and today's war on terror are also hauntingly familiar:

---

[144] For an example of an Army unit learning and adapting in the field, see Peter W. Chiarelli and Patrick R. Michaelis, "Winning the Peace: The Requirement for Full-Spectrum Operations," *Military Review*, July–August 2005, pp. 4–17. See also Nigel Aylwin-Foster, "Changing the Army for Counterinsurgency Operations," *Military Review*, November–December 2005, pp. 2–15. This article is by a British Army brigadier general who believes that

> [t]he U.S. Army's tardiness in adapting to the changing operational environment in OIF phase 4 was indeed a contributory factor in the Coaliton's failure to exploit rapid victory over Saddam achieved in the preceding conventional warfighting phase.

He also points to the difficulty of changing the U.S. Army, noting that it

> has been a victim of its own successful development as the ultimate warfighting machine. . . . [O]ver time the Army has developed a marked and uncompromising focus on conventional warfighting, leaving it ill-prepared for the unconventional operations that characterise OIF Phase 4" (p. 14).

[145] Robert M. Utley, "The Contribution of the Frontier to the American Military Tradition," in Harry R. Borowski, ed., *The Harmon Memorial Lectures in Military History, 1959–1987: A Collection of the First Thirty Lectures Given at the United States Air Force Academy*, Washington, D.C.: Office of Air Force History, 1988, p. 530.

The frontier army was a conventional military force trying to control, by conventional military methods, a people that did not behave like conventional enemies and, indeed, quite often were not enemies at all. . . . [T]he situation usually did not call for warfare, merely for policing; that is, offending individuals needed to be separated from the innocent and punished. . . . [T]he conventional force was unable to do this and . . . as a result punishment often fell, when it fell at all, on guilty and innocent alike.[146]

Although the Army's warfighting preference is shared by all the services, it will be expected—as it always has been—to take the lead in dealing with non-warfighting missions.[147] Nevertheless, given the Army's long history of focusing on conventional conflict, it is difficult to imagine that the institution will be able to reform itself radically to develop the capability to execute warfighting and non-warfighting missions with equal effectiveness without external intervention from DoD or Congress.[148] Indeed, the continued resilience of the Army's belief in the sufficiency of well-trained and equipped general-purpose warfighting forces for other operations is evident in its description of the centerpiece of its Future Force, the FCS-equipped UA: "Although optimized for offensive operations, the FCS-equipped UA will be capable of executing stability and support operations."[149]

Therefore, the final conclusion of this study is that many of the purported lessons learned about the relative roles of air and ground power since the end of the Cold War have been interpreted within

---

[146] Utley, "The Contribution of the Frontier to the American Military Tradition," in Borowski (1988), p. 531.

[147] Clearly, the other services have requirements to support operations across the range of military operations. For example, the Air Force will provide significant lift support.

[148] In this regard, see John A. Nagl, *Learning to Eat Soup With a Knife: Counterinsurgency Lessons from Malaya and Vietnam*, Chicago: University of Chicago Press, 2005. Nagl, describing the effect the conventionally oriented U.S. Army's culture had on organizational learning during the Vietnam War, notes that "[e]ven under pressures for change presented by ongoing military conflict, a strong organizational culture can prohibit learning the lessons of the present and can even prevent the organization's acknowledging that its current policies are anything other than completely successful" (p. 217).

[149] U.S. Department of the Army, *2005 Army Modernization Plan* (2005), p. 32.

service perspectives—perspectives shaped by experience and culture—and this has the effect of sustaining the status quo. Much work remains to attain a truly joint American warfighting system, reinterpreting the lessons from recent conflicts in a broader context. Even more work is needed to adapt American warfighting prowess into capabilities to achieve national objectives after the warfight. This is the strategic realm in which post-warfighting victory is secured for the nation, and it is largely and intrinsically ground centric. Consequently, given the effectiveness of air power in deep operations, perhaps the time has come to assess whether the Army should be redesigned to prepare for winning and not just fighting the nation's wars. Resources for this redesign should come in part from existing or envisioned deep operations capabilities—from across the services—that can be more effectively provided by air power.

Given existing service preferences, the task of reform will be difficult. Nevertheless, these reforms must proceed apace to ensure that the United States has the capacity to deal with the strategic realities of the twenty-first century.

# Bibliography

12th Army Group, *12th Army Group Report of Operations, Vol. 11: Antiaircraft Artillery, Armored Artillery, Chemical Warfare, and Signal Sections*, 1945.

Allard, C. Kenneth, *Command, Control, and the Common Defense*, New Haven, Conn.: Yale University Press, 1990.

———, *Somalia Operations: Lessons Learned*, Washington, D.C.: National Defense University Press, 1995.

Air Combat Command, "Airpower Lessons from Operation Iraqi Freedom: Briefing by Lt Col Mark Simpson, HQ ACC/XPSX, 25 Nov 03," Langley Air Force Base, Va., 2003.

Andres, Richard B., Craig Wills, and Thomas E. Griffith, Jr., "Winning with Allies: The Strategic Value of the Afghan Model," *International Security*, Winter 2005–2006, pp. 124–160.

Apple, R. W., Jr., "Conflict in the Balkans: News Analysis, A Fresh Set of U.S. Goals," *New York Times,* March 25, 1999, p. A1.

"Army Announces Unit Designations in the Modular Army," Army News Service, September 30, 2005.

Army Science Board, *Challenges and Opportunities for Increments II and III Future Combat Systems (FCS)*, Summer 2003.

Arnold, Steven L., "Somalia: An Operation Other Than War," *Military Review*, Vol. 73, No. 12, December 1993.

Aspin, Les, and William L. Dickinson, *Defense for a New Era: Lessons of the Persian Gulf War*, Washington, D.C.: U.S. Government Printing Office, 1992.

Atkinson, Rick, *Crusade: The Untold Story of the Persian Gulf War*, Boston: Houghton Mifflin, 1993.

———, "Night of a Thousand Casualties," *Washington Post*, January 31, 1994, p. A1.

———, "The Raid That Went Awry," *Washington Post*, January 30, 1994, p. A1.

"AWPD/1, Munitions Requirements of the Army Air Forces to Defeat Our Potential Enemies," table 2, section 2, part 3, appendix 2, p. 2, in Joint Board 355, Serial 707, National Archives Microfilm Publication M1080, Washington, D.C.: National Archives, undated.

Aylwin-Foster, Nigel, "Changing the Army for Counterinsurgency Operations," *Military Review*, November–December 2005, pp. 2–15.

Bacevich, Andrew J, *The New American Militarism: How Americans Are Seduced by War*, Oxford, UK: Oxford University Press, 2005.

Bacevich, Andrew J., and Eliot A. Cohen, eds., *War Over Kosovo: Politics and Strategy in a Global Age*, New York: Columbia University Press, 2001.

Barnett, Thomas P.M., *The Pentagon's New Map: War and Peace in the Twenty-First Century*, New York: G. P. Putnam's Sons, 2004.

Bash, Brooks L., "Leadership and Parochialism: An Enduring Reality?" *Joint Force Quarterly*, Summer 1999, pp. 64–71.

Batschelet, Allen W., "Effects-Based Operations for Joint Warfighters," *Field Artillery*, May–June 2003, pp. 7–13.

*Battle Summary, OPERATION IRAQI FREEDOM, 6th Squadron, 6th U.S. Cavalry*, undated.

Bentley, Christopher F., "Afghanistan: Joint and Coalition Fire Support in Operation Anaconda," *Field Artillery*, September–October 2002, pp. 10–14.

Bergerson, Frederic A., *The Army Gets an Air Force: Tactics of Insurgent Bureaucratic Politics*, Baltimore, Md.: Johns Hopkins University Press, 1980.

Biddle, Stephen D., *Afghanistan and the Future of Warfare: Implications for Army and Defense Policy*, Carlisle, Pa.: Strategic Studies Institute, U.S. Army War College, 2002.

———, *Military Power: Explaining Victory and Defeat in Modern Battle*, Princeton, N.J.: Princeton University Press, 2004.

———, "Allies, Airpower, and Modern Warfare: The Afghan Model in Afghanistan and Iraq, *International Security*, Winter 2005–2006, pp. 161–176.

Biddle, Stephen, James Embrey, Edward Filiberti, Stephen Kidder, Steven Metz, Ivan C. Oelrich, and Richard Shelton, *Toppling Saddam: Iraq and American Military Transformation*, Carlisle, Pa.: Strategic Studies Institute, U.S. Army War College, April 2004.

Bolger, Daniel P., *Death Ground: Today's American Infantry in Battle*, Novato, Calif.: Presidio Press, 2000.

———, *Savage Peace: Americans at War in the 1990s*, Novato, Calif.: Presidio Press, 1995.

Boot, Max, *The Savage Wars of Peace: Small Wars and the Rise of American Power*, New York: Basic Books, 2002.

Borowski, Harry R., ed., *The Harmon Memorial Lectures in Military History, 1959–1987: A Collection of the First Thirty Lectures Given at the United States Air Force Academy*, Washington, D.C.: Office of Air Force History, 1988.

Bowden, Mark, *Black Hawk Down: A Story of Modern War*, New York: Atlantic Monthly Press, 1999.

Bowie, Christopher, Fred Frostic, Kevin Lewis, John Lund, David Ochmanek, and Philip Propper, *The New Calculus: Analyzing Airpower's Changing Role in Joint Theater Campaigns*, Santa Monica, Calif.: RAND Corporation, MR-149-AF, 1993.

Boyne, Walter J., *Operation Iraqi Freedom: What Went Right, What Went Wrong, and Why*, New York: Forge, 2003.

Builder, Carl H., *The Masks of War: American Styles in Strategy and Analysis*, Baltimore, Md.: Johns Hopkins University Press, 1989.

Byman, Daniel L., and Matthew C. Waxman, *The Dynamics of Coercion: American Foreign Policy and the Limits of Military Might*, Cambridge, UK: Cambridge University Press, 2002.

———, "Kosovo and the Great Air Power Debate," *International Security*, Vol. 24, No. 4, Spring 2000.

Cain, Anthony C., "Flight Lines: The Transformation of Air and Space Power in Operation Iraqi Freedom," *Air and Space Power Journal*, Summer 2003.

Casper, Lawrence E., *Falcon Brigade: Combat and Command in Somalia and Haiti*, Boulder, Colo.: Lynne Rienner, 2001.

Center for Army Lessons Learned, *Operation Just Cause Lessons Learned*, Vol. I, *Soldiers and Leadership*, Fort Leavenworth, Kan.: U.S. Army Combined Arms Command, 90-9, 1990.

———, *Operation Just Cause Lessons Learned*, Vol. II, *Operations*, Fort Leavenworth, Kan.: U.S. Army Combined Arms Command, 90-9, 1990.

———, *Operation Just Cause Lessons Learned*, Vol. III, *Intelligence, Logistics & Equipment*, Fort Leavenworth, Kan.: U.S. Army Combined Arms Command, 90-9, 1990.

Chairman of the Joint Chiefs of Staff, *Joint Vision 2010*, Joint Chiefs of Staff, 1996.

Chapman, Suzann, "The 'War' Before the War," *Air Force Magazine*, February 2004.

Chiarelli, Peter W., and Patrick R. Michaelis, "Winning the Peace: The Requirement for Full-Spectrum Operations," *Military Review*, July–August 2005, pp. 4–17.

Clark, Wesley K., *Waging Modern War*, New York: PublicAffairs, 2001.

Clodfelter, Mark, "Of Demons, Storms, and Thunder: A Preliminary Look at Vietnam's Impact on the Persian Gulf Air Campaign," *Airpower Journal*, Winter 1991.

Cohen, Eliot A., *Supreme Command: Soldiers, Statesmen, and Leadership in Wartime*, New York: The Free Press, 2002.

Cohen, William S., *Annual Report to the President and the Congress*, U.S. Department of Defense, 1999. As of November 2005: http://www.defenselink.mil/execsec/adr1999/

Cole, Ronald H., *Operation Just Cause: The Planning and Execution of Joint Operations in Panama, February 1988–January 1990*, Washington, D.C.: Joint History Office, 1995.

Conroy, Jason, with Ron Martz, *Heavy Metal: A Tank Company's Battle to Baghdad*, Dulles, Va.: Potomac Books Inc., 2005.

Conversino, Mark J., "The Changed Nature of Strategic Air Attack," *Parameters*, Winter 1997–1998, pp. 28–41.

Cooling, Benjamin Franklin, ed., *Case Studies in the Development of Close Air Support*, Washington, D.C.: Office of Air Force History, 1990.

Cordesman, Anthony H., *The Lessons and Non-Lessons of the Air and Missile Campaign in Kosovo*, Washington, D.C.: Center for Strategic and International Studies, 1999 (September 29, 1999 revision).

———, *The Lessons of Afghanistan: War Fighting, Intelligence, and Force Transformation*, Washington, D.C.: Center for Strategic and International Studies, 2002.

———, *The Iraq War: Strategy, Tactics, and Military Lessons*, Washington, D.C.: Center for Strategic and International Studies, 2003.

Cordesman, Anthony H., and Abraham R. Wagner, *The Lessons of Modern War*, Vol. IV, *The Gulf War*, Boulder, Colo.: Westview Press, 1996.

Costa, Keith J., "Army Crafting Field Manual for Counterinsurgency Operations," *Inside the Army*, August 26, 2004.

Crane, Conrad C., and W. Andrew Terrill, *Reconstructing Iraq: Insights, Challenges, and Missions for Military Forces in a Post-Conflict Scenario*, Carlisle, Pa.: Strategic Studies Institute, U.S. Army War College, 2003.

Cureton, Charles H., *U.S. Marines in the Persian Gulf, 1990–1991: With the 1st Marine Division in Desert Shield and Desert Storm*, U.S. Marine Corps, 1993.

Daalder, Ivo H., and Michael E. O'Hanlon, *Winning Ugly: NATO's War to Save Kosovo*, Washington, D.C.: Brookings Institution Press, 2000.

D'Amico, Robert J., "Joint Fires Coordination: Service Competencies and Boundary Challenges," *Joint Force Quarterly*, Spring 1999, pp. 70–77.

Davis, Lynn E., and Jeremy Shapiro, eds., *The U.S. Army and the New National Security Strategy*, Santa Monica, Calif.: RAND Corporation, MR-1657-A, 2003.

Davis, Mark G., *Operation Anaconda: Command and Confusion in Joint Warfare*, thesis, School of Advanced Air and Space Studies, Air University, 2004.

Davis, Paul K., *Effects Based Operations: A Grand Challenge for the Analytical Community*, Santa Monica, Calif.: RAND Corporation, MR-1477-USJFCOM/AF, 2001.

Davis, Richard G., *The 31 Initiatives: A Study in Air Force–Army Cooperation*, Washington, D.C.: Office of Air Force History, 1987.

Day, Clifford E., *Critical Analysis on the Defeat of Task Force Ranger*, thesis, Air Command and Staff College, 1997.

Deptula, David A., and Sigfred J. Dahl, "Transforming Joint Air-Ground Operations for 21st Century Battlespace," *Field Artillery*, July–August 2003, pp. 21–25.

Deptula, David A., Gary L. Crowder, and George L. Stamper, Jr., "Direct Attack: Enhancing Counterland Doctrine and Joint Air-Ground Operations," *Air & Space Power Journal*, Winter 2003.

DePuy, William E., "FM 100-5 Revisited," *Army*, November 1980.

Donnelly, Thomas, Margaret Roth, and Caleb Baker, *Operation Just Cause: The Storming of Panama*, New York: Lexington Books, 1991.

Dudney, Robert S., "Toward Battlefield Air Operations," *Air Force Magazine*, October 2003.

Dunnigan, James F., and Raymond M. Macedonia, *Getting It Right: American Military Reforms After Vietnam to the Gulf War and Beyond*, New York: William Morrow and Company, 1993.

"An Eaker Colloquy on Aerospace Strategy, Requirements, and Forces," transcript, August 16, 1999. As of November 2005:: http://www.aef.org/pub/eaker/eak16aug99.asp

Echevarria, Antulio, II, "Fusing Airpower and Land Power in the Twenty-First Century: Insights from the Army After Next," *Airpower Journal*, Fall 1999, pp. 66–74.

———, "Interdependent Maneuver for the 21st Century," *Joint Force Quarterly*, Autumn 2000, pp. 11–19.

———, *Toward an American Way of War*, Carlisle, Pa.: Strategic Studies Institute, U.S. Army War College, 2004.

Epley, William W., *Roles and Missions of the United States Army: Basic Documents with Annotations and Bibliography*, Washington, D.C.: U.S. Army Center of Military History, 1991.

Feaver, Peter D., *Armed Servants: Agency, Oversight, and Civil-Military Relations*, Cambridge, Mass.: Harvard University Press, 2003.

Fehrenbach, T. R., *This Kind of War: A Study in Unpreparedness*, New York: MacMillan, 1963.

Fogleman, Ronald R., "Aerospace Doctrine: More Than Just a Theory," *Airpower Journal*, Summer 1996, pp. 40–47.

Fontenot, Gregory, E. J. Degen, and David Tohn, *On Point: The United States Army in Operation Iraqi Freedom*, Fort Leavenworth, Kan.: Combat Studies Institute Press, 2004.

Fought, Stephen O., and O. Scott Key, "Airpower, Jointness, and Transformation," *Air & Space Power Journal*, Winter 2003.

Franks, Tommy, *American Soldier*, New York: ReganBooks, 2004.

Gass, Gregory P., "The Road Ahead," *Rotor and Wing*, October 2003, pp. 24–26.

Giambastiani, E. P., "Remarks for AFCEA West 'Born Joint?' Conference," transcript, February 4, 2004. As of May 2006:
http://www.jfcom.mil/newslink/storyarchive/2004/sp021004.htm

Glenn, Russell W., ed., *Capital Preservation: Preparing for Urban Operations in the Twenty-First Century, Proceedings of the RAND Arroyo-TRADOC-MCWL-OSD Urban Operations Conference, March 22–23, 2000*, Santa Monica, Calif.: RAND Corporation, CF-162-A, 2001.

Gordon, John IV, David Johnson, Walter L. Perry, and Bruce R. Pirnie, "Letter to the Editor: Kosovo and Landpower," *Army Magazine*, April 2001, pp. 4–8.

Gordon, John IV, and Bruce R. Pirnie, "Everybody Wanted Tanks: Heavy Forces in Operation Iraqi Freedom," *Joint Force Quarterly*, No. 39, October 2005, pp. 84–90.

Gordon, John, IV, and Jerry Sollinger, "The Army's Dilemma," *Parameters*, Summer 2004.

Gordon, Michael R., and Bernard E. Trainor, *The Generals' War: The Inside Story of the Conflict in the Gulf*, Boston: Little, Brown and Company, 1995.

———, *COBRA II: The Inside Story of the Invasion and Occupation of Iraq*, New York: Pantheon Books, 2006.

Grange, David L., Huba Wass De Czege, Richard D. Liebert, Charles A. Jarnot, and Mike Sparks, *Air-Mech-Strike: 3-Dimensional Phalanx*, Paducah, Ky.: Turner Publishing Company, 2000.

Grant, Rebecca, "Nine Myths About Kosovo," *Air Force Magazine*, June 2000.

————, "Deep Strife," *Air Force Magazine*, June 2001a.

————, "Wesley Clark's War," *Air Force Magazine*, September 2001b.

————, "The War Nobody Expected," *Air Force Magazine*, April 2002.

————, "The Clash About CAS," *Air Force Magazine*, January 2003a.

————, "Saddam's Elite in the Meat Grinder," *Air Force Magazine*, September 2003b.

————, "The Redefinition of Strategic Airpower," *Air Force Magazine*, Vol. 86, No. 10, October 2003c.

————, "Marine Air in the Mainstream," *Air Force Magazine*, June 2004.

Grinter, Lawrence E., and Peter M. Dunn, eds., *The American War in Vietnam: Lessons, Legacies, and Implications for Future Conflicts*, Westport, Conn.: Greenwood, 1987.

Groen, Mike, et al., *After Action Report, 1st Marine Division: Operation Iraqi Freedom*, Camp Pendleton, Calif.: Headquarters, 1st Marine Division, 2003.

Grossman, Elaine M., "Duel of Doctrines," *Air Force Magazine*, December 1998.

————, "The Halt Phase Hits a Bump," *Air Force Magazine*, April 2001, pp. 34–36.

————, "Left in Dark for Most Anaconda Planning, Air Force Opens New Probe," *Inside the Pentagon*, October 3, 2002.

————, "Was Operation Anaconda Ill-Fated from Start? Army Analyst Blames Afghan Battle Failing on Bad Command Set-Up," *Inside the Pentagon*, July 29, 2004a.

————, "Anaconda: Object Lesson in Ill Planning or Triumph of Improvisation?" *Inside the Pentagon*, August 19, 2004b.

Grossman, Jon, David Rubenson, William Sollfrey, and Brett Steele, *Vertical Envelopment and the Future Transport Rotorcraft: Operational Considerations for the Objective Force*, Santa Monica, Calif.: RAND Corporation, MR-1713-A, 2003.

"Guerrilla Warfare—As the High Command Sees It," *Army*, March 1962.

"The Gulf War: A Chronology," *Air Force*, Vol. 84, No. 1, January 2001.

Haight, David B., *Operation JUST CAUSE: Foreshadowing Example of Joint Vision 2010 Concepts in Practice*, thesis, Naval War College, 1998.

Hall, Dwayne P., *Integrating Joint Operations Beyond the FSCL: Is Current Doctrine Adequate?* Maxwell Air Force Base, Ala.: Air University, Air War College, AU/AWC/RWP071/97-04, April 1997.

Hallion, Richard P., *Storm Over Iraq: Air Power and the Gulf War*, Washington, D.C.: Smithsonian Institution Press, 1992.

————, "Airpower and the Changing Nature of Warfare," *Joint Force Quarterly*, Autumn/Winter 1997–1998, pp. 39–46.

Halperin, Morton H., *Bureaucratic Politics and Foreign Policy*, Washington, D.C.: Brookings Institution, 1974.

Hammond, Grant T., *The Mind of War: John Boyd and American Security*, Washington, D.C.: Smithsonian Institution Press, 2001.

Hammond, Kevin J., and Frank Sherman, "Sheridans in Panama," *Armor*, March–April 1990, pp. 8–15.

Hansell, Brigadier General Haywood S., 'The Development of the United States Concept of Bombardment Operations," lecture presented at the Air War College, February 16, 1951, Maxwell Air Force Base, Ala.: Airpower Research Institute, 1951.

Haun, Phil M., *Air Power Versus a Fielded Army: A Construct for Air Operations in the 21st Century*, Maxwell Air Force Base, Ala.: Air University, Air Command and Staff College, AU/ACSC/054/2001-04, 2001.

————, "Vortices: Direct Attack—A Counterland Mission," *Air and Space Power Journal*, Summer 2003.

Herrly, Peter F., "The Plight of Joint Doctrine After Kosovo," *Joint Force Quarterly*, Summer 1999, pp. 99–104.

*Hilberer, Richard K., John C. Barry*, and *Dawn N. Ellis,* "Go Ugly, Early," *Marine Corps Gazette*, May 2005.

Hines, Jay E., "Confronting Continuing Challenges: A Brief History of the United States Central Command," paper delivered to the Second International Conference of Saint Leo College's Center for Inter-American Studies, March 19, 1997.

Hirsch, John L., and Robert B. Oakley, *Somalia and Operation Restore Hope: Reflections on Peacemaking and Peacekeeping*, Washington, D.C.: United States Institute of Peace, 1995.

————, "Corps Historian's Personal Notes Recorded During the Operation," 1989–1990. As of November 2005:
http://www.army.mil/cmh-pg/documents/panama/notes.htm

————, "Operation Just Cause: List of Participating Units," undated. As of December 2005:
http://www.army.mil/cmh-pg/documents/panama/pdfob.htm

Hoar, Joseph P., "A CINC's Perspective," *Joint Force Quarterly*, Autumn 1993, pp. 56–63.

Hoffman, F. G., *Decisive Force: The New American Way of War*, Westport, Conn.: Praeger, 1996.

Holbrooke, Richard, *To End a War*, New York: Random House, 1998.

Hosmer, Stephen T., *The Conflict Over Kosovo: Why Milosevic Decided to Settle When He Did*, Santa Monica, Calif.: RAND Corporation, MR-1351-AF, 2001.

————, *Effects of the Coalition Air Campaign Against Iraqi Ground Forces in the Gulf War*, Santa Monica, Calif.: RAND Corporation, MR-305/1-AF, 2002.

————, *Psychological Effects of U.S. Air Operations in Four Wars 1941–1991: Lessons for U.S. Commanders*, Santa Monica, Calif.: RAND Corporation, MR-576-AF, 1996.

House, Jonathan M., *Combined Arms Warfare in the Twentieth Century: Modern War Studies*, Lawrence, Kan.: University Press of Kansas, 2001.

Huchthausen, Peter, *America's Splendid Little Wars: A Short History of U.S. Military Engagements, 1975–2000*, New York: Viking Press, 2003.

Hughes, Thomas A., *Over Lord: General Pete Quesada and the Triumph of Tactical Air Power in World War II*, New York: The Free Press, 1995.

Inman, Bobby R., Joseph S. Nye, and Roger K. Smith, "Lessons from the Gulf War," *The Washington Quarterly*, Winter 1992.

Jaffe, Gregg, and David S. Cloud, "Pentagon's New War Planning to Stress Postconflict Stability," *Wall Street Journal*, October 25, 2004.

Jaffe, Lorna S., *The Development of the Base Force: 1989–1992*, Washington, D.C.: Joint History Office, 1993.

Johnson, David E., *Fast Tanks and Heavy Bombers: Innovation in the U.S. Army, 1917–1945*, Ithaca, N.Y.: Cornell University Press, 1998.

————, *Modern U.S. Civil-Military Relations: Wielding the Terrible Swift Sword*, Washington, D.C.: National Defense University Press, 1997.

————, *Preparing Potential Senior Army Leaders for the Future: An Assessment of Leader Development Efforts in the Post–Cold War Era*, Santa Monica, Calif.: RAND Corporation, IP-224-A, 2002.

Johnson, David E., Karl P. Mueller, and William H. Taft V., *Conventional Coercion Across the Spectrum of Operations: The Utility of U.S. Military Forces in the Emerging Security Environment*, Santa Monica, Calif.: RAND Corporation, MR-1494-A, 2002.

Johnson, Douglas V., II, ed., *Warriors in Peace Operations*, Carlisle, Pa.: Strategic Studies Institute, U.S. Army War College, 1999.

Johnson, Lt. Col. Edward C., *Marine Corps Aviation: The Early Years, 1912–1940* Headquarters, U.S. Marine Corps, 1977.

Jumper, John, Testimony to the Military Readiness Subcommittee, House Armed Services Committee, Washington, D.C., October 26, 1999. As of August 19, 2005: http://www.fas.org/man/congress/1999/99-10-26jumper.htm

Kagan, Frederick, "Army Doctrine and Modern War: Notes Toward a New Edition of FM 100-5," Parameters, Spring 1997, pp. 134–151.

Kan, Paul Rexton, "What Should We Bomb? Axiological Targeting and the Abiding Limits of Airpower Theory," Air and Space Power Journal Spring 2004.

Keaney, Thomas A., and Eliot A. Cohen, Gulf War Air Power Survey Summary Report, Washington, D.C.: U.S. Government Printing Office, 1993.

———, Revolution in Warfare? Air Power in the Persian Gulf, Annapolis, Md.: Naval Institute Press, 1995.

Keegan, John, "Please, Mr. Blair, Never Take Such a Risk Again," London Daily Telegraph, June 6, 1999. As of November 2005: http://www.portal.telegraph.co.uk/htmlContent.jhtml?html=%2Farchive%2F1999%2F06%2F06%2Fwkee06.html

Kent, Glenn A., and David A. Ochmanek, Defining the Role of Airpower in Joint Missions, Santa Monica, Calif.: RAND Corporation, MR-927-AF, 1998.

Kirkpatrick, Charles E., Joint Fires as They Were Meant to Be: V Corps and the 4th Air Support Operations Group During Operation Iraqi Freedom, Arlington, Va.: The Institute of Land Warfare, Association of the United States Army, 2004.

Kitfield, James A., Prodigal Soldiers: How the Generation of Officers Born of Vietnam Revolutionized the American Style of War, New York: Simon & Schuster, 1995.

———, "Another Look at the Air War That Was," Air Force Magazine, October 1999. As of November 2005: http://www.afa.org/magazine/Oct1999/1099eaker.asp

Kozaryn, Linda D., "Air Chief's Lesson: Go for Snake's Head First," American Forces Information Service, June 18, 2004.

Krepinevich, Andrew F., Transforming the Legions: The Army and the Future of Warfare, Washington, D.C.: Center for Strategic and Budgetary Assessments, 2004.

Kuehl, Daniel T., and Charles E. Miller, "Roles, Missions, and Functions: Terms of Debate," Joint Force Quarterly, Summer 1994, pp. 103–105.

Kuhn, Thomas S., The Structure of Scientific Revolutions, 2nd ed., Chicago: University of Chicago Press, 1962.

Lamb, Michael W., Sr., Operation Allied Force: Golden Nuggets for Future Campaigns, Maxwell Air Force Base, Ala.: Air War College, 2002.

Lambeth, Benjamin S., The Transformation of American Air Power, Ithaca, N.Y.: Cornell University Press, 2000.

————, "Storm Over the Desert: A New Assessment," *Joint Force Quarterly*, Winter 2000–2001, pp. 30–34.

————, *NATO's Air War for Kosovo: A Strategic and Operational Assessment*, Santa Monica, Calif.: RAND Corporation, MR-1365-AF, 2001.

————, *Air Power Against Terror: America's Conduct of Operation Enduring Freedom*, Santa Monica, Calif.: RAND Corporation, MG-166-CENTAF, 2005.

LaPorte, Leon J., and MaryAnn B. Cummings, "Prompt Deterrence: The Army in Kuwait," *Military Review*, Vol. 77, No. 6, November–December 1997.

Larson, Eric V., David T. Orletsky, and Kristin Leuschner, *Defense Planning in a Decade of Change: Lessons from the Base Force, Bottom-Up Review, and Quadrennial Defense Review*, Santa Monica, Calif.: RAND Corporation, MR-1387-AF, 2001.

Lederman, Gordon Nathaniel, *Reorganizing the Joint Chiefs of Staff: The Goldwater-Nichols Act of 1986*, Westport, Conn.: Greenwood Press, 1999.

Locher, James R., *Victory on the Potomac: The Goldwater-Nichols Act Unifies the Pentagon*, College Station, Tex.: Texas A&M University Press, 2002.

Macgregor, Douglas A., *Transformation Under Fire: Revolutionizing How America Fights*, Westport, Conn.: Praeger, 2003.

Macloud, Jeffrey D. "Letter to the Editor: Land Power Revisionism," *Armed Forces Journal*, December 2005, p. 6.

Mangum, Ronald Scott, "NATO's Attack on Serbia: Anomaly or Emerging Doctrine?" *Parameters*, Winter 2000–2001, pp. 40–52.

Mazarr, Michael, Don M. Snider, and James A. Blackwell, Jr., *Desert Storm: The Gulf War and What We Learned*, Boulder, Colo.: Westview Press, 1993.

————, *Light Forces and the Future of U.S. Military Strategy*, Washington, D.C.: Brassey's, 1990.

McCaffrey, Barry R., "Lessons of Desert Storm," *Joint Force Quarterly*, Winter 2000–2001, pp. 12–17.

McCaffrey, Terrance J., III, *What Happened to BAI? Army and Air Force Battlefield Doctrine from Pre–Desert Storm to 2001*, thesis, School of Advanced Airpower Studies, Air University, 2002.

McElroy, Robert H., and Patrecia Slayden Hollis, "Afghanistan: Fire Support for Operation Anaconda; Interview with Major General Franklin L. Hagenbeck," *Field Artillery*, September–October 2002, pp. 5–9.

McGee, Michael B., Jr., *Air-Ground Operations During Operation Iraqi Freedom: Successes, Failures, and Lessons of Air Force and Army Integration*, thesis, Air War College, 2005.

McNaugher, Thomas, David Johnson, and Jerry Sollinger, *Agility by a Different Measure: Creating a More Flexible U.S. Army*, Santa Monica, Calif.: RAND Corporation, IP-195, 2000.

Mets, David R., "Bomber Barons, Bureaucrats, and Budgets: Your Professional Reading on the Theory and Doctrine of Strategic Air Attack," *Airpower Journal*, Summer 1996, pp. 76–95.

Michaels, G. J., *Tip of the Spear: U.S. Marine Light Armor in the Gulf War*, Annapolis, Md.: Naval Institute Press, 1990.

"The Military Must Be Different," *Aviation Week & Space Technology*, Vol. 141, No. 13, September 26, 1994.

Momyer, William W., *Airpower in Three Wars*, Maxwell Air Force Base, Ala.: Air University Press, 1978.

Morrison, G. A., "Air Power—Maneuver Element or Pretender?" 1992. As of November 2005:
http://www.globalsecurity.org/military/library/report/1992/MGA.htm

Moseley, T. Michael, "Operation Iraqi Freedom—By the Numbers," Central Air Forces, April 30, 2003.

Moskal, Leonard S., *Effective Planning of Joint Air Operations*, thesis, School of Advanced Military Studies, U.S. Army Command and General Staff College, 1996.

Mowbray, James A., "Air Force Doctrine Problems 1926–Present," *Airpower Journal*, Winter 1995.

Murray, Williamson, and Allan R. Millett, eds., *Military Innovation in the Interwar Period*, Cambridge, UK: Cambridge University Press, 1996.

Myers, Gene, "Interservice Rivalry and Air Force Doctrine: Promise, Not Apology," *Airpower Journal*, Summer 1996, pp. 60–64.

Nagl, John A., *Learning to Eat Soup with a Knife: Counterinsurgency Lessons from Malaya and Vietnam*, Chicago: University of Chicago Press, 2005.

Nardulli, Bruce R., Walter L. Perry, Bruce Pirnie, John Gordon IV, and John G. McGinn, *Disjointed War: Military Operations in Kosovo, 1999*, Santa Monica, Calif.: RAND Corporation, MR-1406-A, 2002.

Naylor, Sean D., *Not a Good Day to Die: The Untold Story of Operation Anaconda*, New York: Berkley Books, 2005.

———, "The War's Bloodiest Battle," *Army Times*, March 18, 2002.

Neller, Robert B., "Marines in Panama: 1998–1990," As of December 2005:
http://www.globalsecurity.org/military/library/report/1991/NRB.htm

Neuenswander, Matthew D., "Letter to the Editor: JCAS in Operation Anaconda—It's Not All Bad News," *Field Artillery*, May–June 2003.

Newman, Richard J., "Ambush at Najaf," *Air Force Magazine*, Vol. 86, No. 10, October 2003.

Norman, Lloyd, and John B. Spore, "Big Push in Guerrilla Warfare," *Army*, March 1962, pp. 32–33.

Ochmanek, David A., Edward R. Harshberger, David E. Thaler, and Glenn A. Kent, *To Find and Not to Yield: How Advances in Information and Firepower Can Transform Theater Warfare*, Santa Monica, Calif.: RAND Corporation, MR-958-AF, 1998.

Odom, William O., *After the Trenches: The Transformation of U.S. Army Doctrine, 1918–1939*, College Station, Tex.: Texas A&M University Press, 1999.

Owen, Robert C., "The Balkans Air Campaign Study: Part 1," *Aerospace Power Journal*, Summer 1997a, pp. 4–25.

———, "The Balkans Air Campaign Study: Part 2," *Aerospace Power Journal*, Fall 1997b, pp. 6–27.

———, ed., *Deliberate Force: A Case Study in Effective Air Campaigning* (final report of the Air University Balkans Air Campaign Study), Maxwell Air Force Base, Ala.: Air University Press, 2000.

———, "Operation Deliberate Force: A Case Study on Humanitarian Constraints in Aerospace Warfare," presented at Humanitarian Challenges in Military Intervention workshop, Washington, D.C., November 29–30, 2001. As of November 2005:
http://www.ksg.harvard.edu/cchrp/Web%20Working%20Papers/Owen2001.pdf

Owens, Mackubin T., "Vietnam, Kosovo, and Strategic Failure," editorial, Ashbrook Center for Public Affairs at Ashland University, May 1999. As of November 2005:
http://ashbrook.org/publicat/oped/owens/99/vietnam.html

Owens, William A., and Edward Offrey, *Lifting the Fog of War*, New York: Farrar, Straus and Giroux, 2000.

Pace, James A., "Myths, Misperceptions, and Reality of the Ground Fires Triad," *Marine Corps Gazette*, June 2005.

Pape, Robert A., *Bombing to Win: Air Power and Coercion in War*, Ithaca, N.Y.: Cornell University Press, 1996.

———, "The True Worth of Air Power," *Foreign Affairs*, March/April 2004.

Perry, Charles P., "Mogadishu, October 1993: A Company XO's Notes on Lessons Learned," *Infantry*, November–December 1994, pp. 31–38.

Pirnie, Bruce R., and Corazon M. Francisco, *Assessing Requirements for Peacekeeping, Humanitarian Assistance, and Disaster Relief*, Santa Monica, Calif.: RAND Corporation, MR-951-OSD, 1998.

Pirnie, Bruce R., Alan Vick, Adam Grissom, Karl P. Mueller, and David T. Orletsky, *Beyond Close Air Support: Forging a New Air-Ground Partnership*, Santa Monica, Calif.: RAND Corporation, MG-301-AF, 2005.

Pivarsky, Carl R., Jr., "Airpower in the Context of a Dysfunctional Joint Doctrine," Air War College Maxwell Paper No. 7, 1997.

Plummer, Anne, "Army Chief Tells President Restructuring Force Could Cost $20 Billion," *Inside the Army*, February 9, 2004.

Pogue, Forrest C., *The Supreme Command: U.S. Army in World War II*, Washington, D.C.: U.S. Army Center of Military History, 1989.

Powell, Colin (with Joseph E. Persico), *My American Journey*, New York: Random House, 1995.

"Prepared Testimony by U.S. Secretary of Defense Donald H. Rumsfeld," before Senate Armed Services Committee, July 9, 2003. As of November 2005: http://www.au.af.mil/au/awc/awcgate/congress/rumsfeld_09july03.pdf

The President of the United States, *The National Security Strategy of the United States of America*, The White House, 2002.

"Proponents Defend Army Helicopters," *Columbia (Mo.) Daily Tribune*, August 1, 2004. As of November 2005: http://www.showmenews.com/2004/Aug/20040801News017.asp

Putney, Diane T., *Airpower Advantage: Planning the Gulf War Air Campaign, 1989–1991*, Washington, D.C.: Air Force History and Museums Program, 2004.

Record, Jeffrey, *Making War, Thing History: Munich, Vietnam, and Presidential Uses of Force from Korea to Kosovo*, Annapolis, Md.: Naval Institute Press, 2002.

Reimer, Dennis J., "Dominant Maneuver and Precision Engagement," *Joint Force Quarterly*, Winter 1996–1997, pp. 13–16.

Reimer, Dennis J., and Ronald R. Fogleman, "Joint Warfare and the Army–Air Force Team," *Joint Force Quarterly*, Spring 1996, pp. 9–15.

Reynolds, Nicholas E., *Just Cause: Marine Operations in Panama, 1998–1990*, Washington, D.C.: Headquarters, U.S. Marine Corps, 1996.

Reynolds, Richard T., *Heart of the Storm: The Genesis of the Air Campaign Against Iraq*, Maxwell Air Force Base, Ala.: Air University Press, 1995.

Rice, Frederick, "Army Aviation—Preparing for the Future," Fort Rucker, Ala., undated. As of December 2005: http://www-rucker.army.mil/50th/preparing_for_future.html

Riggins, James, and David E. Snodgrass, "Halt Phase Plus Strategic Preclusion: Joint Solution for a Joint Problem," *Parameters*, Autumn 1999, pp. 70–85. As of November 2005: http://carlisle-www.army.mil/usawc/parameters/99autumn/riggins.htm

Romjue, John L., *From Active Defense to Airland Battle: The Development of Army Doctrine, 1973–1982*, Fort Monroe, Va.: U.S. Army Training and Doctrine Command, 1984.

———, *The Army of Excellence: The Development of the 1980s Army*, Fort Monroe, Va.: U.S. Army Training and Doctrine Command, 1993.

Rosen, Stephen Peter, "Service Redundancy: Waste or Hidden Capability?" *Joint Force Quarterly*, Summer 1993.

Samek, Rocky G., "ATACMS: Fires for the Objective Force," *Field Artillery*, May–June 2003, pp. 20–24.

Scales, Robert H., *Firepower in Limited War*, Washington, D.C.: National Defense University Press, 1990.

———, *Future Warfare Anthology*, Carlisle, Pa.: Strategic Studies Institute, U.S. Army War College, 2000.

———, *Yellow Smoke: The Future of Land Warfare for America's Military*, Lanham, Md.: Rowman and Littlefield, 2003.

———, "The Shape of Brigades to Come," *Armed Forces Journal*, October 2005, pp. 28–32.

Scales, Robert H., Terry L. Johnson, and Thomas P. Odom, *Certain Victory: The US Army in the Gulf War*, Washington, D.C.: Office of the Chief of Staff, United States Army, 1993.

Schein, Edgar H., *Organizational Culture and Leadership*, 2nd ed., San Francisco: Jossey-Bass, 1992.

Schubert, Frank N., and Theresa L. Kraus, eds., *The Whirlwind War*, Washington, D.C.: U.S. Army Center of Military History, 1995.

Schwarzkopf, H. Norman, and Peter Petre, *It Doesn't Take a Hero: General H. Norman Schwarzkopf, the Autobiography*, New York: Bantam Books, 1992.

Scroggs, Stephen, *Army Relations with Congress: Thick Armor, Dull Sword, Slow Horse*, Westport, Conn.: Praeger, 2000.

Sheftlick, Gary, "Army to Reset into Modular Brigade-Centric Force," Army News Service, February 24, 2004. As of November 2005: http://www4.army.mil/ocpa/read.php?story_id_key=5703

Shelton, Henry H., "Peace Operations: The Forces Required," *National Security Studies Quarterly*, Summer 2000.

Sherman, Frank, "Operation Just Cause: The Armor-Infantry Team in the Close Fight," *Armor*, September–October 1996, pp. 34–35.

"Shinseki Hints at Restructuring, Aggressive Changes for the Army," *Inside the Army*, June 28, 1999.

Sinclair, Edward J., "Aviation in Operational Maneuver," briefing, U.S. Army Aviation Warfighting Center, undated.

———, "Army Aviation's Progress Toward Transformation," *Army*, January 2006, pp. 33–37.

Snider, Don M., and Gayle L. Watkins, eds. *The Future of the Army Profession*, New York: McGraw-Hill, 2002.

"Somalia: Operations Other Than War," *Foreign Military Studies Office Special Study*, No. 93-1, 1991.

"Springboard for Airpower," *Air Force Magazine*, Vol. 87, No. 3, March 2004. As of December 2005:
http://www.afa.org/magazine/march2004/0304airpower.asp

Staff of the Marine Corps Center for Lessons Learned, "Operation Iraqi Freedom Lessons Learned," *Marine Corps Gazette*, May 2005.

"Statement of General Tommy R. Franks, Former Commander, US Central Command," before the Senate Armed Services Committee, July 9, 2003. As of November 2005:
http://www.au.af.mil/au/awc/awcgate/congress/franks_09july03.pdf

Strickland, Paul C., "USAF Aerospace-Power Doctrine: Decisive or Coercive?" *Aerospace Power Journal*, Fall 2000.

Stroup, Theodore G., Jr., "Task Force Hawk: Beyond Expectations," *Army Magazine*, August 1999.

Szafranski, Richard, "Interservice Rivalry in Action: The Endless Roles and Missions Refrain?" *Airpower Journal*, Summer 1996, pp. 48–59.

Talbot, David, "How Technology Failed in Iraq," *Technology Review*, November 2004. As of November 2005:
http://www.technologyreview.com/articles/04/11/talbot1104.asp

Taw, Jennifer Morrison, *Operation Just Cause: Lessons for Operations Other Than War*, Santa Monica, Calif.: RAND Corporation, MR-569-A, 1996.

Thomas, Timothy L., "Air Operations in Low Intensity Conflict," *Aerospace Power Journal*, Winter 1997.

Tilford, Earl H., Jr., *Halt Phase Strategy: New Wine in Old Skins . . . With Powerpoint*, Carlisle, Pa.: Strategic Studies Institute, U.S. Army War College, 1998.

———, "Operation Allied Force and the Role of Air Power," *Parameters*, Winter 1999–2000. As of November 2005:
http://carlisle-www.army.mil/usawc/parameters/99winter/tilford.htm

———, "Review of *Fast Tanks and Heavy Bombers: Innovation in the U.S. Army, 1917–1945*," *Naval War College Review*, Winter 2000.

Tirpak, John A., "Enduring Freedom," *Air Force Magazine*, February 2002, pp. 32–39.

Titus, James, *The Battle of Khafji: An Overview and Preliminary Analysis*, Maxwell Air Force Base, Ala.: Air University, 1996.

Toffler, Alvin, and Heidi Toffler, *War and Anti-War: Survival at the Dawn of the Twenty-First Century*, Boston: Little, Brown and Company, 1993.

"Transformation Is the Key," *Army Times*, August 11, 2003.

"UK: 'No Plans' for Kosovo Call-Up," *BBC Online* (online), May 30, 1999.

U.S. 12th Army Group, *Antiaircraft Artillery, Armored, Artillery, Chemical Warfare and Signal Sections*. Vol. XI, *12th Army Group Report of Operations (Final After Action Report)*, 1945.

U.S. Army 3rd Infantry Division, *Third Infantry Division (Mechanized) After Action Report: Operation Iraqi Freedom*, Fort Stewart, Ga., 2003.

U.S. Army Center for Army Lessons Learned, *Operation Restore Hope Lessons Learned Report, 3 December 1992–4 May 1993*, Fort Leavenworth, Kan.: Center for Army Lessons Learned, 1993.

U.S. Army Training and Doctrine Command, *Change 2 to TRADOC Pamphlet 525-3-90 O & O, The United States Army Objective Force Operational and Organizational Plan, Maneuver Unit of Action*, final version, Fort Knox, Ky.: Unit of Action Maneuver Battle Lab, 2003.

———, *Change 3 to TRADOC Pamphlet 525-3-90 O & O, The United States Army Objective Force Operational and Organizational Plan, Maneuver Unit of Action*, draft, Fort Knox, Ky.: Unit of Action Maneuver Battle Lab, 2004.

———, TRADOC Pamphlet 525-3-0, *The Army in Joint Operations: The Army's Future Force Capstone Concept, 2015–2024, Version 2.0*, Fort Monroe, Va., 2005.

———, "TRADOC Futures Center Feedback on RAND Study: 'Learning Large Lessons: The Evolving Roles of Ground Power and Air Power in the Post-Cold War Era'—Part III, Army Aviation Transformation: Army Attack Aviation for a Campaign Quality Army with Joint and Expeditionary Capabilities," PowerPoint briefing, Fort Monroe, Va., August 31, 2005.

U.S. Code, Title 10, Subtitle A, Part I, Chapter 5, Section 153.

U.S. Department of the Air Force, Air Force Manual 1-1, *Basic Aerospace Doctrine of the United States Air Force*, 1984.

———, AFM 1-1, *Basic Aerospace Doctrine of the United States Air Force*, Vol. I, 1992.

———, AFDD 1, *Air Force Basic Doctrine*, 1997.

———, AFDD 2-1.3, *Counterland*, 1999.

————, AFDD 1, *Air Force Basic Doctrine*, 2003.

————, AFDD 2-1.2, *Strategic Attack*, 2003.

————, *United States Air Force Posture Statement*, 2004.

————, *Air Force Concept for Joint Operations*, 2005.

————, *Operation Anaconda: An Air Power Perspective*, 2005.

————, AFDD 2-1.3, *Counterland Operations*, 2006.

U.S. Department of the Army, "Army Campaign Plan Briefing," undated. As of November 2005:
http://www.army.mil/thewayahead/acpdownloads.html

————, FM 100-5, *Operations*, 1976.

————, FM 100-5, *Operations*, 1982.

————, FM 100-5, *Operations*, 1986.

————, FM 6-20, *Fire Support in the Airland Battle*, 1988.

————, FM 6-20-30, *Tactics, Techniques, and Procedures for Fire Support for Corps and Division Operations*, October 18, 1989. As of November 2005:
https://atiam.train.army.mil/soldierPortal/atia/adlsc/view/public/9181-1/fm/6-20-30/toc.htm

————, "Joint Task Force South in Operation Just Cause," Oral History Interview, JCIT 097Z (LTG Carmen Cavezza)," April 30, 1992. As of November 2005:
http://www.army.mil/cmh-pg/documents/panama/JCIT/JCIT97Z.htm

————, FM 100-5, *Operations*, 1993.

————, FM 100-23, *Peace Operations*, 1994.

————, *A Statement on the Posture of the United States Army: Fiscal Year 1996*, 1995.

————, FM 1-100, *Army Aviation Operations*, 1997.

————, FM 1-112, *Attack Helicopter Operations*, 1997.

————, "Army Accelerates Aviation Transformation," press release, September 7, 2001. As of December 2005:
http://www4.army.mil/ocpa/print.php?story_id_key=1425

————, *Concepts for the Objective Force*, 2001.

————, FM 3-0, *Operations*, 2001.

————, "Army RDT&E Budget Item Justification (R-2 Exhibit): 0604768A, Brilliant Anti-Armor Submunition (BAT)," February 2003. As of December 2005:
http://www.dtic.mil/descriptivesum/Y2004/Army/0604768A.pdf A

———, FM 3-04.111, *Aviation Brigades*, 2003.

———, "Memorandum for Record: AH-64 Operations in Iraq Lessons Learned," Headquarters, 11th Aviation Regiment, April 7, 2003.

———, *United States Army Transformation Roadmap, 2003*.

———, *2004 Army Transformation Roadmap*, 2004.

———, *2005 Army Modernization Plan*, Office of the Deputy Chief of Staff, G-8, 2005.

———, FMI 3-04.101, *UEx Aviation Brigade Organization, Training, and Operations*, 2005.

U.S. Department of the Army and Marine Corps Combat Development Command, U.S. Department of the Navy, FM 3-24 and MCWP 3-33.5, *Counterinsurgency*, Washington, D.C., December 15, 2006.

U.S. Department of Defense, *DOD Pam 1-20: The Armed Forces Officer*, 1960.

———, *Conduct of the Persian Gulf War: Final Report to Congress*, 1992.

———, "Joint Statement on the Kosovo After Action Review," news release, October 14, 1999. As of November 2005:
http://www.au.af.mil/au/awc/awcgate/kosovoaa/jointstmt.htm

———, *Report to Congress: Kosovo/Operation Allied Force After-Action Report*, 2000.

———, *Quadrennial Defense Review Report*, 2001.

———, Directive Number 5100.1, *Functions of the Department of Defense and Its Major Components*, August 1, 2002.

———, Directive Number 3000.05, *Military Support for Stability, Security, Transition, and Reconstruction (SSTR) Operations*, November 28, 2005.

U.S. Department of the Navy, MCWP 3-2, *Aviation Operations*, U.S. Marine Corps, 2000.

———, MCDP 1-0, *Marine Corps Operations*, U.S. Marine Corps, 2001.

———, *Aviation Training and Readiness (T&R) Manual, AH-1, Marine Corps Order 3500.48*, U.S. Marine Corps, May 13, 2003.

U.S. Department of State, "Text: President Bush Announces Military Strikes in Afghanistan," Office of International Information Programs, October 7, 2001. As of November 2005:
http://www.globalsecurity.org/military/library/news/2001/10/mil-011007-usia01.htm

————, "Transcript: Rumsfeld, Myers Brief on Military Operation in Afghanistan," Office of International Information Programs, October 7, 2001. As of November 2005:
http://www.globalsecurity.org/military/library/news/2001/10/mil-011007-usia04.htm

U.S. General Accounting Office, *Kosovo Air Operations: Army Resolving Lessons Learned Regarding the Apache Helicopter*, GAO-01-401, 2001a.

————, *Kosovo Air Operations: Need to Maintain Alliance Cohesion Resulted in Doctrinal Departures*, GAO-01-784, 2001b.

U.S. Joint Chiefs of Staff, JP 0-2, *Unified Action Armed Forces (UNAAF)*, 2001.

————, JP 3-0, *Doctrine for Joint Operations*, 1995.

————, JP 3-04, *Doctrine for Joint Interdiction Operations*, 1997.

————, *The National Military Strategy: Shape, Respond, Prepare Now—A Military Strategy for a New Era*, 1997.

————, JP 3-09, *Doctrine for Joint Fire Support*, 1998.

————, JP 3-33, *Joint Force Capabilities*, 1999.

————, JP 1, *Joint Warfare of the Armed Forces of the United States*, 2000.

————, *Joint Doctrine Capstone and Keystone Primer*, 2001.

————, JP 1-02, *Department of Defense Dictionary of Military and Associated Terms*, 2001.

————, JP 3-0, *Doctrine for Joint Operations*, 2001.

————, JP 3-70, *Joint Doctrine for Strategic Attack*, 2001.

————, JP 3-60, *Joint Doctrine for Targeting*, 2002.

————, JP 3-09.3, *Joint Tactics, Techniques, and Procedures for Close Air Support*, 2003.

————, JP 3-30, *Command and Control for Joint Air Operations*, 2003.

————, JP 3-31, *Command and Control for Joint Land Operations*, 2004.

————, *National Military Strategy of the United States: A Strategy for Today; A Vision for Tomorrow*, 2004.

————, JP 3-0, *Joint Operations*, 2006.

U.S. Joint Forces Command, *Joint Forces Command Glossary*, undated. As of December 2001:
http://www.jfcom.mil/about/glossary.htm

————, "What Is Transformation?" Web page, undated. As of January 2006:
http://www.jfcom.mil/about/transform.html

——, *Pamphlet 7: Operational Implications of Effects-Based Operations (EBO)*, Suffolk, Va.: Joint Warfighting Center, 2004.

——, *Commander's Handbook for an Effects-Based Approach to Joint Operations*, Suffolk, Va.: Joint Warfighting Center, 2006.

U.S. War Department, *Field Service Regulations, United States Army, 1923*, Washington, D.C.: U.S. Government Printing Office, 1924.

——, Field Manual 100-2, *Command and Employment of Air Power*, Washington, D.C.: U.S. Government Printing Office, 1943.

Vick, Alan, David Orletsky, Bruce Pirnie, and Seth Jones, *The Stryker Brigade Combat Team: Rethinking Strategic Responsiveness and Assessing Deployment Options*, Santa Monica, Calif.: RAND Corporation, MR-1606-AF, 2002.

Vickers, Michael G., "Revolution Deferred: Kosovo and the Transformation of War," in Bacevich and Cohen (2001).

Vought, Donald B., "Preparing for the Wrong War?" *Military Review*, Vol. 57, May 1977.

Wallace, William S., "Joint Fires in OIF: What Worked for the Vth (US) Corps," briefing, U.S. Army Combined Arms Center, 2003.

Warden, John A., III, *The Air Campaign: Planning for Combat*, Washington, D.C.: National Defense University Press, 1988.

Wass de Czege, Huba, "The Continuing Necessity of Ground Combat in Modern War," *Army Magazine*, September 2000, pp. 8–12.

Wass de Czege, Huba, and Antulio J. Echevarria II, "Landpower and Future Strategy: Insights from the Army After Next," *Joint Force Quarterly*, Spring 1999, pp. 62–69.

Weigley, Russell F., *The American Way of War: A History of United States Military Strategy and Policy*, Bloomington, Ind.: Indiana University Press, 1977.

——, *History of the United States Army*, enl. ed., Bloomington, Ind.: Indiana University Press, 1984.

Wells, Gordon M., "Deep Operations, Command and Control, and Joint Doctrine: Time for a Change?" *Joint Force Quarterly*, Winter 1996–1997, pp. 101–105.

Whitlow, J. L., "JFACC: Who's in Charge?" *Joint Force Quarterly*, Summer 1994, pp. 64–70.

Wilson, George C., *This War Really Matters: Inside the Fight for Defense Dollars*, Washington, D.C.: CQ Press, 2000.

Wilson, John B., *Maneuver and Firepower: The Evolution of Divisions and Separate Brigades*, Washington, D.C.: U.S. Army Center of Military History, 1998.

Wilson, Peter A., John Gordon IV, and David E. Johnson, "An Alternative Future Force: Building a Better Army," *Parameters*, Vol. 33, No. 4, Winter 2003–2004, pp. 19–39.

Winnefeld, James A., and Dana J. Johnson, *Joint Air Operations: Pursuit of Unity in Command and Control, 1942–1991*, Annapolis, Md.: Naval Institute Press, 1993.

———, "Unity of Control: Joint Air Operations in the Gulf," *Joint Force Quarterly*, Summer 1993, pp. 88–99.

Winnefeld, James A., Preston Niblack, and Dana J. Johnson, *A League of Airmen: U.S. Air Power in the Gulf War*, Santa Monica, Calif.: RAND Corporation, MR-343-A, 1994.

Winton, Harold R., "Partnership and Tension: The Army and the Air Force Between Vietnam and Desert Shield," *Parameters*, Spring 1996, pp. 100–119. As of December 2005:
http://carlisle-www.army.mil/usawc/parameters/96spring/winton.htm

Wolf, Richard I., *The United States Air Force: Basic Documents on Roles and Missions*, Washington, D.C.: Office of Air Force History, 1988.

Woods, Kevin M., Michael R. Pease, Mark E. Stout, Williamson Murray, and James G. Lacey, *Iraqi Perspectives Project: A View of Operation Iraqi Freedom from Saddam's Senior Leadership*, Suffolk, Va.: U.S. Joint Forces Command, Joint Center for Operational Analysis, 2006.

Woodward, Bob, *Plan of Attack*, New York: Simon & Schuster, 2004.

Worden, Mike, *Rise of the Fighter Generals: The Problem of Air Force Leadership, 1945–1982*, Maxwell Air Force Base, Ala.: Air University Press, 1998.

Wrage, Stephen D., ed., *Immaculate Warfare: Participants Reflect on the Air Campaigns over Kosovo and Afghanistan*, Westport, Conn.: Praeger, 2003.

Wright, Evan, *Devil Dogs, Iceman, Captain America and the New Face of American War*, New York: G.P. Putnam's Sons, 2004.

Zook, David H., *The Fire Support Coordination Line: Is It Time to Reconsider Our Doctrine?* thesis, U.S. Army Command and General Staff College, 1992.

# Index